W9-CCH-611

WICKED
GAME

WICKED GAME

AN INSIDER'S STORY ON HOW TRUMP WON, MUELLER FAILED, AND AMERICA LOST

RICK GATES

Post Hill
PRESS

A POST HILL PRESS BOOK
ISBN: 978-1-64293-792-3
ISBN (eBook): 978-1-64293-793-0

Wicked Game:
An Insider's Story on How Trump Won, Mueller Failed, and America Lost
© 2020 by Rick Gates
All Rights Reserved

Cover art by Cody Corcoran

Post Hill Press
New York • Nashville
posthillpress.com

Published in the United States of America

1 2 3 4 5 6 7 8 9 10

To my wife and children, whom I adore.

CONTENTS

Preface

IT WAS TIME FOR DONALD TRUMP TO MAKE HIS EXIT.

He had not only won the Indiana primary that night, but more importantly, Trump's last remaining Republican rival, Senator Ted Cruz, had bowed out.

Which meant that Donald J. Trump had just become the Republican Party's "presumptive nominee" in the race to become the next president of the United States.

He celebrated the victory as he always did, surrounded by the comfort and loyalty of his family, behind a modest podium, not in Indiana but in front of a crowd full of press and a few hundred well-heeled supporters in the heart of Manhattan—where the rousing chorus of The Rolling Stones' "Start Me Up" now echoed off the pink marble walls in the cavernous lobby of Trump Tower.

Trump had shown remarkable restraint during his victory speech that night. He didn't lob any personal attacks against Cruz. He didn't disparage the "rigged" primary system or the Republican establishment. He didn't say anything remarkably over-the-top about how he'd beaten the entire Republican field at their own game to become the last man standing.

To the contrary, he *praised* Cruz as one of the toughest competitors in the field. He *thanked* the voters, recognizing their hard work and efforts, proudly stating that "[w]e won with women, we won with men, we won with Hispanics, we won with African Americans, and we won with everybody." He talked about healing our divided country and how "[w]e are going to love each other" and "[w]e are going to cherish each other."

Instead of going negative, he relished the victory and allowed the power of the moment to speak for itself.

Paul Manafort and I were beyond elated as we accompanied our candidate and his wife, Melania, on the walk from the Trump Tower hallway to the residential elevator. He moved deliberately, waving and nodding at a few people in the back of the lobby and shaking a few hands along the rope line on the way.

As we reached the elevator bank, the four of us quickly stepped in. The door closed.

There was a long silence.

Trump put his head down slightly, staring over at Melania as we rose toward his three-story penthouse on the sixty-sixth floor.

After a few seconds, Paul looked at Trump, proud that the outcome he had predicted for him in late March had now come true. "Well, Donald," he said, "you are now one of only two people who will become the next president of the United States."

The weight of Paul's sentence was enormous. But Trump barely glanced up.

It was the first time ever in the history of this country that a political outsider, a businessman and celebrity who had never held a political office in his life, had become the presumptive nominee from either party. I fully expected to see and hear some elation from Trump, some gratitude, some gravitas, or maybe some joy—*something*.

Instead, Trump just nodded his head and said, "Oh."

After essentially winning the biggest upset in the history of the Republican Party, disrupting the protocols and expectations of more than two hundred years of precedent in presidential politics, achieving something almost no one in Washington (or anywhere else) imagined possible, and drawing the attention of the entire world while he did it, Donald Trump's response was "Oh."

On hundreds of occasions since his campaign began, Trump had defied expectations and assumptions like no one I had ever encountered. At times when I expected he might react strongly, his reactions were often measured. When something seemed insignificant, he might treat it like the most important moment in the world. Then on other occasions, he would do exactly the opposite.

The task of figuring out what made Donald Trump tick, of trying to anticipate what he might say or do, of trying to work with him while attempting to understand why he acted and reacted in the very unique ways he did, had proven to be one of the most intense and formidable challenges I had ever faced in my entire career in politics.

Yet clearly, I still had a lot to learn.

Looking back now, knowing what's happened to our country since that turning point on the night of May 3, 2016, I sometimes wonder if Trump *knew*. While his detractors wound up stunned and bewildered in his wake, I sometimes wonder if he knew exactly what he was doing—and just how massively he was about to upend the world of politics as we knew it.

It's staggering to think about. But I wasn't the only one who had a lot more to learn.

In order to make sense of Trump—how he wins, and how he loses; how to work with him, or what it's like to work against him; in order to be able to predict how he leads, where he might take us, and just where his followers might be willing to follow—we *all* had a lot to learn.

And we still do.

★　★　★

Donald Trump has forever changed the political landscape of the United States of America.

He has utilized skills learned over decades in business and transformed them into political tools that have enabled him to galvanize supporters and soundly beat establishment politicians on *both* sides of the political aisle. And it seems no matter how hard he punches—or how hard his opponents try to knock him down—he always winds up on top.

No matter which side you happen to be on, there is one truth we all need to grasp: Donald Trump isn't going away, and the impact of his actions, his words, and his style of winning will continue to impact this country—and the world—for decades to come, if not more.

Whether we want to understand Trump as a means to learn to survive and thrive in the world in which he operates, whether we want to reelect him or defeat him, we first have to understand him. How he got elected, how he wins, how he challenges the media and talks directly to his base in a way that no one ever thought possible; what he's thinking, what he's not thinking, how he's influenced (or not influenced) by the voices around him; why he seemingly embraces other world leaders who are enemies to the United States; what it all means to the present and future of our complex political system, and how he exposes our long-established institutions in ways that hardly anyone ever sees coming—all of it *matters*.

Americans have largely ignored this notion of "learning" about Trump. His opponents have derided him. They've complained about him, loudly, while his supporters have rallied around him. But during the 2016 campaign and election, the Democrats and many establishment Republicans alike refused to acknowledge Trump's strengths and instead determined that he was not going to be around politics long enough to care.

That attitude was a mistake.

The disruption that Donald Trump brought to Washington exposed and amplified everything that is wrong with our political system, in all of its divisiveness, on both sides. And that amplification has now spilled over into our justice system, and our media, and into the social and financial fabric of our everyday lives to the point where nearly everything we cherish as a nation is fraught with tension, dysfunction, division, and in some cases, outright hatred. We can't even talk about our political differences anymore without breaking into arguments at the family dinner table or tearing each other apart on social media. Or, in some cases, confronting each other right out in the streets.

If we want to fix it, we first have to endeavor to understand how we got here. If we don't? If Liberals keep busy blaming everything on Trump, and the Republicans keep blaming everything on the Liberals, we will only continue to *lose*. And right now, in the current state of global chaos, we're losing our economic power, any semblance of our democratic values, and our country's dominance and respect around the world.

I know this is difficult for some readers to hear, but Trump didn't "do this" to us. *We* did this. We, the American people. Through our overall lack of participation in the political process, we allowed a dangerous status quo to grow for decades, a state in which many Americans were (and still are) so completely fed up with their own government that they were willing to take a chance on a political outsider, a celebrity businessman who promised to "drain the swamp" and "Make America Great Again."

Donald Trump stepped into that role with ease. And while some may say he's only exacerbated our problems ever since, we cannot ignore the fact that Trump's presence has exposed many of our government's (and our society's) shortcomings and failures in ways that they've never been exposed before now.

My hope is that by sharing my experience inside Donald Trump's campaign for the presidency, as well as my experience as a target of and key witness for the Mueller investigation on Russia collusion, readers from both sides of the political aisle will open their eyes to just how broken our systems actually are, so we can put an end to the infighting, and begin to repair the damage that has been done.

In the government's sentencing memo in their case against me, federal prosecutors took the unusual step of praising me for my "extraordinary assistance" in their efforts. "Gates has worked assiduously to provide truthful, complete, and reliable information," they wrote. The government concluded that "under exceedingly difficult circumstances and under intense public scrutiny, Gates has worked earnestly to provide the government with everything it has asked of him."

I hope and earnestly pray that no person is ever subjected to the process that I experienced. But with that same forthrightness and truth, what I offer to you in this book is a factual account, to the best of my recollection, of the rise of Donald Trump, how and why he won, the campaign operations that brought him to victory, and a look behind the curtain of a justice system that acted against him—and, by proxy, *me*—for what I firmly believe were purely political motives.

Why do I believe that?

One: Because there's ample concrete evidence to support it.

And Two: Because it's nothing new. This is how Washington has always worked.

Politics is a tool that is often weaponized for personal gain.

Almost from the beginning of our existence, politics has acted as the crucible that determines those chosen to lead our country. And presidential politics have always been fraught with a degree of gamesmanship, including more than a few dirty tricks and "October surprises" along the way. Even in February of 1796, while Vice President John Adams was preparing to run in the very first election that didn't include George Washington, he penned a letter home to his wife, Abigail, stating that he wished to remain a "silent spectator in this silly and wicked game."

Of course, in certain games, silence is a strategy.

Historians suggest that behind the scenes, John Adams made more than a few "silent" moves to try to ensure his win over Thomas Jefferson— that he may have strong-armed a few members of the Electoral College (who were congressmembers, in those days) in order to sway their votes— to ensure that they voted for him instead of siding with the voters of their own states.

In the final results, after a campaign full of insults and innuendos that set the stage for every campaign since, Adams won the presidency by an electoral vote of seventy-one to sixty-eight.

The magic number of seventy-one votes was exactly the number Adams needed in order to secure the win, and if any two of the three Adams electors in Pennsylvania, Virginia, or North Carolina had voted with their states, Jefferson would have received nine more electoral votes.

Which means Jefferson would have been our second president.

Just four years later, the 1800 election battle between Thomas Jefferson and John Adams was once again fraught with slander, acrimony, and behind-the-scenes attacks. As a result of a tie in electoral votes, the House of Representatives was once again tasked to select the president, as directed by the Constitution. After thirty-five ballots cast with no winner, one person—Alexander Hamilton—was able to use his tremendous skills as a political operative to persuade a few congressmen to change their minds. And just like that, Thomas Jefferson became our third president.

Some might say Hamilton was a hero. Some might argue he was diabolical.

Either way, the precedents were set.

When Donald Trump, the penultimate political outsider, made a bid for the presidency in 2016, he did so while ignoring any semblance of political tradition or decorum. He put all of his personal motivations, his hatred of the system, and his nationalist desires and personal feelings about politicians and others right out in the open, for everyone to see. He approached the "wicked game" like no candidate before him, and forced everyone else to play the game on *his* terms.

And he won.

His victory sent shockwaves through a political system that hadn't changed in more than two hundred years. A system that did not want to change. And as that system has attempted to reject him ever since, Trump's very presence in the White House and the unprecedented dynamic it unleashed in Washington have shaken our country to its core.

As a student of politics who studied government at William & Mary before earning my master's degree in public policy at George Washington University, I always had a passion for the subject. I even thought I might run for office one day. But after getting involved in my first presidential campaign in 1996, and seeing firsthand just how ugly the process was—exactly two hundred years after Adams gave the election process its "wicked game" moniker—I knew I never would.

It takes a certain disposition, demeanor, and detachment to run for the presidency, knowing that the media, other politicians, adversaries, and the world at large will invade every part of your life.

Trump was better prepared for all of it than anyone ever expected. More than that, he knew how to counter the invasions, on all fronts, and turn them to his advantage.

As a result, his opponents, in all reaches of the government, were forced to adapt to Trump in ways they never imagined. Even some formerly mild-mannered politicians and bureaucrats have gone to new lows or extremes in search of their own victories in this wicked game.

I have written this book, in this pivotal reelection year, after everything I've endured, because I love this country—and because I know that we cannot stand for this "wicked game" to continue unabated. If we do, there is a very good chance that the democratic values we stand for as a nation will soon be in jeopardy, if they are not already. Not for a presidential cycle or two, but forever.

By sharing my experiences with Donald Trump, along with insights about the political landscape that allowed him to rise in the first place, and by exposing the truth about the opposing forces that caused every one of us to endure the chaos of these last few years, my hope is that we can begin to make some real changes.

To bring an end to the divisiveness that grips our nation.

We must learn from our mistakes, consider where we stand, and determine where we want to go as a nation.

We are not only Republicans or Democrats.

We are Americans, first and foremost.

THE ELECTION CAMPAIGN

CHAPTER 1

The Job I Never Saw Coming

IN LATE JANUARY OF 2016, PAUL MANAFORT ASKED ME TO START BUILD-
ing a detailed memo on the Republican presidential primary process.

Paul didn't tell me which candidate the information was for,
but what he wanted seemed pretty straightforward: a breakdown of the
Republican Party delegate system, state by state, pinpointing the number
of delegates needed in order to win the nomination, and the rules and
procedures that those delegates would have to abide by at the Republican
National Convention in July.

That's how it all started for me. With a research assignment for an
anonymous client.

The request itself caught me off guard. I had no indication until that
moment that my boss wanted to dive back into American politics. Paul
had a long and storied career as a political consultant, having guided both
Gerald Ford and Ronald Reagan to their respective wins. But the last presidential campaign he'd worked on in any official capacity was Bob Dole's
bid in 1996. Since that time, he'd been working almost exclusively overseas, as he and his business partner, Rick Davis, consulted with and ran
campaigns for major international candidates and political parties in a

total of seventy-two countries over the years. Their clients included major political dynasties, such as the Kirchner family in Argentina, and such prominent individuals as President Juan Carlos Varela in Panama and Prime Minister Benazir Bhutto in Pakistan.

I had met Paul briefly, and Rick as well, in the summer of 1995, when I worked as a full-time intern for Charlie Black, one of Paul's partners in their public affairs firm—Black, Manafort, Stone and Kelly—one of the largest bipartisan political affairs firms in the world. I did so while simultaneously going to night school, where I was working on my master's degree in public policy at George Washington University. I spent nearly a decade after that working as a government relations consultant in the gaming industry, addressing issues both in the U.S. and abroad before I agreed to join Rick Davis at their new firm, Davis Manafort Partners, in 2006. Soon after, Rick left the firm to work on John McCain's presidential campaign, and I started working with Paul, whom I barely knew at the time. I'd had the privilege to work directly on political campaigns and elections globally, including in parts of Europe and Latin America. But for the last ten years, most of our work had been in Ukraine; and most recently Paul had been actively working to rebuild the political party of ousted Ukraine President Viktor Yanukovych.

In all of these instances, Paul's reputation for political strategy preceded him. It is no exaggeration to say that in the rest of the world, it was generally assumed that if Paul came on board with his expertise at building candidates and political parties using an American campaign model, whichever candidate or party he worked for was likely to win. He was *that* good at what he did. Running international electoral work was challenging but more profitable than U.S. campaigns—a compelling reason why so many U.S. political consultants take their tradecraft abroad. In addition, many years earlier, Paul had helped found the precursor to the National Democratic Institute to promote democratic values in foreign countries. Paul always believed that U.S. presidential elections were the pinnacle of global politics, and winning a U.S. presidential election at this stage in his career would give him the accolades he so desired after being on the outside of U.S. campaigns for so long.

This was going to be his swan song.

In mid-February 2016, Paul finally told me who my research project was for: Republican candidate Donald J. Trump.

My first question was, "Why would Trump need this sort of basic research when primary season is already almost halfway over?" It was the kind of research that would typically be done at the very start of a campaign, even before a candidate announced that he or she was running. But in the coming weeks, the answer would become glaringly clear: Donald Trump and his staff did not fully understand how the process worked.

Even after successfully bulldozing his way through twenty-one state primaries, winning the vast majority of them while knocking all but five of his sixteen Republican opponents out of the race, he had little understanding of the intricacies of the primary system.

He didn't understand the various rules and technicalities concerning how state delegates would cast their votes at the Republican National Convention, which is pivotal to actually winning the Republican nomination.

He did not fully grasp that unless all of the other leading Republican contenders dropped out and united behind him, he would go into a "contested" convention and could potentially lose the nomination at that point—despite winning the majority of primaries.

Ever since he had announced his candidacy in June of 2015, Trump had moved forward under the assumption that the primary process was simple: that whenever he won a state, he actually *won* that state; that all of the delegates from that state automatically were pledged to him. Whether his staff never explained it to him, or whether he'd simply ignored the complex details of the delegate process, he kept on assuming that whichever way the people voted, the delegates were bound to follow the will of the people; that a win was a win, and therefore the convention was nothing more than a celebration and coronation of the nominee.

Of course, that isn't how presidential primaries work at all, on either side of the political aisle. The national conventions are much more than just TV events. The delegates who come to the convention from certain states can attempt to vote their conscience or to switch their blocs of votes to support a candidate other than the one their state's voters chose.

It's not all that dissimilar to what happens in the general election, in which—as most people are quite aware today—the Electoral College and not the popular vote dictates the winner. But the primary process is much more complicated, and *purposefully* so.

To put it bluntly: The nominating systems of both major parties in the United States of America are not designed by the people, for the people. Instead, they're systems designed by the few, to benefit the few. Specifically party leaders. And the last person these systems were built to benefit is an outsider—like Trump.

Lucky for him, he had a couple of friends and close advisors who recognized this particular blind spot. Political operative Roger Stone and billionaire real estate investor Tom Barrack were both trying to persuade Trump that he needed to hire an experienced political operative to help get him through the convention. And they both told him the best man for the job was none other than their friend, Paul Manafort.

I was Manafort's right-hand man at that point. A "junior partner" at Davis Manafort, one of five employees. I wasn't an equity partner in the firm. I mostly worked from an office in my home in Richmond, Virginia, while Paul did more of the traveling back and forth to Ukraine.

There was just one problem: despite Stone and Barrack's prodding, and Trump's apparent admiration of Paul's political skills, the man showed little to no interest in hiring Paul, or even taking a meeting with him initially. The media was salivating over the idea that the Republican National Convention was going to be a contested convention, but given Trump's success in January and February and his status as the growing front-runner, he thought he had it all under control. Trump was winning "more primaries than anyone." He already had "the best people" on his team. He was doing "unbelievable." He was "going to win," he told them.

Trump's optimism came crashing down in March.

Trump won the Louisiana primary on March 5, but a few days later, he read a headline that drove him crazy: more than half of the Louisiana delegates came out and publicly stated that despite his primary win, they would not vote for Trump at the convention.

Instead of meeting with Paul and discussing our research, instead of stepping back and trying to understand the process, Trump immediately went on the attack. He went on TV and chastised the RNC, saying they'd put together a "sham system." He tweeted that the party system was in "shambles" and that the Louisiana Republican Party executives were a bunch of "crooks."

He attacked first. And then he called Paul.

Paul agreed to fly down and meet Trump at Mar-a-Lago on March 25, the Thursday before Easter weekend. By that time, news was spreading that some of the delegates in states outside of Louisiana that Trump had handily won wouldn't support Trump at the convention either. Paul instructed me to pull together all of the research and other data I had gathered into a brief presentation, not only to show Trump how the delegate and nomination process worked, but more importantly to show Trump how the nomination could be stripped away from him. If Trump didn't protect his success, certain people within the Republican Party would use a contested convention to select *their* candidate instead of him.

By the time he met with Paul in March, Trump was basically *bleeding* delegates.

What Paul confirmed during his meeting at Mar-a-Lago is that prior to reading the headlines about the delegates in Louisiana, Trump had no idea that the primaries and convention could be stolen from him. He mistakenly believed that if he won a state with fifteen delegates, he won all fifteen delegates automatically. He thought that once he won a sufficient number of primaries, he would just go to the convention as a sort of formality. As if the convention was just a big show. A press opportunity. A political rally on a massive, nationally televised scale. A press conference to the world to announce he had "won."

He did not know that he would receive some delegate votes from the proportional states he'd lost, or that other candidates would receive delegate votes from the proportional states he had won. He didn't know that some states gave their delegates the right to change their votes at the convention itself. And no matter how Paul tried to explain that the RNC had a set of national rules governing the process, he couldn't seem to get Trump to understand that each state still had the flexibility to make their *own* rules and that in many cases it was the governors or other high-ranking political officials who chose the delegates and could therefore sway those votes as well.

He didn't know any of this because he had never spoken to anyone at the RNC. At this stage, he didn't have a relationship with the RNC, at all, and he told Paul more than once that he didn't care to.

Hearing the truth from Paul at that meeting, Trump's reaction wasn't that he wanted to get a handle on this mistaken perception or learn how to do better moving forward. His reaction was that the whole primary system was "rigged."

To Trump, the hundreds of years of precedent and protocols that had lent themselves to the creation of the primary process were a "problem" that he wanted "fixed."

Paul returned from Florida that night and told me to plan to join him in New York on Monday, right after Easter. "The meeting went very well," he said. He wasn't able to make our full presentation at Mar-a-Lago, but that single meeting with Paul convinced Trump that he needed to understand how this "rigged" primary system worked.

"He wants us on his team," Paul said. "*Here we go.*"

Early Monday morning, Paul and I flew separately to New York City and headed straight to Trump Tower. I had been inside the building a couple of times in the past, as a guest at political fundraisers for other candidates. But that only gave me access to the marble and gold-accented lobby area of Trump's infamous black skyscraper. I'd never been upstairs, to either the residences or to the office space, and I had never met Trump, even in passing at one of those events. However, Paul had met Trump on a number of occasions over the years. And coincidentally enough, he had an apartment at Trump Tower, and other partners in his firm had even done some lobbying work for Trump back in the early 1990s. He gave me a few pointers on the way in.

"I'm one of the few people who call him Donald, but most people call him Mr. Trump," he noted. "And he probably won't give us a lot of time. The meeting will be short."

We rode the elevator to the twenty-sixth floor, where a receptionist let us in through a set of glass doors. We entered the office space, where two more assistants sat at their desks and never got up as we walked right up to the open doorway to Trump's personal office. He was on the phone with someone. His longtime assistant Rhona Graff called out from her office next door, "He'll be with you in a minute!"

It was surprisingly informal, as was Trump's office itself. From our standing point outside, I could see that the view over Fifth Avenue and Central Park was impressive, but the office was strewn with papers. There were so many framed photographs and awards, many on the floor, leaning against walls instead of hung up since the walls were already full. His desk was toward the back of the office, near the window overlooking Central Park, and when he got off the phone Trump yelled, "Paul! Come on in."

Paul made a quick introduction. Trump's campaign manager, Corey Lewandowski, and his press director, Hope Hicks, were already in the room. Trump yelled to Rhona to bring him some papers he wanted us to see and then yelled to anyone listening outside, "Somebody bring me a Diet Coke!" All the yelling was just so New Yorkish. Only in New York do people yell for things. It's not rude, or angry, it's just a style of inter-office and even inter-family communication that is unlike anything that goes on in most other parts of the country.

Trump didn't bother with any small talk. He jumped right into talking about the delegates as if we were already in the middle of a conversation.

"It's a sham system! If you win a state, the delegates should be yours," he said as I opened my notebook and pulled out our detailed presentation on how it all worked. Paul only got about two minutes into taking them through it when the meeting stopped for Trump to take a phone call. He picked it up on the speakerbox on his desk, which looked like something out of the 1970s, on a cord. Like the speakerbox in *Charlie's Angels*, but with the speaker on top instead of on the side.

It was a business call.

I didn't know much of anything about his business dealings at the time, other than recognizing some of the real estate he owns, including the hotels and golf courses that bear his name. I had watched a few episodes of *The Apprentice* too, but who takes a call in the middle of a high-level political meeting?

When the call was over, Paul continued the presentation for another few minutes. Trump quickly seemed disinterested in the background and jumped in with a few questions about what could be *done* about the delegates. Paul said we could find ways to protect the delegates Trump won. He had done this many times in the past, through many presidential contests. Plus, Paul could organize a strategy for the rest of the primaries to help ensure that he would not only win the number of delegates needed to secure the nomination but do everything in his power to get them committed—so there were no "political games" at the convention itself.

Paul assured him that even if he went into a contested convention, he could handle things there as well. Sometimes delegates do not follow through on their commitment to support the candidate that won, but Paul was determined to prevent it. Trump already knew that Paul was one of the few political consultants alive and working today who had actually been through a contested convention before, the last one this country had ever seen: with Gerald Ford in 1976.

We weren't even a quarter of the way through the presentation yet, but that's when Trump cut us off.

"Great," he said. "Go make it happen."

He wasn't interested in hearing the rest of the details of our plan.

"Do it. Work with Corey, work it out," he said. "You guys get what you need and make sure we win the delegates."

The whole thing lasted less than fifteen minutes.

We said goodbye, and Corey Lewandowski took us down to the fifth-floor campaign headquarters. He told us on the way down that the space they were in formerly served as the production offices for *The Apprentice*, and as soon as we walked through the metal doors we realized the space was raw: concrete floors, open ceilings with exposed pipes and wires, no individual rooms, no real offices, no privacy. There were a couple of major areas marked out on the floor, one where campaign staff was sorting mail and correspondence, and another with plastic tables bearing taped signage on pieces of paper designating "Advance" or "Travel" or "Delegates."

Corey took us to a barely walled-in "office" in the back, with a desk for Paul, and a table for me. It was maybe twelve by six feet. When Corey stepped out for a moment, Paul told me the office space was not going to work. There was no way to have any private conversations with anyone. He decided then and there to work primarily from his apartment upstairs, even though it was difficult to get to. There is only one crossover floor between the residential and office sides of Trump Tower, on the twenty-fourth floor. Which meant lots of tedious up-and-down elevator rides with a wait in the middle. But at least his apartment was nice and would provide a haven away from the chaotic environment of the day-to-day campaign operations, he said.

Which meant I would be Paul's eyes and ears on the campaign floor, working from that makeshift headquarters while he dealt with high-level matters from upstairs.

I should mention that Paul joined the campaign as a volunteer. He was never placed on Trump's payroll. Neither was I.

It struck me as odd that the headquarters had very few landlines. Everybody was using personal cell phones and computers. Where were the call centers and the phone banks? And over the course of the first day, the oddness continued. Paul and I spoke to the "delegates" team and realized even *they* had no idea how the national convention worked. They were largely clueless and had no real plan to navigate through the process. The number of delegates they thought they had locked up were nowhere near "locked up" at all. And in talking with Corey, we realized that it was more than Trump who had failed to do any outreach or communication with the RNC since the campaign began; the campaign itself had done no liaising at all with the RNC. They hadn't connected to anyone on top, including RNC Chair Reince Priebus, or anyone below, either. Which meant they had little to no idea at all that the Republican Party establishment, as a whole, was backing Ted Cruz and eschewing Donald Trump, which would ultimately mean big trouble in the weeks and months ahead. If he wanted to win, and especially if he was serious about wanting to win the general election, he would need the RNC on his side.

Given the fact that Trump had started publicly bashing the RNC for its "rigged" system, it quickly settled in that we weren't just starting from the ground level on these things. We were starting from a ditch.

Generally, this is not the way you want to start a campaign. But if anyone was up for the challenge, it was Paul. When Paul came on board, his official title was "convention manager" and I was introduced as the deputy convention manager. On March 29, a press statement was released to make the announcement. Immediately the response from the press was positive: "Trump finally hires an expert," the talking heads said, referring to Paul as Trump's "first true campaign consultant." Paul was "seasoned," an "expert" at what he did. He was going to bring "structure" to an otherwise disorganized campaign effort. The media called him "one of the best," and Trump loved that. "Paul's a killer," he started saying, and he immediately began referring to Paul as "the greatest political consultant you could have on your team."

Late that evening Paul returned to his apartment upstairs, and I continued to work through the night. At this point, my belief was this would all be temporary. We were only hired to manage the convention, which was set for July 18-21 in Cleveland, Ohio, and I knew there was a possibility that our work would end whenever the Trump campaign came to a close. And from what I was looking at, despite Trump's wins so far and his rising poll numbers, a big part of me imagined that could come sooner rather than later.

I should point out here that initially I wasn't a Trump supporter.

It's not at all unusual for political operatives and staff members to not personally support the candidate with whom they wind up working. During primary season, when one candidate drops out, many of the staffers from that person's campaign often go find work at competing candidates' campaigns, and so forth. Everyone gets it. It's normal. So it surprised me when a number of my friends and colleagues got upset when they learned that I was working for Trump. Never had I experienced a situation in which so many people were angry at me for working on a political campaign. I expected that the 2016 election was going to be intense. A level of divisiveness had long marked the nature of major elections in our country, and the passions on either side had grown more and more heated since the 1990s. But I was not prepared for the rabid emotional feelings people had about the candidates this time around.

Friends came right out and told me that Trump "didn't stand a chance." Those were my *better* friends. Others were more abrasive and told me I would "never work in Washington, D.C.," or even in "politics" again, just because I was working for Trump. Some friends stopped talking to me altogether.

The reactions were unusually personal in a business that had become mostly *impersonal*.

Politics has become a business in which "the best people" are not willing to serve, or never get far enough to win. At the end of the day, we're all left with one of two people to choose from, and sometimes we make a choice not because we want to, but because we feel compelled to.

Honestly, I didn't agree with the way he bullied people, personally, on the national stage, and I didn't like some of the hurtful rhetoric he delivered, but I was impressed that Trump had managed to get as far as he had, and I liked the idea of a political outsider bringing change. No other politician had ever accomplished so much so quickly, and he had done it with no advertising budget whatsoever.

Later on, we did the math based on airtime and figured that Trump received around $5 billion of unpaid network and cable coverage during the primaries alone. Five *billion*! That is an astonishing amount of free advertising for a political election. It was hard for anyone to compete with that.

The more time I spent with him the more I got to see the person behind the camera. Despite the wave of emotions he evokes with his policies and his tweets, one observation stood out among all others: he loves his country. And I saw this as the driving force for the reason he was running in this race.

Still, it was all I could do to muster my personal support for *any* political candidate at that point in my life and career. I was tired of politics.

Like a lot of Americans, I was discouraged by witnessing too many years of government inaction. I was sick and tired of watching politicians say one thing on the campaign trail only to do something different, or worse, do nothing at all once they were in office. They routinely made promises they didn't keep, and in the end, the American people suffered for it.

For far too long I'd been telling myself, "This is my last foray into politics," and this time, I meant it: after my work on the Trump campaign ended, it would be time for me to go do something else. I wasn't sure what that something else would be, but I was convinced it was time to change careers.

I felt that if this didn't work out, or if Trump dropped out of the race the next week, it wouldn't matter much to me either way.

Even with all the ground he'd broken, and even with Paul's help—knowing that Paul really *was* the best, a political strategist like no other—I was not sure he had a shot at winning. Not because of him, but because the system would not allow for it. The rules of the game were just too well established. And historically speaking, in order to become president, you had to check off a long list of boxes.

First of all, you had to have political experience: a record of climbing the political ladder to a mayorship or a governorship, or serving in the House or Senate at the very least. You had to have an established record on and understanding of the issues—*all* of the big issues, from the economy to social issues to foreign policy. You had to have an effective political fundraising operation in place because presidential elections cost a fortune. You had to have a ground game, with offices and operatives in place in every state, and nearly every significant *region* of every state. And you had to have the backing of at least some of the party elite: the people who hold the reins of power in the process.

Trump checked none of those political boxes. Not a single box. But it was worse than that: on our third day in the office, Trump made an off-the-cuff remark in an interview with MSNBC, saying "there needs to be some form of punishment for women who have abortions."

How could someone who says things like this win? He was brash and aggressive, and some of the things he said were offensive to millions of people. But some of these statements were not offensive to millions of others. Despite the extreme nature of some of his statements, the fact that he spoke his mind was refreshing in politics, and it almost drove people to react in a way that showed them how they truly felt. He drew very clear lines, which made people decide if they were on one side or the other. And I could not believe that the establishment would ever get behind a guy who talked like this.

On the campaign trail, he'd already made divisive comments about immigrants, climate change, and healthcare. Not to mention the fact that he had a number of lingering allegations thrown at him about his treatment of women, and he'd been married three times. I kept thinking: *How is any of this going to win over a Republican Party that once sold itself as the party of "family values"? How could Trump ever expect to win over Evangelicals and Conservatives in the Midwest, or the South, or anywhere else?*

He'd even gone so far as to attack his Republican rivals in ways no candidate had ever attacked members of their own party. Ever. I remembered watching one of the first few Republican debates, where Ted Cruz, who was basically the front-runner among hardcore Conservatives, gave this long set of introductory remarks, talking about the issues and the serious changes he wanted to make, and when he was done, and it was Donald Trump's turn to speak, Trump just turned to Cruz and called him "Lyin' Ted!"

And it *worked*. Two words out of his mouth and he knocked Ted Cruz off his game. Poor Cruz couldn't shake it. The nickname stuck, and Trump kept hammering with it at every debate and every campaign rally from that moment forward.

He had an uncanny ability to attach biting nicknames to just about every one of his Republican rivals, and he used that tactic again and again. (Remember "low-energy" Jeb Bush?) No one in politics had ever *dared* to do something like this, and it was incredibly effective on TV. Surprisingly, viewers loved it. They were sick of politics as usual and Trump added some reality-TV-style drama to the proceedings. But inside the Beltway? Republican elites, the people who really control the party, couldn't *stand* Trump. Many made it clear, in public, early on, that they would *never* cast a vote for him, let alone throw their public support behind the man or encourage their constituents to vote for him. And that's important: in the history of presidential politics, no candidate has ever won without the support of Senators and House members (and more) whose endorsements bring voters to the polls in their home states.

Even setting all of that aside, a lot of Republicans didn't like him simply because Trump wasn't a lifelong Republican. It was well known by this point that he had registered as an Independent, and even a Democrat, at various times in his life. Just a few years earlier he had donated to Hillary Clinton's U.S. Senate campaign in his home state of New York. That kind of behavior and history wasn't going to fly with the "true" Republicans.

Stepping foot into Trump Tower did nothing to convince me he could win, either. His campaign staff simply wasn't experienced, starting at the top: Corey wasn't schooled in presidential politics and he had never worked on a presidential race. The biggest campaign he'd ever run was a primary race for U.S. Senator Bob Smith in New Hampshire—and they'd lost. He was one of only a handful of salaried people on the entire campaign staff, which was made up of mostly college-aged hourly workers who had never worked on a political campaign in their lives. They hadn't set up any state offices. They had no ground game. And the whole operation was unstructured and disorganized, right down to the most basic calendar items.

In the first few days, Paul and I realized that Trump hadn't properly registered for upcoming primaries in some of the remaining states. Every state has a different process, and many require in-person signatures from a candidate or his designate, meaning someone from the campaign, if not the candidate himself, has to physically go to the state and register. It was now April, and neither Trump nor his staff had managed to do that, in *numerous* states, and we were right up against the deadlines in most of them.

If he had missed those registration deadlines, his name would have been left off the ballots in those states—and that alone could have prevented him from winning the Republican nomination.

Paul and I started to work on it immediately and get it all sorted out. At the level of presidential politics, it is essential that a campaign team understands the nuances and intricacies of campaigning. Experience matters.

By the end of our first two weeks, Paul and I were mostly up to speed on where things stood. So we turned our attention to putting Trump's delegate house in order in preparation for the convention, which is what we were hired to do.

Then, on April 5, the Wisconsin primary happened.

Internally, everyone on Trump's team had assured him that he was going to win, and win big—and they were *wrong*. He got destroyed.

It was the most dramatic loss Trump had faced to date in the primaries, losing to Ted Cruz by 13 percent.

That's when Trump blew a gasket.

That night, he called Paul and told him he wanted him to get more involved in the overall state operations. Paul wasn't sure yet what that would entail because there were only a few people working on it. All he knew was that Trump was angry. He didn't want to face a surprise like that—or a loss like that—ever again.

Early the next morning Paul met with Trump at his residence. Trump was fuming over the headlines about losing Wisconsin. "They lied to me," he said. "My own team told me I would win. They lied to me. Can you believe it?" Paul gave me the rundown the moment he walked out, and his message to Paul was: "My team has no idea what they are doing." This was a pivotal moment, a fracture in the campaign, and Paul knew exactly how to fix it. In fact, he already had a plan mapped out.

As I boarded a plane for Iowa two days later for my first official campaign event, it all seemed like too much. Privately, Paul and I both had serious concerns about whether we could do what Trump needed us to do in such a short amount of time. If we couldn't? Trump was bound to get crushed by his own party at the convention. And even if he somehow managed to survive the coming Republican backlash and rebellion, would Trump and his team have what it took to go up against the gigantic power of the Clinton machine and the organizational prowess of the DNC in the general election?

In those first few days, there was one recurring thought that kept rattling around my head: *This is chaos.*

CHAPTER 2

Candidate Trump

The Outsider No One Expected

THE 2016 IOWA CAUCUSES TOOK PLACE ON FEBRUARY 1, NEARLY two months before Paul and I joined the Trump campaign, but they were still a thorn in Trump's side. He'd lost to Ted Cruz, and both Trump and then-candidate Ben Carson accused the Cruz campaign of "stealing" the caucuses by deceiving caucus-goers on the ground—telling them that Carson had dropped out of the race the night before the caucuses, when he hadn't, and other tactics that, if true, very well could have worked in this particularly unusual contest that kicks off every election season in earnest.

The media said Cruz won because he connected better with Iowa evangelicals and Conservatives. Personally, I would say that Trump's pulling out of the Republican debate on Fox News two nights before the Iowa caucus might have had more to do with Cruz's win than anything else. In politics, showing up is half the game. Which is why Paul dispatched me to go to Iowa in person as a representative for the Trump campaign at the Iowa Republican District Committee meetings on April 9. The committee meetings aren't something most Americans are aware of because they're mostly a formality. It's when the state formally picks its delegates to send to the Republican National Convention and when statewide candidates are chosen in other races outside of the presidential election. But the event offered an early opportunity for me to get a feel for voter intensity—to see how much passion Trump supporters had for their candidate, and whether they were coming out for him and willing to stand up for him, even in a situation where he hadn't initially won the caucuses earlier that year.

The meetings were set to unfold at four locations across the state, and I decided to check out the scene in Cedar Falls, where Senator Chuck Grassley was scheduled to speak as a cautious surrogate for Trump in front of an audience of hundreds of potential delegates at Northern Iowa University.

I arrived at the convention and was immediately taken by the scene, as hundreds of people milled about wearing shirts and buttons with candidates' names on them, dressed in red, white, and blue hats, and carrying little flags. These people were passionate about their involvement. Passionate about this process. It was refreshing to see people who wanted to make a difference.

I met up with some Trump supporters who had a table in the lobby, where they were handing out Trump bumper stickers, and no sooner did I introduce myself than people started coming over to talk to me. "We love him!" they said. "I'm so glad he's running." Disabled veterans, even a few people who identified themselves as lifelong Democrats, said, "He's real. He's authentic. He speaks his mind."

People said they wished he didn't use profanity but said they forgave him because he was so fed up at the government—and so were *they.*

I sat in meetings and briefings, and I listened to potential delegates make their two-minute speeches from the small stage, and I was floored by the passion they showed. They spoke about farming and protecting the Constitution. Almost every speech had God in it. Many spoke about the America we were leaving for our children and grandchildren. One lady opened with, "Obama changed my life." She then proceeded to attack just about every policy President Obama had enacted in the last eight years. She believed those policies hurt our country. These people had paid attention.

I went to lunch at a BBQ joint up the street and saw guys in Harley shirts talking about Trump, and how they couldn't wait to vote for him. But there were whole families there, all eating together and smiling, and so many people nodded and smiled and said hello to me—the only guy dressed in a suit in the whole place.

I called around to our team members at the other three locations, and they all had similar experiences. They saw lots of Trump supporters, and the enthusiasm was strong. These Iowans believed that Trump could make a difference in their lives. Not that it made a big difference that day. Cruz won the majority of the delegates at the district committee meetings— eleven of the twelve that go to the national convention. So Cruz walked away with a small victory. And in Iowa, the rules for the national convention stated that those delegates had no choice but to vote just the same as the people of Iowa had voted—at least for the first round of voting. If there was a second round? Anything goes. And the support we saw on the ground that day could sure come in handy if anyone tried to push Trump out at the national convention.

I didn't get back to the hotel until after 9:00 p.m., and I still had work to do. I'd been put in charge of keeping the master schedule for Trump's activities, and I was firming up plans for a series of campaign rallies in the week ahead. After getting Trump's personal schedule from Rhona, it was my task to make sure everything was set. Paul tried to get Trump to set a monthly calendar, or more, but he wouldn't do it. The furthest out we could schedule anything was a week, and most of the time he preferred not to book events more than forty-eight hours in advance. Even big events. Which meant we were always scrambling, always adjusting, always dealing with issues at the very last minute.

I barely blinked and I was back in New York boarding the private jumbo jet, aptly nicknamed Trump Force One, to fly with him to my first Trump campaign rally, in Pittsburgh, Pennsylvania. It was the first of a series of near-daily rallies that wouldn't stop for the whole month of April and beyond. And what I learned in an instant, the moment we touched down, was that the "voter intensity" I'd glimpsed in Iowa, even the Trump support I'd seen born out on TV and in primary results so far, barely scratched the surface of a volcano of support that was building under the surface.

These weren't campaign rallies. They were rock concerts. It was like nothing I'd ever seen before. I'd attended political rallies for George W. Bush at the height of his popularity, and Mitt Romney at his peak in the past, and they were *nothing* like this. People had lined up for six hours just waiting to see him. There were overflow areas in the arenas, and even the overflow areas were packed. We're talking five thousand people, growing to ten thousand people as the campaign went on, and even upwards toward thirty thousand by the time we were finished.

Trump had already fallen into a pattern when it came to rallies, and Paul and I worked to solidify the pattern into a solid, predictable routine—one of the few predictable, routine things we would encounter during the entire campaign.

First of all, Trump largely refused to stay in hotels. That meant we flew back to New York City after every rally, no matter where it was, so he could sleep in Trump Tower.

His rallies were almost always held in the afternoons. And the routine included a pretty basic format: He'd fly in, motorcade to the rally site, and wait in a holding room, signing a few photos or other memorabilia for certain dignitaries or donors or friends of the organizers—but not many, and not in person with them. While he waited, a surrogate would fire up the crowd. It might be General Michael Flynn talking about Trump's tough stance on eliminating ISIS, or Rudy Giuliani, or Newt Gingrich, or sometimes early on in the campaign his speechwriter Stephen Miller would take on the task. Whoever it was, their one task was to talk red meat issues and get the crowd on their feet—so Trump walked out to a standing ovation.

At some rallies during the campaign, I was tasked with walking out ahead of him, making sure the microphone was adjusted to the correct height and everything was ready to go. The blue backdrop was in place—the exact Pantone shade of blue that Trump picked out and insisted upon—with a series of American flags in front of it. That was it. No video screens or fancy backdrops. Just blue cloth and flags. The microphone was a single mic, not the traditional double-gooseneck mics you see at most political speeches. That was also at Trump's insistence. The lighting was just so. The media was the correct distance from the stage. He oversaw every bit of minutia when it came to the optics of the rallies, and the only thing that really ticked him off was that CNN and other "mainstream" television networks refused to ever turn the cameras around and show the full size of the crowd. Trump was convinced it was because his rallies dwarfed the turnout at Hillary Clinton's rallies, and the mainstream media was on her side. He called them out on it. Publicly. Which made the crowds go wild and get angry at the media too.

He called out the RNC as well, telling these gathered crowds that the Republican primary system was "rigged," and how together they were going to change things. His message was, "The Republican Party has done nothing for you, and nothing for me. We're going to win big, we're going to change Republicans, we're going to change Washington, we're going to change the entire system!" And the crowds ate it up. They were as fed up with the political process as I was, with the added fire of feeling like they'd been cut out of the whole process for far too long. The message even resonated with Democrats, and especially Independents, who saw Bernie Sanders getting forced out of the process on the DNC side of things, while the media refused to show the size of his crowds, either. So the people were angry, on *all* sides.

Later on in the campaign, a Reuters/Ipsos poll showed more than half of Americans believed the primary process was "rigged." It didn't hurt that Bernie Sanders picked up the same mantra on the Dem side. But it was one example of how Trump's repeated messaging and simple "branding" of subjects could almost single-handedly sway beliefs, nationwide.

So many Americans felt that no one was speaking to them, or to their issues. And now? Here was Trump. Talking directly to them while bashing the media, crushing the politicians, and verbally destroying anybody else who'd been standing between them and the way they ought to be treated in the America they loved.

I was stunned to witness the visceral anger on the faces of the people in these crowds. They were angry at politicians who said they were going to do things but never did them, and the wasteful spending in Washington, and how useless Congress had become—this mostly geriatric group of lifetime politicians who, collectively, had even lower approval ratings than the president. (Congress's approval rating under Paul Ryan hovered at a dismal 13 percent.) That anger gave them a level of voter intensity I had never witnessed in my political life. An intensity that I started to believe would push them to get to the polls and vote, whether or not they had ever voted in an election in their lives.

The proof? As part of the admission process to every rally, our campaign collected voter data—names, email addresses, and cell phone numbers—and by the end of May, our campaign had accumulated a list of almost four million potential voters that the RNC didn't have on their rolls. Four million voters, many of whom had never voted, some of whom hadn't voted in years, many of whom were registered Independents, and some of whom were Democrats ready to flip to the other side specifically because of what they saw in and heard from Donald Trump.

Over the course of the campaign, the RNC *begged* us for that list. They swore that by sharing the list, they could help us. But Trump and our campaign refused. He wasn't about to betray his potential voters like that. Not when he was at war with the system itself, and those voters were his soldiers.

The way these rallies unfolded threw the Democrats for a loop as well. Even the seasoned Clinton team didn't know how to counter the effects of these rallies, or the media coverage of these rallies, because they'd never seen anything like them. They also couldn't predict what was going to happen, because we planned these events so last minute, all the time. They couldn't get ahead of us.

At the first few rallies, I assumed people might get tired of listening to Trump after two hours. I was wrong. I thought, just as any political operative might think, that flying in and out of rally locations across the country on a daily basis would be far too much for any candidate to handle. He might get exhausted. But that never happened, either. In the end, the rallies were what gave Trump his energy. It was the only real factor in the campaign that I ever got the sense was something he wanted to do, and actually *loved* to do. He soaked up the energy and adulation.

For all of the organization and routine that went into the staging of the rallies, once Trump was on stage, we never knew if he would stay up there for thirty minutes or three hours. And we also had no idea what he was going to say. Ever. Sure there was a boilerplate speech and some talking points. He knew it. He'd studied it. But I quickly learned that he prepared most of his speeches on the plane on the way to whatever rally he was going to, and he finished them up in the car on the way from the airport to the venue. He gathered his talking points from watching TV on the plane too, simply by watching whatever they were talking about on the news, not only on Fox News (his go-to information source, for sure) but on CNN and MSNBC as well. As much as he said he didn't watch those networks, he actually watched them all the time. He would flip between them. He wanted to know what they were all talking about. But Fox was the one he focused on for important issues.

When we tried to give him specific talking points for the regions where his rallies were held, it didn't go so well. I quickly learned that Trump wouldn't focus on any written document that was more than a half page in length. He preferred to see no written documents at all. He wanted to talk, engage, ask people their opinions. This is the way he absorbed information. And once he felt he had a message to deliver, he got up on stage or in front of a camera and delivered it. And from that point forward, in his mind, whatever he said was fact. Even if he wasn't correct.

It was clear that he could do these rallies *endlessly*.

Paul and I tried setting him up with a few small but important meetings with potential donors and some members of an evangelical group at Trump Tower in our first couple of weeks, and in those small group settings we could physically see him get cooped up, turned off, tired, anxious, and ready to walk out after just a few minutes. But at the rallies? He was *himself*. No matter what spin the media put on it, no matter how much juggling we had to do to try to explain something after he said it, it was worth it. Once we saw the reaction from the crowd, we knew it was a net positive.

Pretty soon, we stopped fighting him on it because there wasn't any point.

His way of talking was *winning*.

By April 10, according to all of the major polls and all of the primary results so far, Trump had become the clear front-runner for the Republican nomination.

Paul was a Republican Party guy. He believed strongly that Trump would absolutely need that party to be on his side in order to win the general election, and he took it upon himself to act as a bridge between them. Paul was thinking that far in advance. This wasn't just about winning over the people at the rallies or in the primaries. It wasn't just about securing delegates at the national convention. It was about beating Hillary Clinton.

Behind the scenes, Paul was making plans to build that bridge.

Trump however still had no interest in the party establishment. The people he respected were law enforcement, veterans, and first responders. And at the rallies, that meant he would only leave after he shook the hands of law enforcement and military personnel who had come out to protect him that day.

We could hardly ever get him to shake a governor's hand, or the hand of a Republican donor. But police officers? Veterans? He would stop and shake the hand of every law enforcement officer and veteran he encountered from the time he left the podium to the time he boarded the plane. Whether it was in the hallway of the arena, or in the motorcade, or at the airport, he talked to nearly every one of them.

At one of our rallies in Florida, more than a hundred motorcycle cops showed up to lead Trump from the airport to the arena. These weren't mandated motorcades. These officers were volunteering their time to show up off duty but in uniform to participate. And Trump shook their hands and spoke to them. All of them. There were times when the campaign would lose him to the law enforcement handshaking for an hour, in the middle of an incredibly busy schedule. It drove me nuts at first, but it was the way it was going to work. It was the way *he* wanted it to work. And after a while, it became clear to me that we weren't really "losing" anything.

This was Trump talking directly to the people. His people. His audience. And that audience was growing in the most grassroots way possible— person to person. It was different than any other "grassroots" campaign in history, of course. But it really was sort of grassroots and personal in its own uniquely Trumpian way.

As was well known by this point, Trump ran his own Twitter account too, where he spoke directly to his then-thirty-five million followers. (He has eighty million now.) The power of that is unfathomable—and completely unprecedented.

There has never been a politician whose social media wasn't controlled by his or her campaign staff. In other campaigns, anything a candidate wants to be posted is first cleared by others in his or her organization. Most politicians don't want anything to do with social media. It's too overwhelming, too risky, too easy to make a mistake.

With Trump? If we wanted something posted on his Twitter account, we had to clear it with *him*. And unless he asked for input, nothing he ever posted was vetted, proofread, or cleared by anyone on his team.

One of the first things anybody who joined the campaign (including Paul and me) wanted to do was to try to control what he put on Twitter, because it mattered. And every one of us failed. Trump saw it as the one part of the campaign where, as he said, "I don't need anybody." He loved that he could communicate directly to his followers and say whatever he wanted to say, however he wanted to say it. He insisted on no interference from anybody.

To protect the candidate and the campaign, Social Media Director Dan Scavino put a system in place to receive a copy of his tweets and an alert as soon as one was sent so we would know instantly what Trump had said. But it only helped us marginally since even in the space of a few seconds Trump's tweets went global, leaving us little time to react, much less change the message. On multiple occasions, this led to 2:00 a.m. "Oh *?&@! We've got a problem" calls from Dan.

Trump would occasionally have other people write his tweets. He would dictate them to Hope or me or whoever was in earshot. But then he absolutely reviewed them before he posted them himself. And if you suspect that you can tell which ones he writes vs. which ones somebody else has written, you're correct. It's easy to tell. But what moved the needle, both on Twitter and in person, was when he challenged people, when he took them on, when he said something directly from his voice.

Like the day in April when he stood at a press conference at Trump Tower and said, "Frankly, if Hillary Clinton were a man, I don't think she'd get 5 percent of the vote. The only thing she's got going is the women's card. And the beautiful thing is, women don't like her."

On a subject most candidates would readily avoid, he opened up the "woman card" like he was opening up a letter bomb. That brought all kinds of hateful comments from the Left, and from women's groups, and from a slew of celebrities, including Rosie O'Donnell—Trump's old nemesis, whom he sparred with all over the media in the mid-2000s, calling her "my nice, fat little Rosie" in an article on People.com, and threatening to sue her over some comments she made about him and his businesses on the talk show *The View*. Trump *loved* the controversy. He ate it up. It kept people talking about him for weeks on end back then, and it keeps people talking about him for weeks on end now. Same strategy, same players, only raised into this new arena where his political opponents never seemed to know what to do in response.

His audiences devoured it. In the history of presidents and candidates, almost everything has been scripted. The rule, especially in campaigns, is always: the message drives the candidate.

Trump was the first person in three decades, maybe longer, that actually drove the message himself. Even Reagan was scripted, to a large extent, when compared with Trump. They *all* are.

Being careful and strategic, thinking about timing, following a plan, staying on message—all the sorts of things that most people cared about in terms of running for president, Trump ignored. He didn't care about those things at all. Reagan, Obama, Bush, Clinton—any candidate in the past spent all sorts of time learning about foreign policy and other issues; he didn't do any of that. Connecting to the people was what was going to get him the win.

He played the traditional media game better than any of them too.

In a traditional campaign, the campaign manager and communications director would do everything in their power to keep 90 percent of the press at bay, at all times, while putting the candidate directly in touch with the 10 percent of the press that they considered friendly. With Trump, it was the polar opposite approach.

From the day I came aboard, I noticed that Trump almost never said no to reporters' requests. He had reporters calling him directly. He had reporters calling Rhona, who would shout over to him to let him know, and he'd shout back, "Put him through!"

Some reporters would call his longtime security guard, Keith Schiller, and thankfully he'd run most of those requests by us before bringing them to Trump—at least when they had something to do with the campaign. But most would just go ahead and call his political press coordinator Hope Hicks because Hope would bring him all of the requests she received.

And the way Trump handled the press was remarkable to watch. He famously called out reporters by name, lashing out at them when they wrote things he didn't like. And yet, even the press that Trump lashed out at, if they called back for an interview on another story the next week, Trump would pick up the phone and speak with them directly. He played the media game on a personal level unlike anything I'd ever seen.

Honestly, after going to Iowa, after attending his rallies, after watching the way the press breathlessly covered his every move and reported his every word, and every tweet, I started to question my assumptions about what winning the Republican nomination might take—and whether, at this juncture in our nation's political history, this completely unorthodox, chaotic approach to running a campaign might in fact be a strength instead of the weakness I'd assumed it was in the beginning.

After a couple of weeks in the Trump universe, and especially after witnessing the enthusiasm of his crowds up close, I started to fully believe that the answer to whether Trump could pull this off was a resounding "Yes."

CHAPTER 3

The Political Party Battle

Trump vs. the Republican Establishment

W HILE TRUMP WAS EMBRACING HIS RALLIES, PAUL WAS WORK-
ing behind the scenes to secure delegates—a task that often
involved meeting delegates and key Republicans to convince them to support Trump based on a range of issues. And as part of
that effort, he asked me to put together a PowerPoint presentation on
the subject of "Why Donald Trump Can Win." He specifically planned
to make that presentation to the annual meeting of the RNC, in Florida,
in late April.

Paul knew lots of people at the RNC. They had concerns. They flat
out said they could never support Trump.

Paul had encountered this kind of resistance before, in countries
around the world. He knew what to do. He quickly put a long-term strategy together—one which, if Donald Trump followed his lead, could get
the Republican establishment on board, and in his corner.

In the PowerPoint, we showed how Trump was tackling long-ignored
issues on the economy, as a business leader who had gone through bank-
ruptcy and faced the sort of hard decision-making that Obama and the
Clintons and even the Bushes had never encountered. We showed how

he was self-financing his campaign, and not taking money from special interests, and paying attention to budgets, noting that Trump always hand-signed all the paychecks for the people on his staff. I witnessed him doing this in his office while we were having one of our earliest campaign meetings. Signing every check, one by one.

Paul showed how Trump talked aggressively when it came to immigration in public, but stated that his private stance was more pragmatic: He had no problem with legal entry, with people earning their citizenship and staying, but he felt that America had a set of laws, and those laws needed to be obeyed. We left out the fact that while illegal immigration was one of Trump's signature issues, something he was vowing to eradicate, he didn't have a major plan to do so other than building the wall, and he actually had little idea of the bureaucracy of what building such a wall would entail. Instead, we showed them how we ran some quick polls in Arizona, Texas, and New Mexico and found that even people who were offended by the way Trump spoke about the issue were very much supportive of Trump's stance when we put it in context of "What if illegal immigration results in increased healthcare costs for you and your family?" or "What if illegal immigration costs you a job, because illegal immigrants are being paid under the table?"

We showed poll numbers that indicated just how strongly his anti-Obamacare healthcare platform was resonating with voters, despite their misgivings about possibly losing certain positive parameters of the Obamacare legislation, like putting an end to insurance companies denying coverage for those with preexisting conditions.

The overall point of Paul's presentation was to show that while Trump was all bluster on stage and on screen, his message was resonating with voters and winning him votes—and that after the convention, Trump would "pivot."

This is what great candidates often do. They go Far Right or Far Left in the primaries, and once they get the nomination, they pivot on certain issues to appeal to a wider swath of voters.

There was just one problem with that: Paul hadn't yet spoken to Trump about this "pivot" plan at all.

The RNC as a whole was receptive to Paul's presentation. Paul came back feeling great. He'd made inroads. He was building the much-needed bridge with the party.

But no sooner did Paul brief Trump on how well the meeting went than Trump turned on him. "I hate the word 'pivot,'" Trump said. He went on and on about how he didn't believe in pivoting, and it was nothing but a political screw word. He hated the whole idea that politicians would "say something and not mean it." He associated the word "pivot" with the worst of what politics was all about and wanted nothing to do with it. He wasn't going to soften his stance or rhetoric on immigration. He wasn't going to stop attacking Obamacare. He wasn't going to change. And most importantly, he said to Paul, "Don't ever speak for me. Nobody speaks for me but me."

It was the first chink in Paul's armor.

Paul is a man who single-handedly led Ukraine's Viktor Yanukovych from a 13 percent approval rating in 2005 to winning him the presidency in 2010, against all odds, against all sorts of internal opposition, by strategizing just the way he was strategizing now for Donald Trump. The fact that Trump was already rejecting a part of Paul's long-term strategy was a problem. At the time, we thought it was more of a problem for Trump than for us, but it was a problem, nonetheless.

It became clear in that one moment that Paul wasn't going to have constant and direct input into Trump's messaging. That was something new to him

Paul understood that Trump was creating his own messaging and understood how well it had worked for him so far. But what about going forward? Paul was concerned about the topics Trump hadn't thought about, that he would surely need to address over the course of the campaign—including foreign policy.

The only foreign policy issues he had addressed were destroying ISIS, improving America's "lousy" deals with China (using tariffs), and the truly obscure issue of taking money back from the UN and NATO—an issue no one was talking about or cared about before Trump started obsessively bringing it up at nearly every campaign rally.

He was right: the U.S. was piling more money than other countries into those organizations, and other countries weren't ponying up their fair share. But it was nothing anyone was focused on. Yet, the more he talked about it, the more it started showing up in polls as an issue Americans wanted to see fixed; just another example of the federal government wasting our precious tax dollars. Once again, Trump turned something into an important issue, single-handedly, just by talking about it again and again.

As long as the cameras were pointed at him, he controlled the narrative.

But how would he ever manage to stand up to former senator and secretary of state Hillary Clinton in a presidential debate in the fall when he had no handle on any other foreign policy issues at all? Paul was right to worry about that, and he was thinking that far ahead.

Paul needed help.

He needed to understand how to get Donald Trump's ear when it truly mattered, and get him to pay attention to things he might not want to pay attention to. Otherwise, Paul thought, this campaign was going to fail.

He'd learned the hard way that reason didn't matter, experience didn't matter, and even bringing Trump positive news didn't matter if it was something Trump didn't care about—and he did not care about making friends at the RNC.

The only people who seemed capable of getting his attention and influencing his decision-making process better than any of us were his closest allies, his most-trusted sources: his family. But there was one small issue. Ivanka, Don Jr., and Eric—who all worked right there on the twenty-fifth floor of Trump Tower, one floor beneath their father—had told us they weren't really interested in being involved in the campaign at that moment. In fairness, they were involved in their businesses and had young families of their own.

Even before he met with the RNC in Florida, Paul had made up his mind that it was time to get them involved. He asked them to come together for weekly meetings on Monday mornings, to discuss issues and share some insight into their own thoughts on their dad's campaign.

By the time Trump became the clear front-runner on April 10, setting those meetings became easy to do. In fact, Ivanka's husband, Jared

Kushner, made his presence known as well. He was still working out of his family skyscraper at 666 Sixth Avenue and never wanted to take a campaign email address—but he wanted to be a part of this. He wanted to come to those meetings, and he started joining us on Trump's plane when we went to rallies.

The first time we met on the plane, Trump said, "That's Jared. That's my son-in-law. I could've had Tom Brady as my son-in-law, but I got Jared."

Jared had clearly heard that joke about a thousand times, but Trump never got tired of telling it.

Jared was a shrewd businessman. But the fact that he ran a real estate empire, and the fact that he owned the iconic *New York Observer* newspaper on Long Island, didn't preclude him from openly admitting that he knew little about running a political campaign. Unlike some of the other players in the Trump universe, though, Jared spent hours doing research, listening to experts, taking other people's opinions, and piecing it all together. He was a quick study. Actually, I give Jared and Trump's kids a lot of credit, because they all admitted they didn't know what they didn't know. Most people in politics don't do that. Politicians usually try to say they know more than they know.

Paul got along with Jared well until his departure, and Jared liked strategy, so he respected Paul and his approach to the early stages of the campaign. They formed a good bond early on. Paul saw the value of Jared becoming more and more involved, even though he wasn't viewed as a "true" Republican and didn't typically travel in those circles.

However, in one early strategy meeting, Jared made his alignment with Trump perfectly clear: "We need to get away from the party and go to the people," he said to Paul and me. "Screw the party. Let's keep going directly to the people."

And later in the month, when Trump was confronted with some negative polling data during another meeting that Jared attended, Jared knew just what to do. Trump was angry. He started lashing out: "The polls are bogus. They're rigged. More Dems are interviewed than Republicans so of course they're not going to show in my favor."

"Political consultants are worthless," he continued. "Can somebody please tell me why I need all these political consultants? I think I will fire them all."

We were sitting right there!

"Donald," Jared said, glancing at Ivanka, Don Jr., and Eric, "Four of us you *can't* fire."

Paul and I held back our shock at Jared's response. But it was clear that Jared and Ivanka were very good at knowing how Trump operated, and there was an absolute trust with family regardless. That was a strength we wanted to tap into, and which we both also recognized might be his Achilles' heel if any of them were to make bad decisions down the road. But in this case, Jared knew exactly what to do and how to do it.

Instead of continuing to erupt, Trump said, "Yeah, yeah. These polls are useless," and we moved on.

That one disarming, familial comment made Trump nod his head and move on from what might have resulted in the rash firing of me, or Paul, or our new political pollster, Tony Fabrizio. Maybe *all of us.*

On a side note, Paul suggested bringing Tony Fabrizio in. He's a top-notch pollster, one of the best in the business, and Paul used him for polling projects around the world, but when Paul first brought up his name, Trump went apoplectic. He went to unusual lengths to describe how much he hated pollsters, and especially Fabrizio, he said. He didn't want anything to do with the guy. I was surprised he even knew who he was, and I backed off until I learned why Trump was opposed to him joining the team: back in 2013, when Trump was flirting with the idea of running for governor of New York against Andrew Cuomo, Trump called Fabrizio—and Fabrizio never called him back.

Three years later, Trump was still steamed by one unreturned phone call.

That was a lesson I tucked away for later: *When he takes something personally, Trump never forgets.*

He does forgive, though. When we pressed upon him that Tony really was the best guy for the job, Trump relented. And clearly he's been okay with that decision. Fabrizio is still working for Trump as of the writing of this book.

What Fabrizio's polling showed us was exactly why Trump was winning.

Trump's opponents kept assuming that he could "never" win because he didn't act like a president, or speak like a president.

They completely missed the reality of what was happening: candidate Trump was winning specifically *because* he didn't act like a president, and because he didn't speak like past presidents always *had*. According to our polling data, the fact that he said what he wanted to say, no matter how outrageous it might seem, made him "authentic" in the eyes of voters. And in 2016, authenticity *mattered*.

One of Trump's favorite songs to play at his rallies (and which he personally selected for his inauguration) was Paul Anka's "My Way," a song popularized and frequently sung by Frank Sinatra.

It was the perfect choice for Trump because it pretty much summed up the theme of his entire campaign, and maybe his entire style of leadership.

"My Way."

Where most political candidates in the history of politics have adapted to the way things are supposed to be done, adapted to the expected norms and protocols of the systems that were already in place, adapted to the expertise of their campaign managers and the parade of top-notch political advisors and experts at their fingertips, in Trump's case, none of that applied. Within the first few weeks of our employment, it became very clear to Paul and me that we were *never* going to get Donald Trump to adapt to us, because Donald Trump doesn't adapt to, or for, anyone.

Which meant that we would have no choice but to learn to adapt to *him*.

★　★　★

I can understand why an outsider looking at the chaos that kept unfolding around Trump during the month of April might've thought, "There's no way this guy's going to make it."

Republican candidates have always struggled with the archaic party process, just as Dems do with the DNC party procedures, but there has always been a belief that everybody in the race will eventually play nice and do what politicians do: smile for the cameras and do their backstabbing behind closed doors. With Trump, his every gripe was thrown right out in the open, shared with the people at rallies and on TV, and it left the Republican Party reeling. They didn't know how to deal with him, how to quantify him, how to make sense of whether or not he really meant what he said when he attacked his own political party.

Trump's way of handling things so publicly meant he wasn't just fighting against his fellow candidates; he was fighting battles on all fronts. He was battling the party, Ted Cruz, and John Kasich, as well as the media, *and* the system, *and* the Democrats, including both Hillary and Bernie at this point—and he was doing it all at once.

He was also battling his own personal history.

While no one could attack him on policy issues, since he wasn't a politician and therefore had no record, his biggest vulnerability was on the personal front. And after he raised the "woman card" in late April, we started getting calls from reporters who were fielding reports of Trump's alleged history of harassment of women.

We kept track of them and brought every allegation to Trump directly, and we hoped—as any campaign would—that none of the alleged claims or stories would rise to a level of seriousness that would derail the campaign. By the time the campaign ended, we would tally a total of forty-five women in Trump's past who claimed he'd crossed a line. He denied all of their allegations, and we took him at his word. These types of personal attacks, which have been a part of politics for two centuries, are often untrue, and so in the political arena they are viewed with skepticism until there is verifiable proof, unless of course a candidate confesses. In this case, neither of those things happened. In order to do our jobs, we simply had to set it aside, and move forward.

Around all the chaos, Paul was doing his best to look ahead and strategize for the long-term. He was already pursuing the idea of who might serve as a strong running mate to Trump should he receive the Republican nomination, and one of the earliest names he floated was the one he truly thought would do Trump the most good: Indiana Governor Mike Pence.

Pence was a strong Conservative from the Midwest, a man who could help stabilize the bridge Paul was trying to build between Trump and the rest of the Republican Party. Plus, Paul believed a boost in the Midwest was exactly what Trump would need to secure key parts of the Republican base and push him over the top in terms of electoral votes come November.

Trump didn't have much of an opinion about Pence at first. He didn't know Pence. He didn't really know *many* politicians. In April he was still so caught up in the primary fight that he didn't pay attention to anything Paul tried to share with him about Pence, either, until he saw the news on TV one day that Pence was 10 percentage points behind in his polls for reelection for governor.

"Why would I want a guy like that to be my VP?" Trump asked out loud on his plane, as we flew to yet another rally. "He's losing!"

Paul had his work cut out for him.

So did the rest of us.

On April 16, as we were heading to Pennsylvania for a rally, Trump was rifling through a cardboard box of papers he carried on the plane every trip. For a man that could have had any briefcase he wanted, he carried all of his important papers in a simple beaten-up box. He caught a segment on Fox News about Hillary Clinton and her "lack of character." I do not know if he came up with it on the spot or if he had been mulling it over for a few days, but at a rally that afternoon, he rattled off a brand-new nickname for his presumptive Democrat rival in the upcoming general election: "Crooked Hillary."

He said it once, and the crowd cheered wildly. He started using it in tweets—more than a dozen in the course of the next week. The nickname could have applied to any number of scandals Clinton had been involved in, going back years, including Benghazi. But Trump attached it to the latest investigation into a private server Hillary Clinton used for State Department business. It was tied to an investigation that began way back in 2014 and which was still hyped on a daily basis on Fox News—because Hillary had failed to turn over somewhere between thirty-one thousand and thirty-three thousand supposedly "personal" emails to investigators, and as time went on, it had become clear that those emails were not just held back. They'd been erased. Wiped clean. The emails were scrubbed from her server using "BleachBit" and even the FBI's forensic computer experts were unable to dig them up.

To call his opponent "crooked" was seen as crossing an unspoken line, of Trump hitting below the belt in presidential politics. The media and plenty of his fellow Republicans hit Trump hard over that nickname. And yet, none of this controversy slowed him down. In fact, the more controversy and chaos he created, the more the press kept saying his name on TV, every minute of every day. And every bit of that coverage and discussion, whether for or against him, helped to amplify the enthusiasm of his supporters.

On April 26, Trump swept the Acela primaries—nicknamed "Acela" because they cover multiple states in the Northeast that are accessed by the Amtrak train of the same name—winning five out of five states, and essentially clinching the Republican nomination. There was no path for Ted Cruz to reach the 1,237 delegates he needed going forward. But that still wasn't enough to force Ted Cruz to drop out of the race. If Cruz won Indiana on May 3, he could perhaps gain enough delegates to take Trump into a contested convention in July. Cruz vowed to fight on, even though he was hanging on by a thread. So did Ohio Governor Kasich— not because he had a shot at the nomination, since he ran a distant third in all of those contests, but maybe out of a personal vendetta, or just to be a thorn in Trump's side.

Part of Trump's victory that day was specifically attributable to Paul's strategic approach and planning. In Pennsylvania in particular, Paul worked to have ballot cards printed with the Trump campaign logo and banner, listing the names of delegates we knew supported Trump. Our team handed those cards out to voters going into the polling stations. In a state in which the voters actually choose the specific names of the delegates to send to the convention, Paul arranged for the delegates themselves to be hand-selected by our campaign—a list of solid Trump supporters who would be listed first on our ballot cards. This meant that those delegates were more likely to get chosen by voters at the voting locations, simply because they were identified Trump supporters.

And it worked brilliantly.

In a complex primary system, it's this sort of attention to small details that can help a candidate win big. And without a longtime expert like Paul in the mix, Trump likely would not have swept that day. If even a few of the chosen Pennsylvania delegates had gone the other way and pledged their support to Cruz or Kasich, it would have made it that much harder for Trump to secure the nomination, and it wouldn't have provided any security in a second round of delegate voting should Trump go into a contested national convention come July.

For all intents and purposes, Trump became the presumptive nominee on that day. But there was too much risk in announcing such a thing until his opponents dropped out of the race. Jumping the gun could have persuaded voters in upcoming states to vote against him, just to have their voices heard, and that would have all but ensured that he would face a contested convention. Trump didn't come out and announce his victory quite yet. He listened to Paul and Jared and understood that there was just too much at stake.

At the same time, during the lead-up to the Acela primary, Paul and I worked with Jared behind the scenes to arrange for Trump to make his first major speech in Washington. Not a speech to the public, but to senators, House members, and select invitees from various corners of the Republican Party.

Just like Paul's April trip to the RNC gathering in Florida, this trip was for one purpose: to prove to doubters inside the Beltway that Trump not only had what it took to win in November, but that he had what it took to lead the party, and to lead this country, as president of the United States.

We debated extensively over which policy area to focus on in this speech, and we all agreed that the biggest missing piece so far in Trump's campaign platform was foreign policy. Which got us thinking: If he could deliver a speech on foreign policy that dealt with a long list of serious issues beyond his three tried-and-true topics—ISIS, the budgets for the UN and NATO, and his desire to go after China on trade—it would go a long way toward building a bridge with the Washington elites who, for the most part, were still decidedly anti-Trump.

Had it not been for Jared's influence, I'm pretty sure Trump would have treated this speech like any other: he'd have gone in and winged it without much preparation after reading a half page of notes on the subject at hand. But Jared and Ivanka impressed upon Trump how important this was, how serious it had to be, how different this audience was than an audience full of his die-hard supporters. He also insisted that Trump should use a teleprompter as a way to make sure his message was clear, concise, and impressive to the people in the room, most of whom were experts on foreign policy themselves.

To our surprise, Trump listened—and agreed.

As for the content of Trump's first foreign policy speech, Trump largely left that to the campaign in the initial stages. The speech fell first to Trump's policy director and speechwriter, Stephen Miller, along with Jared, Paul, and me. It was an important speech, and we knew it would be used to define Trump moving forward in the campaign.

I always called Stephen "The Silent Assassin." He was easily the most surgical guy in the group, someone who stayed in his lane and knew that his most important audience was Trump himself. Jared liked him because he was a good writer, and Trump liked him because he thought overall Stephen captured his voice accurately and authentically. And while Stephen was a super ideological guy, he rarely talked publicly about his policy ideas. Instead, he would slip ideas into Trump's speeches now and then, especially about his hardline stance on immigration, which Trump would wind up following very closely because he felt the same way.

It wasn't what typically happened in a presidential campaign. In most campaigns, a foreign policy advisory team of a dozen or more experts in the field would assemble to discuss every stance, every speech, every move a candidate made. Corey Lewandowski had pulled together a haphazard advisory team for Trump early on, of which Jeff Sessions was by far the most seasoned expert on the panel, but Trump never considered them serious players. Paul would work to pull together a true foreign policy advisory panel later on—but for now, we were pretty much it.

We specifically arranged the event so there would be no Q&A after he made the speech. Our fear was there might be a moment of some-one asking him, "What's the name of the president of such-and-such country?" A question that, if he blundered it, could turn into a major disaster, which history has shown has happened to many a previous presidential candidate.

Overall the speech was well balanced, talking about how he would deal with Vladimir Putin in Russia, and Kim Jong Un in North Korea, and some thoughts on the Middle East, and more—but the only parts that Trump really cared about were what he said on China and ISIS. That's where his focus had been, and that's what he wanted to focus on here.

In the days before the speech, the stakes were high, and the expectations were low. Several reporters told me they were certain that Trump was going to bungle this so badly that it would knock him right out of the race.

But something big happened on the day of the Acela primaries: as exit polls were released and it became clear that Trump was going to sweep all five states and gather enough delegates to push him over the top, we suddenly received RSVPs and new attendance requests from more than five hundred people wanting to attend.

It was almost as if all of Washington suddenly woke up to what was happening, that the guy they'd written off as a candidate was actually going to win.

The stakes were high—and about to get a lot higher.

CHAPTER 4

Building Relationships Trump's Way

The Foreign Policy Speech That Surprised the World

AS WE PREPARED FOR THE MOST CRUCIAL SPEECH OF TRUMP'S entire campaign so far, Jared brought in a sponsor to make sure everything was paid for and presented in the most professional way possible. That sponsor was the Center for the National Interest, a Washington, D.C.-based public policy think tank established by former U.S. President Richard Nixon. The center, formerly known as the Nixon Center for Peace and Freedom, was led by an executive director named Dimitri Simes, who, as I would later find out in the course of the Mueller investigation, allegedly had relationships with various Russian oligarchs, some with connections to Vladimir Putin. I didn't know anything about Simes then, and the concept of questioning how a prominent think tank founded by a former U.S. president might have gotten its funding never occurred to me. The center was covering the cost of the room and staffing of the event, and that was all.

I wouldn't even bother mentioning any of this were it not for the fact that this day would be brought up and investigated again and again as the Mueller investigation unfolded over the course of the following two years. (I'll speak more about that in later chapters.)

The Russian ambassador attended the speech that day as well, along with ambassadors from nearly a dozen other nations, many of whom stuck around after the speech and shook Trump's hand.

General Mike Flynn was present for that speech as well. After serving as a surrogate and warm-up speaker for Trump on the campaign trail, he wanted to be there, and it made sense for him to be there. He knew a number of these ambassadors, including the Russian ambassador and others, from the work he performed in counterterrorism for the Obama administration, and from his work in the private sector.

When it came to foreign policy, Russia was not one of Trump's primary focuses, at all. But, interestingly enough, Trump and I (along with others on the plane) did discuss Putin on the plane ride down. I was curious about why, in Trump's view, he thought it was a good idea to try to build a relationship with the Russian leader— or any known enemy of the United States.

And Trump's stance was basically this: If you're the president, why would you *not* want to work on improving relations with the leader of any country in the world?

He was fully aware that past presidents had tried to build such relationships, behind the scenes if nowhere else. After they met at a summit in 2001, President George W. Bush boasted that he'd "looked into Putin's eyes" and had seen his "soul." And during his first term in office, President Obama famously talked to Russia's then-prime minister Dmitry Medvedev about Putin and told him that "this is my last election. I will have more flexibility" after the reelection. So they also were trying to build a relationship with Putin.

The difference in Trump's eyes was that the last two presidents put on a façade and disguised the relationships they were trying to build. In this, as in everything else (except maybe his taxes), he wanted to put everything out in the open. His gripes about policies, his disdain for politicians, his hatred of the RNC primary system—he didn't play nice or cover up his true feelings about any of it.

He told me he couldn't understand why anybody *wouldn't* want to develop a relationship with the leaders of *any* other country, including North Korea or China, even if you have issues with them. "I'm the best negotiator in the world," he said, "so whatever it is, we'll find a solution, so long as everybody sits at the table."

Trump didn't understand that it doesn't work that way in the world of politics.

In politics, if the president of the United States picks up the phone when Putin calls, that sends a signal to the entire world that Putin is being taken seriously by the United States—and that increases Putin's power, and Russia's status.

Trump's approach was basically, "This is ridiculous. If he calls me, I'm going to pick up the phone and talk to him!"

That stance put him in a position of butting heads with the diplomats of the world, especially at the State Department as it had been organized under President Obama and Secretary of State Hillary Clinton over the course of the previous eight years, and more specifically in the wake of the 2014 Russian invasion of Crimea (in southeastern Ukraine). Plus, the protocols of American foreign policy are deeply entrenched in the State Department, and for the most part, they outlast and tend to supersede any individual president's policies. I knew, as Paul knew, as nearly everyone around Trump with any political experience knew, that his stance would rub a lot of people in Washington the wrong way.

Trump didn't care. Just like with everything else, if elected, he would do things his way, and he wanted everyone to know it.

Just to be clear, I do not believe from any of the conversations we had that Trump had any actual relationship with Putin whatsoever. I would later learn that the two had briefly crossed paths some years earlier when friends and business associates with ties to Putin paid Trump's Miss Universe Organization $20 million to bring the pageant to Moscow in 2013. (This was the infamous Miss Universe pageant that Trump attended in Moscow, the one that brought him to stay at the Moscow Ritz-Carlton, which would lead to a number of salty allegations that would appear in the now-debunked "Steele dossier," years later.) But how the media managed to spin that thin connection into the idea that "Putin and Trump are friends" is beyond me, particularly when Hillary Clinton's long-standing relationships with Russian oligarchs who made sizeable contributions through the Clinton Foundation and the Clinton Global Initiative have been mostly ignored.

The foreign policy stance that Trump presented on Russia in his speech that day was based on his principles of deal-making and relationship building. And in all of these cases in which the foreign leaders in question were not considered allies of the United States, Trump's stance was firm: behind the scenes, he *routinely* stated that he wanted to "talk to them."

That was all.

"But we're not going to get bullied," he insisted. "I'll do whatever I need to do to make sure America's interests come first. But I'm not gonna go out and make enemies, either."

Unfortunately, the latter part of Trump's overall message never seemed to get out to the public. He hardly ever talked about it in public himself. As a rule, whenever Trump spoke, he rarely seemed to deliver a complete message. Some pretty important pieces of his thinking and reasoning were always left out of any speech or interview response. And even when Paul, or General Flynn, or his other surrogates tried to explain it on TV or elsewhere, it seemed to get overlooked or under-reported.

The media seemed more interested in supporting the titillating idea that Trump was more of a friend to Putin than he was to the United States, or that Putin "had something" on Trump that kept him under his thumb. I saw nothing in my time with Trump that led me to believe either of those things were true. But at this point in his campaign, Trump had said so little about foreign policy that the media and the Democrats tried to define Trump on these issues.

That made his delivery of this foreign policy speech all the more important.

And he delivered.

At a crucial moment, Trump stuck to the speech as it scrolled on the teleprompter. The only places where he went off-script and expounded a little bit were when he was talking about China and ISIS, and he knew those areas well. He'd been talking about them for months.

Everyone on the campaign was thrilled with his performance.

All in all, the media reported that he came off as intelligent, thoughtful, even nuanced—not words that had been associated with Trump so far on the campaign.

Even some of his most ardent critics reached out to Paul and me afterward and complimented us on it, some saying it was the best speech Trump had ever given. They said they were glad to see the professionalism of a "real campaign" finally kicking in.

To be so well received in Washington after winning five primaries the night before, Trump was flying high.

He went into the Indiana primary on May 3 feeling like nothing could stop him.

He felt this way even though Cruz had outspent Trump four to one in advertising in Indiana. And even though on April 29, Cruz's good friend, Indiana Governor Mike Pence, had gone ahead and endorsed Ted Cruz for president.

Paul and I were both upset and frustrated. We were getting ready to make the hard push to encourage Trump to pick Pence as his running mate. But after reading Pence's tepid endorsement of Cruz, we realized it was nothing but a political move that Pence felt he had no choice but to make: he was so far down in the polls for his gubernatorial race, he thought that endorsing Cruz might give him a much-needed boost with Conservatives. Still, how he went about it made us laugh. In his endorsement, during a local TV interview with WIBC, Pence started out by saying he was "grateful for Trump…for his voice in the national debate."

"I'm not against anybody," he said, "but I will be voting for Ted Cruz in the Republican primary."

Talk about a weak endorsement. Still, the fact that he didn't come out for Donald Trump directly created another hurdle he'd have to get over to get on Trump's good side in the days ahead—because Trump didn't see anything as purely political.

And on that day, Trump called Mike Pence "a loser."

Nonetheless, Trump won the primary that day, besting Cruz with a solid 53.26 percent of the vote to Cruz's 36.63 percent, and Kasich coming in under 8 percent.

Reince Priebus, the head of the RNC who for more than a year had routinely told his fellow Republicans in private, "Hey, don't worry, Trump can't win," went ahead and tweeted that night that Trump had, in fact, become "the presumptive nominee."

Ted Cruz dropped out of the race instantly, followed by Kasich, who waited till the next morning.

We celebrated at Trump Tower, and I expected Trump would be happy. Instead, in the coming days, he grew angry.

He turned on the TV expecting to receive all kinds of praise and attention, and instead, he saw prominent Democrats, and even some prominent Republicans who'd stayed mostly silent during the primaries, suddenly speak up and speak out against him. One of the more vocal Democrats he noted was New York Senator Chuck Schumer—a man whose campaign Trump had personally donated money to in the past. He had even hosted events for Schumer at Trump Tower. Trump considered him a personal ally. After all, they're from the same state and had worked together on projects. He could not understand why Schumer would suddenly turn on him, and he started fuming about it.

He took Schumer's attack, and other attacks, personally. He repeatedly said that he could not understand why people he thought were his "friends" would treat him this way.

I think it was his first introduction to the fact that in political life, you have no "friends."

We should have been basking in the glow of the big win. Instead, we were dealing with an angry candidate who was gathering new grudges that he would never forget.

And less than a week later, the media let loose.

Back in the 1990s, Trump had made calls to press outlets under the false pretense of being a "Trump publicist" named John Miller (or occasionally named John Barron), a man who was quoted in numerous publications on all sorts of topics surrounding Trump's marriages, divorces, and dating life. The *Washington Post* broke the story on May 13. They quoted respected journalists who'd been contacted by "Mr. Miller" back in those days, who stated on the record that the pretend publicist was absolutely Trump himself. They posted tape recordings of one of the reporter's interviews online. The story even referenced a lawsuit in which Trump *admitted* to making phone calls to journalists under the false name of "John Barron." But when we brought the story to Trump for comment, shortly before the *Post* put it on their website, Trump denied it was him. He said the story wasn't true.

As a staff, we had no choice but to echo his denials in response to the *Post*'s reporting, or any of the hundreds of other press outlets that picked up and ran with the story over the next few days.

I listened to the tapes myself and spoke to people who knew Trump in those days. If it was Trump, it made sense to me, because no one speaks for Trump except for Trump. I think if he had just admitted it, most voters would have shrugged their shoulders and said, "Who cares?" But instead, Trump continually denied it.

On that very same day, Friday the thirteenth of May, Trump said something in public that was even more outrageous than his two-decades-old antics with the New York press: in response to a question about an ongoing civil lawsuit, which claimed that his Trump University was a fraud, Trump commented that the federal judge assigned to the case, U.S. District Judge Gonzalo Curiel, had a "conflict of interest"—because he was Mexican.

"I'm building a wall," Trump said. "It's an inherent conflict of interest."

To call out a federal judge and claim he was biased because of his heritage was so far outside of anything considered acceptable or normal in the world of politics, it tested every one of us.

Paul was regularly going on TV to defend Trump against one thing or another, and he was exhausted. By all of it. It just never let up. But this felt like it would do him in. The press used this very personal attack on a judge as an example to try to prove, once and for all, that Trump was a racist, a talking point born out in his lack of compassion for Dreamers and others in his hardline immigration stance, they said.

I was on the plane with Trump right after he said it, just as the ripple effects were starting to surface on every cable news channel he flipped to. He wanted to prove this was a biased judge. He turned to me, Hope, Stephen, Dan Scavino, and Corey and directed us to go find evidence in court records.

Right away we realized the judge was not "Mexican." He was born in Indiana to parents of Mexican descent, but he had always been an American citizen, and his court record looked good.

But Trump wouldn't let it go. Weeks later, on June 3, he called Judge Curiel a "hater" in another tirade about Trump University, questioning why the case was still ongoing.

Honestly, any other politician might have been knocked out of the game by this one controversy, let alone the double controversies that hit that Friday the 13th. But not Trump. We'd all learned by this point that he was resilient and spoke his mind. Despite the offensiveness of his words in some cases, his appeal laid in his unconventionality. And while the media focused on and stressed the outrage of his comments, most Americans were more concerned with issues that actually impacted their economic standing.

Those of us who follow politics assume everyone else follows politics too. But over the course of the campaign, the average CNN audience was about three million people. Fox's audience was about 3.8 million. That's less than 2 percent of the population combined. Which means that most of this "controversial" news and commentary was only resonating in the D.C. bubble, and the media bubble in and around a few large cities.

In general, people were far more incensed over ineffective politicians ruining their lives and the legacy of this country than they were about one guy going around saying a few awful things about a judge. It was not an issue that impacted them on a daily basis, so it did not impact his campaign. In fact, as our polls kept showing, the vast majority of Republicans in key border states including Texas, New Mexico, and Arizona didn't think what he was saying about this judge or stopping "illegals" was terrible at all. The majority of Americans understood the impact of illegal immigration, and the hard work that was required to become a legal immigrant. Trump would often say he had no problem with immigrants coming into the U.S. as long as it was done by the book.

What our data showed was that voters were willing to take a chance on someone as seemingly outrageous and unconventional as Trump, because it would break the monotony of do-nothing, arrogant, selfish politicians in Washington who seemed to be in it only for themselves.

And Hillary Clinton was included in that group of established politicians, which so many of Trump's supporters, and Bernie's supporters, were lining up to vote against.

Trump's routinely referring to her as "Crooked Hillary" throughout May and into June was working. It was a moniker that stuck to her as hard as "Lyin' Ted" stuck to Ted Cruz. And we all saw firsthand what that kind of name-calling did to Cruz: even where he outspent Trump four to one, Cruz lost.

Trump's instincts for beating the press and other politicians at their own game combined with Paul's instincts for political strategy—which were focused now well past the convention and onto the various roadmaps to winning enough Electoral College votes to secure Trump's victory in November—seemed almost unstoppable.

This was why Trump promoted Paul to the role of campaign chairman in the third week of May, essentially demoting Corey Lewandowski at that point. Four weeks later, Trump fired Corey outright. Or, to be accurate, I should say Don Jr. fired Corey.

Ironically, Trump never fired anyone directly himself. The man who made a name for himself on reality TV with his catchphrase, "You're fired," never fired anyone the whole time I worked for him. Instead, he always had somebody else do the firing. Rather than burn a bridge, Trump made it a practice to leave a rope line out in the water—just in case he ever needed or wanted to pull somebody back into the fold.

In this case, Don Jr. was eager to fire Corey. The two just didn't get along during the campaign. But Paul didn't necessarily want Corey fired. Corey had a punkish and demeaning attitude and constantly felt threatened by Paul. He exhausted Paul with his juvenile antics and made life difficult for most everyone on the campaign. Paul would have preferred if Corey had just followed his directions, and he told me on more than one occasion that he could have made Corey the most successful campaign manager in presidential politics. However, Corey constantly worked against most everyone in matters big and small. He personally targeted Paul, Jared, Ivanka, and others with negative attacks in the media. We never understood his approach. But we were short on time and resources, and we were all working toward a common goal of getting Trump elected. In the end, Corey needed to go so the campaign could function efficiently.

Paul was placed in the role of campaign chair, and I became deputy campaign chairman—taking over even more of the day-to-day tasks than I'd been handed in my first two months, and the job wasn't getting any easier.

Trump himself kept making it tougher than it needed to be, and the RNC was still dismissive of him. That bridge had not been built yet, no matter how hard Paul had tried.

Honestly, the thought that Trump was going to be the nominee seemed to be causing a sense of unease throughout the entire Washington establishment. It was an organ rejection, as if this man just did not fit and did not belong, and a whole bunch of people on all sides still wanted to find a way to ensure that it wouldn't come to pass.

Trump didn't care. He believed he didn't need to worry about any of "them." He believed in his campaign—now more than ever—and he believed that he could easily beat Hillary come November all on his own.

As we were flying to the final rallies before the convention, we showed Trump some of Obama's anti-Hillary ads. They were scathing—and Trump loved it. The more he saw, he said, the more predictable she seemed. He started to predict the types of attacks she might levy against him, so he could prepare to go on the attack against her before she ever had the chance.

He was absolutely convinced he could slaughter her in the general election.

Did he need help to accomplish that? Did he need more ammunition than what he already had to use against her, given her long track record in politics, and the way Fox News and right-wing radio had been attacking her and her husband for years? No.

Would we welcome some additional ammunition if it came? Sure. Who wouldn't? This was a contest, and she was our opponent. Opposition research is an important part of any campaign. And the remarkable thing was, after Trump became the presumptive nominee, it seemed as if everybody and their brother was calling to say they knew how to help us destroy her.

At this point, I started receiving more than 450 emails per day, plus dozens of phone calls, so it was hard to keep track of it all, but many of the emails and calls that weren't directly campaign-related were from people all over the world who claimed they had dirt on Hillary Clinton. Some went so far as to claim they had Hillary's missing emails—and they were willing to share them with us if we'd meet with them, and if they could meet the candidate.

Paul and I knew the odds of these individuals delivering on their claims were highly unlikely. We didn't entertain their pitches and rarely returned their emails or calls. These were mostly just people trying to gain access to the candidate.

And in the middle of it all, rumors were swirling about Wikileaks, and what *they* might have on Clinton, based on reports that, at some point, a DNC server had been hacked. The information we kept hearing was that the Chinese or North Koreans had been responsible for the hacking, and possibly the Russians. But none of it was more than rumors.

Adding intrigue to the rumor mill, Roger Stone kept bragging to Paul that he had a relationship with Wikileaks founder Julian Assange, and that Assange had told him that they definitely had something on Clinton. He kept telling us over and over, "More will be coming."

We didn't know if he was talking about Hillary's missing thirty-three thousand emails—which was the only topic Trump himself really cared about when it came to finding any "dirt" on Hillary. Stone never said anything about Wikileaks having Hillary's emails to me directly, and as far as I know he never talked about what Wikileaks might actually have with Paul, or Trump himself, or anyone else. He just kept bragging that "more was coming."

One morning, I walked into Paul's apartment when he was on the phone with Stone, and Paul looked at me and rolled his eyes as he put Stone on speaker for my amusement. Stone was going on and *on* about some items that Paul wasn't paying attention to, until Paul finally jumped in and said, "Hey, Roger? Rick's here. We've got a meeting in a few. I've got to go."

"All right," Stone said, and he hung up.

Paul laughed.

"Guess who Roger had dinner with last night?" he asked me.

"The pope?" I said.

"No, even better: Julian Assange."

Assange was holed up at the Ecuador Embassy in London at the time, seeking asylum and refuge from international arrest warrants. He certainly wasn't going out to dinners.

"Ummm, where is Roger now?" I asked.

"I'm pretty sure he's still here in New York!" Paul said.

We both shook our heads at Roger's antics, and we moved on with our day.

We'd grown used to it: whenever Roger called with an update or information, Paul and I took him at his word, which was, for the most part, worthless. Roger flourished in the absurd. He used it as a political tool to generate enthusiasm and intensity among core voters. Three years later, the world would learn from the Special Counsel's investigation that Stone never had dinner with Assange. He admitted that it was "pure shtick" and that he "simply milked the joke." This type of behavior and bravado was commonplace in Roger's toolkit of political tactics. And Manafort was attuned to the antics having known Roger for more than forty years.

We were dealing with similar distractions from a tangential member of the Trump team, George Papadopoulos, whom Sam Clovis and Corey Lewandowski had hired in March as an advisor on foreign relations. George came over from the Ben Carson campaign after Carson dropped out of the race, and while he was traveling internationally for personal business he met with several figures about the possibility that Russia had acquired a series of damaging emails on Hillary Clinton. These figures just wanted to meet with Trump, and Paul, Jared, and I were constantly trying to block these overtures. Not only would they have wasted Trump's time, and our time, but the very perception that Trump was talking to foreign diplomats during his campaign could be extremely damaging.

We knew this.

It's why Paul and Jared had agreed, and then directed the campaign, and Trump himself, that this was not the time to entertain any foreign meetings.

After receiving another communication in a series of emails from Papadopoulos, this time suggesting that the Greek minister of defense wanted to broker a meeting between Putin and Trump soon, Jared, Paul, and I got together with Senator Jeff Sessions to deal with all of this foreign interest as forthrightly as we could. Trump didn't want to meet with *anyone* at this stage from other countries anyway. He wanted to stay focused on "America First." But we decided to put Sessions in charge, as an intermediary, to handle the protocols necessary to meet with foreign diplomats of any kind, and any foreign leaders, should it ever be required during the campaign. But none of that would come to pass. It was all precautionary.

Trump's kids didn't know any of this was going on. They weren't involved in the day-to-day activities. Once Trump became the presumptive nominee, though, they wanted to get more involved with the campaign. At that time, they were inexperienced. They had little to go on when it came to understanding who to trust and who not to trust in politics.

So when someone connected to a wealthy Russian family, a man who had been involved with helping his father bring the Miss Universe pageant to Moscow a few years earlier, emailed Don Jr. to say he had some "dirt on Hillary," Don responded. Positively. He said he'd be happy to see that dirt. He went so far as to set up a meeting to discuss the information with this individual and his associates in a conference room at Trump Tower, on June 9.

He mentioned this to us at our weekly family meeting, on Monday, June 6, and Paul and I just looked at each other. Paul smiled slightly and then warned Don that we'd seen plenty of these sorts of "offers" before, and they never panned out. He hinted that these people might be trying to trap him. Unbeknownst to me, instead of canceling the meeting, Don Jr. proceeded anyway.

Of course, the people he met with didn't have Hillary's emails. It was a longshot for him to believe that they might have access to *anything* we didn't already know about the Clintons. In terms of opposition research that a campaign might want, they had nothing. Paul sat in on the meeting, which only lasted about forty minutes, and there was nothing noteworthy that came from the meeting. Just as we'd suspected, it was nothing but an excuse for these people to try to get closer to our campaign.

To entertain these types of people carrying these types of "offers" was a waste of everyone's time.

Paul and I *knew* this. And many others on the campaign did as well.

But on that day, Don Jr. learned his lesson firsthand—and the consequences of his naiveté would later play out in ways none of us could have predicted.

CHAPTER 5

The Presumptive Nominee

The Russia Narrative and Vetting Vice Presidents

A FEW ROGUE RUSSIANS WEREN'T THE ONLY ONES TRYING TO better their own positions through association and proximity to Trump. Paul Manafort wasn't immune to using the power of that proximity for himself.

The fact that Paul was now leading the presidential campaign of an American businessman and political outsider who just happened to be a celebrity known all around the world, combined with the fact that Paul's strategies for the Trump campaign were working, was a major achievement. It could quite possibly raise his status overseas like never before, earning him consulting contracts in Ukraine and elsewhere around the globe that would be much more lucrative going forward. And in Paul's case, it might also serve as leverage to help him get paid for some work he did for Ukrainian clients who had stiffed him on bills in years past. Any of his old clients who wanted to remain close to Paul, which could be perceived as their having an "in" at the White House in the future, would certainly want to step up and pay their overdue bills in order to get back into Paul's good graces.

In the interest of all of that, to make sure his associates back in Ukraine knew exactly how well Paul was doing, he decided to share some of our positive polling data with a man named Konstantin Kilimnik.

Kilimnik had worked for Paul for years. We called him "KK" for short, and the two of us shared an office in Ukraine. At 4'11", this forty-something political operative used to tell me all sorts of Russian and Ukrainian jokes and spent time asking me to explain certain American phrases that he found funny or interesting. Born in Ukraine while it was still part of the Soviet Union, Kilimnik was one of only a handful of Russians who were sent to a specialized language school on merit, where most of his classmates were sons of high-level politicians. Although initially schooled in Finnish, he spoke English extremely well, and when the wall came down, he stepped out publicly as a proponent of Democracy.

Kilimnik was easygoing. A nice guy to be around. And despite his background and connections, which could have lent themselves to suspicion that he might have worked for the KGB (now the FSB), KK was the last guy anyone would suspect of working as any sort of spy or secret operative, for Russia or anyone else. His personality just didn't lend itself to suspicion, which may have been why so many people at the U.S. Embassy trusted him. He introduced me to his family several times over the years. And his American ties went back to his work with the International Republican Institute—a U.S.-backed think tank that supports Democratic efforts in former communist regimes. In fact, he had worked to help open the Moscow office of IRI, which I'm sure was no easy task, back when the institute was headed by John McCain. McCain's right-hand man at that time was Rick Davis, Paul's business partner, and that's how he and Paul met (even though McCain and Paul were not friendly).

KK was the perfect person to help spread news of Paul's success to people of influence—including Paul's former clients—back in Ukraine. So Paul instructed me to send KK copies of the *New York Times* story announcing that Paul had been hired by Trump, and later Paul had me send him some ad hoc polling results just to prove how well Paul was performing. The numbers came from both our internal daily polling data and some public data, but were always a couple of days old. This wasn't deep polling research. It wasn't the binders full of detailed breakdowns (called cross tabs) on polling stats and demographic alignments by state and region and town and household that our digital team would use in the general election to better target our political ads online. It was just top-line polling data, saying things like, "Ohio: Trump 48, Hillary 42...."

Paul knew that those numbers were all KK needed to spread the word, and Paul was excited about the business prospects of his post-election future because of it.

It's no secret that there's a lot of money to be made in political consulting in Ukraine and other emerging democracies, and Republicans aren't the only ones capitalizing on the opportunities. Not only is there high demand for American political operatives to help individuals and parties win elections, but once those elections are won, bringing anywhere from four to eight years of new political stability to a particular region, those same political operatives are then in a perfect position to work as consultants to American, European, and Asian companies that want to come in and do business with the new regimes. They have the connections and knowhow to walk companies in and help them get the contracts, tax breaks, and whatever other assurances they need to do business in those countries. And in a place like Ukraine, none of this is considered illegal, unethical, or unseemly. Not at all. There is also nothing in U.S. law or trade policy that blocks it.

Muddying the waters even further, in Ukraine, it is perfectly acceptable for a leading businessman—say the head of a major solar energy firm—to also serve as prime minister. Simultaneously. No one bats an eye that an individual is performing both roles at the very same time.

And if American companies want help moving into a certain region, who better to turn to than an American consultant? Whenever a new U.S. president is elected, you can bet that the consultants behind that campaign—from either political party—are going to get the majority of these foreign contracts.

When Obama won in 2008, his chief strategists, David Axelrod and David Plouffe, made millions doing the same kind of work that Paul had been doing. There were no fewer than eight different major political consultants from America actively working in Ukraine during the ten-year period while we were there. And the truly ironic and amazing thing about it is that when we export the American political model, the party lines fade away.

In Ukraine, Paul brought in Tad Devine, who was on the 2016 Bernie Sanders campaign and who'd worked for Al Gore and John Kerry in the past, to write speeches and do all sorts of high-level work for us. Our media team was all Dems. Our pollster leaned Republican. The digital data team we used in Ukraine in 2012 was made up entirely of Obama data gurus from his 2008 presidential campaign.

When we weren't fighting with each other the way we do under the brutal divisiveness of American politics, we could actually partner and align with each other in the rest of the world to get things done.

But here in America, the divisiveness persists. While people from other countries were scrambling to get close to Donald Trump and we did our best to keep them at bay, here in the States, there was still a ton of hesitation to associate with Trump at all. Not just across political divides, but because of the fight Trump himself had created within the Republican Party.

A big part of the bad blood stemmed back to the primary debates when Trump was the only Republican who refused to sign a pledge to support the Republican nominee at the end of the race, no matter who won. Trump wouldn't sign it. Instead, he said that if he didn't win, he "might have to take a look at Bernie."

The establishment Republicans would not support that kind of behavior.

In June, as we marched on toward the July convention, Trump started to soften up a little bit to Paul's idea that he wanted and needed the party on his side. After all, Paul had proven himself to be a winner in Trump's eyes. So he met with Reince Priebus again, this time on his own turf, at Trump Tower, and agreed to let Reince work more closely with our campaign. He also pulled back some of his anti-RNC rhetoric, just a touch. He realized it wasn't as necessary now, anyway. He kept his focus instead on "Crooked Hillary," and asked his crowds and the television cameras, not so rhetorically, "Where are the emails? Where are they?"

His crowds cheered more than ever.

Internal polls showed Hillary's trust level dropping over the course of the summer.

The nickname was sticking.

Unfortunately, so were the "racist" accusations being hurled at Trump. And he didn't make things any better when, on July 4, he sent a tweet featuring an image of Hillary Clinton in front of a great big pile of cash, with what looked to me (and pretty much anyone else who saw it) like a six-pointed Star of David. Inside the red star were the words: "Most Corrupt Candidate Ever!"

The image was interpreted as anti-Semitic.

I was one of the first people notified about the tweet that morning, and I immediately reached out to Paul. He directed me to draft a press release, affirming that Trump was not a "racist" or an "anti-Semite"—a short "apology" without it being an overt apology, since we knew that Trump would never apologize for something he tweeted. I ran it past Paul and then ran out to find Trump on his golf course in Bedminster, New Jersey, to get his approval.

Mike Pence, his wife Karen, and their youngest daughter Charlotte had secretly flown in on July 2 to meet with Trump and Melania for some time to get to know each other, arranged by Paul. Melania hadn't participated in the campaign much at all up to that point. But when it came to meeting potential VPs and their wives, she stepped into the role easily and gracefully.

Pence had come into that weekend thinking he had no shot at landing the VP slot. When I met him that evening, he was proud but humble and was honored to meet with Trump. He hoped maybe it would lead to a good relationship down the road, and possibly help him in his own bid for reelection as Indiana's governor. The plan was to meet for breakfast the next morning, after which Trump and Pence were going to play a round of golf.

Trump greeted the Pence family with the enthusiasm and graciousness I always saw him show at his resorts. He wanted to make sure they were taken care of and had everything they needed. When we sat down to eat, the Pences were equally polite and were very down to earth. After a few pleasantries, and without missing a beat, Trump looked over at Charlotte and said, "You know your dad endorsed Ted Cruz over me, right?"

Pence smiled back and said, "You were right, and you won Indiana and they love you." Trump, still looking at Charlotte, responded while smiling, "It was a weak endorsement anyway." And just like that, Pence won some points with Trump for owning it and acknowledging Trump beat him (and Cruz).

So you can imagine Pence's surprise when I drove a golf cart over to Trump later that same morning and asked if I could speak with him—and Trump said, "Just tell me. What have we got?"

Trump sat with Pence at his side while I informed him about the controversial tweet. And when I handed him the draft press release, he glanced at it quickly and then handed it to Pence. "What do you think?" he asked. "Should I send this out?"

I knew instantly that this was a test. Trump's body language said clearly that he didn't want this press release to be issued. He handed it to Pence to see what kind of a response he'd give. Trump loved to test people. He'd make it seem like he wanted your opinion when what he *really* wanted to know was if you agreed with him or not.

I knew this.

Pence didn't.

"What do you think?" Trump said. "I'm not apologizing, but what do you think?"

I could see the struggle on Pence's face. He didn't know how to respond. Finally, he answered, "Yes, yes, Mr. Trump, you know, I think that you're right on this. I think this is the right approach, to not send out the press release."

Good answer for Pence.

Terrible answer for me.

"Okay," I said. "I'll let Paul know."

I walked away, called Paul, and Paul simply felt we had to respond. In what he thought was a "compromise" solution, rather than issue the press release, Paul made the decision on his own to pull the tweet down from Trump's account.

By the time Trump came off the golf course, I was waiting for him. I told him what we'd done. And Trump went nuts: "Why would you do that? We have nothing to apologize for!"

I hesitantly tried to explain the trope of Jewish people and money, and what the Star of David represented—

"What 'Star of David'? It's just a *star*!" he yelled.

He said it looked like a sheriff's badge, and what Paul had done was "the wrong response. It makes us look *weak*!" He wanted us to put the image back up on his Twitter account, and we did—only we replaced the star-shaped graphic with a circle. It didn't help. The media noticed. It only made it worse.

The next morning, Paul flew in and we gathered at Trump's cottage at Bedminster to watch the fallout on TV. CNN in particular kept hammering on the issue. Not only had their reporters seen the tweet, and noticed that we'd taken it down and replaced it, they had done some research. They aired a scathing report, noting that the very same image that Trump tweeted had appeared on an anti-Semitic, white supremacist website a few weeks earlier.

Trump insisted the image didn't come from that site. He had seen it on some guy's rabidly anti-Clinton Twitter account. I looked it up, and sure enough, he was correct, it was on the anti-Clinton tweet.

As we watched, Melania sat in the room with us. Trump started yelling at the TV. Then he yelled at me and Paul. He said we needed to *fix this*. This was on *us*. Then he told us both to get lost.

"Have a nice Fourth of July weekend," I said with sincerity on the way out.

Trump exploded when I said it and continued to yell at us from the side door of his cottage.

"I can't believe you just said that," Paul whispered.

We worked for the better part of the weekend trying to come up with a response that might quell the controversy. Dan Scavino took the fall and claimed he had posted the tweet himself, and that of course it wasn't anti-Semitic because his wife was Jewish, and he had been celebrating Jewish traditions with her and her family for the past sixteen years. He said the star was a Microsoft stock image that was clearly labeled "Sheriff's

Star." But the media just wasn't buying it. Neither was the Clinton campaign. They issued a harsh statement, reprimanding Trump for his behavior. To which Trump came out Monday bashing Hillary all over again.

The whole thing set off an alarm for Karen Pence. Through Paul, I got word that she wanted her husband to remove himself from VP consideration. She knew that her husband had long-term goals to run for the presidency himself, and she believed that his association with someone as volatile and lacking in "good Christian values" as Trump would end his chances for good. She promised to support him if he decided to stay in, but from what Paul said, she was not happy about it.

No one was happy about it.

Why did we need to fight this hard? Why did we need to endure this kind of chaos? It certainly didn't help us to gather the surrogates we needed. No one wanted to go out and have to defend this sort of behavior. And it certainly wasn't helping us to build bridges with the RNC as we inched closer and closer to the convention.

It wasn't helping our VP search, either. If Pence dropped out, Paul didn't have a solid Conservative on the bench to take his place.

Later Trump would tell me he was impressed by the way Pence backed him up at Bedminster over the whole tweet debacle, but he was not sure about Pence as a running mate. He wanted to choose a running mate that was more "like him," he said. "Someone that was more aggressive and willing to fight."

Since May, he'd been pushing for either Chris Christie or Newt Gingrich—neither of whom Paul wanted because Paul knew neither of them added any value to Trump's ticket. Both of them had such huge personalities, and they were both angling for the presidency themselves. Paul believed they would have attempted to sideline Trump once inside the White House. So we used the influence of the kids and any other tactics we'd learned about how to best approach Trump to persuade him to look elsewhere. He mostly backed down by early July without telling Christie or Gingrich that they were out of the running, of course. He wanted to keep the tow lines in the water, even as he started talking about bringing a general on board instead.

Early on, I heard him ask people what they thought of General Flynn, mainly because he had defied Obama and was a Trump supporter early on. He asked about General Jack Keane, a retired four-star general in the U.S. Army and a noted national security analyst, and General Stanley McChrystal, also a retired four-star who commanded the U.S. and international forces in Afghanistan. He didn't bring them up in detail, though. There didn't seem to be a seriousness to any one of these suggestions he made. So we didn't vet them.

Honestly, we knew a general wouldn't necessarily help him fill a void anyway. Trump already looked strong to his base in terms of his rhetoric on ISIS and China. So we tried to deflect with other, more innovative ideas.

One suggestion that he was very open to considering was the possibility of bringing in Condoleezza Rice, who served as secretary of state under George W. Bush. The thinking was that having an accomplished woman on board, and a minority woman at that, would throw Hillary completely off her game, instantly taking away the power of the "woman card," and simultaneously diffusing any racist accusations. But Rice turned us down for personal reasons, saying she didn't want to be vetted for the role.

In mid-June, Trump took us down a completely unexpected path. During a VP discussion that included Jared and the other kids all assembled in one room, Trump said, "I think it should be Ivanka. What about Ivanka as my VP?"

There was silence.

"Ivanka should be vice president," he said again.

All heads turned toward her, and she just looked surprised.

We all knew Trump well enough to keep our mouths shut and not laugh. He very well might have been joking. He sometimes did that. Then again, he might not have been joking at all. He might have been perfectly serious.

No one knew what to do, what to say, how to react.

He went on, "She's bright, she's smart, she's beautiful, and the people would love her!"

Okay, I thought. *He's not joking.*

Ivanka was all of those things. So are a lot of other young women in business in New York City. Unfortunately, that is not enough to make someone a viable candidate for vice president of the United States. Nobody would ever believe that a candidate would pick their daughter as a VP possibility. But there it was.

Looking around the table, there were lots of pursed lips and furled brows and raised shoulders and inquisitive nodding, but we somehow moved on quickly to another topic.

Trump didn't stop.

A few weeks later, after looking at Tennessee Senator Bob Corker (whom Trump liked a lot at that moment, but who took himself out), and Iowa Senator Joni Ernst (whose inexperience drew harsh comparisons to Sarah Palin), and Alabama Senator Jeff Sessions (whom Trump called "Mr. Magoo" often), Paul subtly pushed once more for someone who could bring balance to the ticket, like Pence. But Trump said, "Look, I don't *like* any of these people."

Again and again we had learned that he only trusts family, he values loyalty above all other traits, and that seemed to be the reasoning he was placing behind his choice for VP when, once again, he said, "I think it should be Ivanka."

He must have sensed the reservation in the room when he said it, because he kept trying to sell Ivanka to us on her own terms, listing her credentials, her likability, trying to get us on board. He actually took a measured approach every time he brought her up over the next few weeks, and that said a lot since this was not how he normally did things. His own approach to this made us realize just how serious he was about putting his politically inexperienced daughter just a heartbeat from the presidency. So as a way to move on, we decided to field test her on one of our favorability polls—placing her name next to a dozen or so other names of potential VP candidates. These polls gave us an indication of her name recognition, and in rough terms whether people liked or disliked her and the idea of her as a possible VP candidate. She didn't poll tremendously high, but higher than we expected, and that only added to the seriousness of her consideration.

Trump said he believed that Ivanka was a good choice, and we knew that he believed his instincts were great. They *were* great. So we couldn't help but listen. He thought she would be "loved by the people," especially by his Republican base. And there were people on the team who thought, "Who knows? If we push it—maybe!" As crazy as it sounds and as ridiculous as it might have been, it wasn't that far off the rocker in the context of everything else that had happened so far.

We included her in a second poll, and her numbers were higher than the first time. Still low double digits, which showed that people did not really know her or couldn't see her in that position, but she polled higher than some of the other names we were floating.

As we headed into July and Trump still seemed cool to Pence, the Ivanka idea started to catch some momentum. People on the team argued that Ivanka brought a balance to her father. "She's more moderate." "She could help with Independents!" The fact that she was focused on childcare programs and social issues that leaned a little left, if not *fully* left, gave some people the idea that she might bring voters with her that would bolster her father.

By early July, I wasn't the only person on the team who realistically wondered if all the discussion and vetting and polling in the world would ever be enough to make him reconsider. As with so many other decisions, we had to ask ourselves if we were going to wind up standing at the convention shaking our heads, saying, "Wow. He's really going through with this."

That notion was definitely on our minds as we brought Trump to Washington, once again, to try to build bridges in a meeting with the Senate Republican Caucus on July 7.

We kept this meeting closed to press. We needed our candidate to be focused, reasonable, agreeable, even friendly. Paul had counseled Trump numerous times that he would be speaking not only to the most powerful Republicans but to some of the most powerful people in Washington. "You want them on your side," Paul said.

But the whole plane ride down, Trump kept expressing his anger over the way some of these senators had treated him throughout the primaries. Many of them had verbally attacked Trump over the preceding months for his rhetoric and campaign style. Now, as the presumptive nominee, they had to listen to him, and he said he was "going to *unleash* on these people."

We feared the meeting could create a greater divide, but we needed to try. Especially since we were busy trying to get a handle on a new problem that had surfaced within the party.

Ever since he'd become the presumptive nominee, a movement had been afoot. The most vocal anti-Trumpers—the Never-Trumpers—had been organizing, aggressively. A long list of seasoned politicians and former politicians, military generals, governors, cabinet secretaries, and bureaucrats had banded together into a movement. It wasn't all that unusual for parties to splinter, for anti-nominee sentiment to cause a quiet fracturing within one party or the other if certain politicians were unhappy with the nominee. But rarely has intra-party, anti-nominee sentiment grown so organized within either party in the history of this country.

We were slowly getting word from operatives and friends in the field that the Never-Trump movement was focusing strategically on targeting delegates—much in the same way Paul and I had been lobbying delegates to get them to commit to voting for Trump at the convention. And the intel we had suggested that they had made some serious headway, with Never-Trumper delegates now numbering in the hundreds. There are only 2,472 delegates in total. "Hundreds" of defectors could mean they had enough to prevent a legitimate nominee from securing the nomination. It was certainly enough to upset the apple cart and turn the convention into a circus, at the very least, and that could hurt Trump's chances in November.

If on top of that, Trump burned bridges rather than building them at this July 7 meeting—a meeting in which the caucus members would finally be able to ask Trump questions and hear his responses for themselves—we knew he would be in serious trouble.

The room was pretty full when we got there. I think the Republicans had forty-four members in the Senate at that time, and thirty-eight of them showed.

Mitch McConnell got up and gave Trump a very lukewarm introduction, and I stood in the back of the room with my heart pounding, wondering what Trump would have to say to him in response.

But Trump got up on the dais, he politely thanked Senator McConnell for the introduction, and the first words out of his mouth were all about how he wanted "to unite the party."

He echoed many of Paul's themes and talking points *perfectly*.

He said he wanted to "build relationships" with everyone in that room, and move toward "the common goal of beating Hillary Clinton."

I could hardly believe it.

Once again, when it really mattered, when he stood in front of an elite audience of Washington insiders, he rose to the occasion of the seriousness of the office he sought.

Looking back, it seems that he used his staff to vent, rage, argue, and test. And then when the moment mattered, knowing his audience, he was able to do what we thought was the impossible: he delivered.

Over the next hour, he fielded pointed questions on healthcare, on the economy, and on national security, and throughout it all, he kept his cool. He kept his composure, even knowing some in the room despised what he had accomplished. He made a joke about how he and McConnell "didn't talk much," which lightened the mood. Overall, he didn't give very definitive policy responses, but he kept turning back to the fact that he grasped the understanding of what it would take to beat Hillary. "Like nobody else," he said. He told the senators in that room that he would bring his massive wave of supporters out to vote—for them too. And together, they would *win*.

It was, I think, the closest Trump would ever come to building the bridge Paul wanted him to build during the campaign.

Back at campaign headquarters, it was time to go all in on convention planning and double down on our efforts to make sure our delegates wouldn't flip on Trump.

Members of our campaign had been lobbying delegates for months. I'd personally met with certain, more influential delegates three or four times by now. But after realizing how strong the Never-Trump movement had grown, we started asking delegates to put pen to paper—to pledge their loyalty, and sign their names as supporting Trump. These weren't legal documents of course. But the symbolic act of putting pen to paper made some of these people take the pledge more seriously. It was us saying, "It's now or never. Trump is the nominee. We need you to step up."

For delegates in states where they were bound by party rules to vote for Trump, we made it clear that they were "legally obligated to vote for Trump." If not, then we would "pursue legal options." But in reality, these state regulations binding delegates in each state had never been tested. We had no idea what might happen.

We updated our spreadsheet every day to keep track of who was solidly on our side and posted the numbers on a whiteboard. It was wild. In any other campaign, once everyone else in the race has dropped out, your candidate becomes "the nominee." The term "presumptive nominee" isn't something anyone ever bothers saying. The fact that we were using that term showed how dicey this all was: there were *that many* influential Republicans who didn't support him as a candidate, and the Never-Trumpers kept reminding them that it "wasn't over."

Their message to delegates was, "The nomination hasn't been formalized. He still has to get through the convention. You can *stop* this."

While keeping up with all of that, we were rushing to plan the logistics, the staging, the hotels, the signage, the speakers, the nearby fundraisers, and parties for the convention itself, while still trying to narrow down a VP choice, all with the smallest staff I had ever encountered on any presidential campaign.

Usually the nominee's campaign works closely with the RNC, and despite the recent history, we needed to come together. I was on the phone or in person with them no fewer than what seemed like ten times per day. But given the state of the tensions that still existed, instead of making things easier, Trump's imprint on the partnership made it all the more difficult.

The RNC had already negotiated TV coverage for the convention, which meant we needed our best speakers on stage between 7:00 and 10:00 p.m. on all four days of the convention—that was when the networks (outside of cable) would be broadcasting the proceedings. In a traditional convention, a good number of those speakers would've already been preselected based on party position, and in this case, that would have meant McConnell, Ryan, other members of the congressional leadership, Reince Priebus, and so forth, would automatically get primetime slots.

That became one of our first of many fights.

"I don't want any politicians speaking at the convention," Trump told me. "None."

Although he was trying to build bridges through Paul, he also believed that if it looked as if he "pivoted" to embrace the party, he would lose the support of voters who didn't *like* the party. And there were many of them, but we had to remind him that few of them would actually be at the convention. Those at the convention were largely the party faithful. We didn't want to alienate them.

A part of me loved it. I thought, "Here's the first time a guy is truly breaking down the old system."

I truly believed that most Americans were tired of the old staged theatrics of the conventions, with speeches by safe (i.e., boring) politicians, and maybe one or two good keynotes other than the candidate themselves. But the fact is that I was the one who was going to have to relay this news back to Paul and Reince, and it was not going to be well received. I knew it. And I questioned, once again, "Why does this have to be so difficult?"

Two of the first people Trump asked me to secure to speak at the convention were Serena Williams and LeBron James—two sports stars who had previously attended or spoken at Trump Organization events, such as the opening of the Trump International Tennis Center in D.C.

"Do you think they'll do it?" I asked.

"Of course!" he said. "They'll *all* do it!"

He still had no clue that politics and celebrity weren't the same business, and that even where celebrity and the business world mixed, there was no such mixing in politics unless everyone's ideologies were well aligned.

We took Trump's list of speakers back to his kids, and even *they* were concerned. "What is he thinking? These people aren't going to talk at a political convention!"

He wanted Don King to speak too, and Reince and his team went ballistic. Trump kept pushing it. He pushed it harder every time they pushed back until the RNC finally came back and threatened to cancel the convention rather than let someone convicted of manslaughter speak. They weren't bluffing. It took that big of a threat for Trump to eventually back down.

The convention is a political spectacle. Other politicians would be thinking about choosing speakers based on all sorts of criteria and points they wanted to make, even vetting the individuals to make sure there was no chance they would go rogue on live TV. All Trump cared about was bringing in speakers who *weren't* politicians.

After weeks of negotiation, Trump was just beginning to ease his stance and open up to the idea of letting some top Republicans have slots at the convention as a show of good faith as we were getting ready for that July 7 caucus meeting.

Ted Cruz specifically wanted a primetime speaking slot, and he wanted it bad. As the runner-up in the primary race, he thought he deserved it. He thought it would be the spotlight he'd need to help project him into the possibility of running for president again in the future. That's usually how it works. But Trump didn't want to give it to him. So we set up a sort of summit meeting between these two rivals on July 7, right after Trump's caucus meeting with the Senate Republicans.

We were feeling good about it as the caucus meeting ended. *One bridge built*, Paul and I thought. At least *partially built*. This alliance with Cruz would get us a few feet closer to spanning the gap.

I had worked with Paul to negotiate the terms for weeks, to try to make the Trump-Cruz meeting one-on-one. Trump was a dealmaker. We figured he'd be able to find some way to work this out with Cruz and make everybody happy, as long as they were alone in the room. But Paul was planning to be in the room as well, so of course, Cruz's campaign manager, Jeff Roe, wanted to be in the room too. He wouldn't let it go as a condition. We finally agreed to it and moved forward with the planning. I knew the presence of others would change the conversation, but hopefully not in a bad way. If the number of people in the room grew beyond that, chances were Trump would take to posturing more than he would one-on-one.

But on that day, when Trump came out of the caucus meeting, Jared and Ivanka followed Trump and Paul, and a nervous-looking Reince

Priebus, straight into the room where Cruz was waiting, which triggered a seriously glaring look from Jeff, directed at me.

"Oh, no," I thought.

They closed the door, and a few minutes later Trump emerged shaking his head. I found out what happened as we all headed for his plane. The deal he offered to Cruz was this: the only way he would let Cruz speak at the convention was if he came out and formally endorsed him publicly. Flatteringly. He thought Cruz would jump at the offer. It was easy! It was the same thing Trump wanted from anyone else, he told him. But Cruz didn't jump at it. Instead, Cruz and Roe hemmed and hawed and said, "Give us some time to think about it."

So Trump walked away.

Then, as we were boarding the plane, Cruz's team put out a press release announcing that Cruz was now "scheduled to speak" at the convention.

Trump was furious. He thought he'd made it clear that "nobody" from the party was going to speak without endorsing him. (Which was still better than his original stance of "no politicians" on the convention stage at all, I thought.)

He took his anger out on Paul, and told Paul to "fix it."

So Paul called Cruz's team that instant. But instead of shutting Cruz down completely and telling them they'd broken the deal and lost their slot, Paul believed that it still made sense to find a way to make it work. He told Jeff Roe, "It's okay to put out that you *might* be speaking, but we need that endorsement. We *need it.*"

Paul wanted to make it look like the meeting had gone well, in the interest of continuing to mend fences on what had otherwise been a very good day with the Republican Party. He was still angling to get Trump an endorsement from Paul Ryan, and others, which would have gone a long way toward bringing some of the more conservative members of the caucus and party faithful into the fold, for certain.

His intention was absolutely wanting to help Trump, but he got mired in a gray area—and because of that, he wound up angering Trump more than anything else.

As the plane took off, Trump turned to us and announced, "This is not going to happen. Cruz is *not* going to speak at the convention. In fact, forget it. McConnell, Ryan—none of them are speaking!"

The convention was ten days away.

CHAPTER 6

The Convention Begins

*Choosing Pence, the Never-Trumpers' Last
Stand, and Clinching the Nomination*

Back in New York City, Paul impressed upon Trump that we absolutely needed to decide on a VP by week's end. We needed to make an announcement. We needed to get his choice up to speed and ready for the convention.

Fortunately for us, Ivanka pulled herself out of the running. She went to her father and said, "No, Dad. It's not a good idea." And he capitulated.

All of Trump's other potential VP picks had been made public already. Usually, VP candidates are under lock and key; no information is shared until the appointed day. The media constantly played the speculation game about who it might be, and they did it poorly since they never had enough information to complete the picture. In Trump's case, he *encouraged* his potential VP candidates to go out and tell people they were being considered, and then he kept every one of them thinking they were still in the running.

Jared and Ivanka were fond of Newt Gingrich as a choice, but Trump had already told us, privately, that he thought "there was something wrong and off" with Newt. He would constantly hit Trump with a barrage of policy ideas, and Trump did not have the appetite or patience to deal with him. Trump kept throwing bones to Christie too, although Trump had already agreed that the fallout from his "Bridgegate" scandal and Christie's own media-hungry presidential ambitions meant he would never be seriously considered as the top pick for the job.

There was almost no one left on the VP list when Trump flew to Indiana on Tuesday, July 12, to attend a rally in Westfield. So we arranged for Trump to meet with Pence again as part of a bigger campaign tour out West, where Trump would hold rallies but also continue vetting some of the VP candidates. And when Trump arrived at the governor's mansion, the two had an okay meeting. It was cordial, and it was clear that Pence wanted the job and would stand by Trump as a loyal soldier. But Trump still wasn't sold.

Ten days earlier, on the way to Bedminster on July 2, Trump asked about our vetting of Pence and whether there was anything in his past that might hurt him. So I gave him a copy of the vetting report and showed him: the vetting on Pence came back so squeaky-clean that Trump didn't believe it was real.

"Come on," he said. "This guy must be hiding something."

Trump simply did not trust politicians, and even after this second meeting on the twelfth, he felt he still did not know Pence well enough to bring him on board.

That's when I got a call from Johnny McEntee, a hardworking young aide to Trump, with some unexpected news: there was a mechanical issue with Trump's plane. The issue was serious enough that they weren't going to be able to fix it before morning—the brake on one of the wheels had malfunctioned and popped the tire in the process. Trump was in disbelief.

Looking back, it almost feels like some kind of divine intervention, because the chain of events that followed could not have happened without it.

We scrambled to try and get Trump's smaller jet out to Indiana, but he was traveling with too many people to fit on it. So Pence offered to host Trump in Indianapolis for the night, and although Trump was not thrilled with the prospect, he accepted the offer and ended up staying at the Conrad Hotel.

That night, Trump had an impromptu dinner with the Pences at the Capital Grille, which was located inside the Conrad. They made a plan to meet for breakfast the next morning at the governor's mansion. Originally, Pence was supposed to travel back to New York City following the rally with Trump to meet with Trump's kids so they could get to know him better, but the mechanical issue upended that plan. So at 1:00 a.m., Jared called me to see if I could find a private jet to get the kids to Indiana so they could meet Pence there instead. We scrambled a jet, and fortunately for us, the kids flew to Indianapolis undetected by the press.

The next morning, over breakfast at a table decorated with flowers that Mike and Karen had picked themselves from the garden, Trump witnessed something he had never seen before: the normally exceptionally polite and subdued Pence verbally ripped into Hillary Clinton in a vicious and extended monologue. He focused on both Bill *and* Hillary, and all of the "corruption" he saw in the Clinton administration in the 1990s, which he believed persisted to this day.

Trump thought it was great. He responded in agreement with almost everything Pence said, and he clearly liked seeing some fire in the guy.

When breakfast was over, the whole group moved to another part of the mansion, and Trump got down to business. Trump wanted to know why Mike Pence wanted the job of VP, and Pence continued to step up his answers. His staff told me he was well aware of some of the statements that Trump had made to others about Pence struggling in his gubernatorial race, referring to him as a "loser" when he was down 10 percent and throwing his endorsement to Cruz. Knowing how Trump kept score, Pence knew he needed to perform on this day. And it was arguably one of the best performances of his life.

Trump's instincts were that he needed "a killer" as his VP. It was a concept we had discussed many times as we worked through the VP candidates. Paul didn't see it that way: "Donald, the vice presidential candidate is usually the hatchet man," he said. "But on your ticket, *you* are the hatchet. *You* are the killer. So why do you need a killer?"

Trump posed this very question to Pence after their breakfast meeting. And as might be expected, Pence declared to Trump that he was "not" a killer, but rather an "ardent worker" who would be a great governor in support of Trump and his policies.

So, Trump pressed Pence once more. "Why do you want this job, Mike? Why are you going through this process?"

Pence looked at Trump and assertively said, "Well, you tell me. You're in *my* home."

Trump responded, "Wow," and for the first time he saw a strong side to Pence that he had not before seen. Trump was clearly impressed—and so were the kids.

He didn't offer Pence the VP slot then and there. He flew on to California later that morning for more rallies and a few roundtables. But on the plane ride, he phoned Paul to update him on the meeting and remarked that Pence "looked the part" of a vice president. "The guy's straight out of Central Casting," he said.

I knew enough to know that Trump was still not completely sold.

Encouraged by Jared and Ivanka, later that night, Trump called Pence and told him, "I want you to be ready," implying that he was going to be Trump's VP candidate. But I knew he had used that exact same phrase when talking to Chris Christie and Newt Gingrich about the VP slot in the past. Still, there wasn't much time left. We went ahead and invited Pence to come to New York that weekend to participate in campaign events already scheduled, just in case.

The next day, in private, Trump struggled with his decision and started unwinding it. Then he called in to Greta Van Susteren's show on Fox that day, and when she asked him if he'd made his VP pick, he said, "I still haven't made my *final* final decision yet."

Fortunately, the kids weighed in again. It seemed to me that Trump often wanted multiple reassurances about his choices. He would second-guess his own decisions long after the rest of us thought they had been finalized, and he generally wanted to know that his family was on board with any decision he made. In this case, Jared, who Trump knew had been a proponent of Newt's for a long time, stepped up and gave his full support to Pence. So did Eric, Don Jr., and Ivanka.

Melania had already given him her endorsement of the Pences too.

So instead of waiting to make the formal announcement of his running mate at a press conference, which had always been the protocol for an announcement this important, he tweeted out his selection of Pence on the morning of July 15. The following day, at a previously planned campaign event in Manhattan, Trump announced his selection to the gathered crowd and brought Pence out on stage to rousing applause.

With less than forty-eight hours to go before the start of the convention in Cleveland, the VP selection process was finally *over*.

Now we just had to make sure that Trump actually secured the nomination.

A number of anonymous sources had kept tabs for us on the Never-Trumpers' every move. They had informed us that we needed to have a strong presence at the party's Rules Committee meeting one week prior to the official convention itself. The Rules Committee, made up of a group of 112 Republican National Committee members, generally meets every four years to determine the rules for the next convention, which won't occur until four years after the current one. I suppose it's similar to the way the Olympics Committee might meet to determine rules for future Olympics, four years in advance. It would be unusual, and frankly unfair, for anyone to attempt to change the rules for the Olympics a week before they began. It seems obvious that it would be unfair for anyone to attempt to change the rules of what goes on in the procedures of the presidential nomination process just one week before the convention kick-off too. But that's exactly where the Never-Trumpers were planning to make their stand.

We discovered that certain members were going to try to bring about changes in the way the formal nomination process unfolds, to change the technical process of the way delegates are counted at the convention. In essence, the Never-Trumpers intended to stage a coup.

Thankfully, we were able to talk to enough of the 112 Rules Committee members ahead of time to ensure such a rule change would never come to a vote.

But isn't it kind of insane that 112 die-hard Republicans, many of whom have held their positions on the Rules Committee for twenty years or more, are the sole arbiters of the rules surrounding the choice of who becomes the Republican nominee for president? Frankly, the possibility of the rules changing every four years seems insane. That small group of individuals holds too much power. This is the very essence of the "rigged" system that Donald Trump railed against, and which so many Americans want to see ended. When a system is this complicated and this insular at every stage, then every stage opens up a new possibility of corruption.

Our effort worked, but the attempted coup wasn't over.

There was still a possibility that a Never-Trumper could call for a rules change from the floor of the arena, at the very start of the convention come Monday. And that was the plan: for one state's chair to call for a roll call vote then and there, which could trigger a rule change—and all it would take to enact such a rule change was for nine state delegations to support it.

Given how much anti-Trump sentiment there was, we knew the Never-Trumpers had a shot at possibly securing nine states' worth of support, and we were not going to take any chances that this might occur.

The convention takes place over a grueling four-day schedule. There's no way that one chairman could possibly be expected to oversee it all. So the RNC uses a rotating cast of prominent Republicans to take over as the party's "presiding chairman" for various periods of time throughout the official proceedings.

Reince Priebus was in charge of that schedule. So we worked with him to ensure that a Trump supporter would serve as the presiding chairman at the opening of the convention—at the only moment in the four-day proceedings when a rules change could be enacted.

We chose Steve Womack, a pro-Trump congressman from Arkansas.

We let Steve know about the pending coup attempt, so he'd be ready for it if it came.

In the opening minutes, in a packed arena in Cleveland, Ken Cuccinelli, the chair of the Virginia delegation and one of the leaders of the Never-Trump movement, made a motion asking for roll call votes.

Womack, in his role as presiding chair, acknowledged the motion: "There's a motion on the table," he said. He then followed the established parliamentary procedure of calling for a voice vote from the Virginia delegates on the motion their chair had put forth.

"All those in favor?" he asked.

A good number of delegates across the convention floor called out, "Aye!"

"All those opposed?" Womack asked.

An equally solid number of delegates called out, "Nay!"

"The Nays have it," Womack said.

Cuccinelli immediately stood up and objected to Womack's ruling. He called for a roll call on the voice vote, and Womack replied, "No. The Nays have it. Next order of business."

Cuccinelli was visibly incensed, and the Never-Trumpers around him and from various seats all over the arena started yelling: "Fraud!" "Sham!" "It's *rigged!*"

I was standing next to the Virginia delegation as it all unfolded, and to my ears, the Nays really did have it.

Cuccinelli tried to continue arguing for the roll call vote, saying that there were nine states that supported his motion, and that according to procedure, those nine states should be heard from next. But Womack simply declared that three of those states had backed out. As chair, it was up to him to decide whether to hear from those states, and he chose not to.

"The chair recognizes that three states no longer support that motion, so motion is denied," he said.

It was pure parliamentary finagling.

Cuccinelli was furious. He knew this was the last possible stand to muster, and the Never-Trumpers fell. He threw his credentials on the ground and stormed out of the arena.

If we didn't have Womack in place as the presiding chair, it all could have gone down very differently. Whoever controlled the mic controlled the process. But because *we* controlled it, we were able to quickly quell the Never-Trumpers' attempt at subversion.

When I look back and think of the number of months, the twenty-hour days, the resources dedicated to ensuring this one thing—the convention would not be contested—it astounds me that it all ended in a single three-minute exchange on the floor.

After all of the threats, the rumors, the subterfuge, and a barrage of drooling media reports saying that the Never-Trumpers had something up their sleeves, in less than five minutes, we destroyed them. There was nothing more they could do to stop Trump from becoming the nominee, and in the end, we squashed them with a procedural measure.

It also astounds me just how close this country came to *not* seeing Donald Trump make it through the convention. It all could have ended then and there. And hardly anyone outside of a small, intensely politically minded circle had any idea what had occurred.

Donald Trump never got into the minutia of it all. He didn't ask us about what we were doing to stop the Never-Trumpers. He had no idea of the lengths we'd gone to, to put Trump supporters in charge of the sub-committees of the convention Rules Committee itself, or how important Paul's relationship with Reince Priebus and the party apparatus actually was to his success.

When he did ask about it, we told him, "We won. We've got it under control," and that was good enough for him.

When he flew into Cleveland on the evening of July 18, secretly, in order to walk on stage and make a surprise appearance to introduce Melania at her speech, we didn't brief him on every detail of what had taken place on the floor. We just told him that the Never-Trumpers had been defeated.

"The way is paved for you to get the nomination," Paul said.

"Great," Trump replied. "Great job."

An hour later, I was standing backstage with Trump as all the lights in the arena went down, and a hush fell over the crowd.

During our Convention 101 talks with Trump and his family, Paul and I had explained to him that traditionally, the nominee doesn't arrive in the city of the convention until Wednesday night, the night before his speech. When his wife speaks, usually on the first night of the convention, she would be introduced by a close friend or other family member.

But Trump said, "What if *I* introduce her?"

Paul and I looked at each other and he said, "*Different.* Okay. Let's do it."

As we got into production meetings, weeks before the convention, Trump described exactly what he wanted. "I want the whole auditorium dark, and then I want to simply come out, in the middle, and I'm going to introduce her," he said. I wrote several lines for him to say, and he read them, and he told me, "This is good, but I'm just going to go out and say, 'Ladies and gentlemen, my wife, Melania Trump.'"

The production guys, who Trump knew from his *Apprentice* days, thought it might be cool to add a smoke element, and some backlighting, so when he first stepped on stage the only thing the audience would see was his silhouette, and Trump loved that idea.

He picked the music too: the latter part of Queen's "We Are the Champions."

And now, it was happening. The smoke machines billowed. The music started. The lights came up, and he turned to me and said, "Watch this."

Trump stepped out through the smoke, and the backlighting came up, and the audience caught one glimpse of his distinctive silhouette on that stage, and they went *nuts*. Nobody in the audience knew he was there. He wasn't supposed to be there. It was a complete surprise, and they gave him a long standing ovation.

"Thank you," he said. "Thank you. We're going to win so big. Thank you." He had to repeat it a few times until the crowd calmed down. And then, riding the energy, he said, "Ladies and gentlemen, it is my great honor to present the next First Lady of the United States, my wife—an amazing mother, an incredible woman—Melania Trump."

As she walked out, they feigned a kiss without actually touching, so as not to mess up her makeup. She walked to the podium wearing an all-white dress and she just wowed everyone. She had never stood on the international stage like this. Ever. She had never been asked to speak in a political environment for more than a single minute in her entire life. But she was poised. She read from the teleprompter with ease. She connected with the audience. Trump came back behind the curtain and watched her on a TV monitor, alongside me and Paul, and he just kept saying, "Fantastic. *Fantastic*. This is great!"

The applause at the end of her speech was huge.

Honestly, our first day could not have gone any better.

Melania planned to head straight home to Trump Tower after her speech, and so did Trump. We ushered them to the motorcade, they rode to the airport, and our program ended around 10:00 p.m.—and by 10:30 p.m., our moment of first-day campaign bliss ended.

Suddenly my phone started blowing up with text messages from reporters. "Hey. Who wrote Melania's speech? There are some big similarities to Michelle Obama's speech from 2008."

Paul got on the phone to Trump, just before the plane took off. "We've got a problem," he said, as I held up my phone and showed him one part of Michelle Obama's speech that seemed way too close for comfort to what we had just heard from Melania on the stage in Cleveland. "It appears Melania might have used excerpts from Michelle Obama's speech."

"It was a great speech," Trump said. "Everyone loved it."

Once again, when we should have been taking a victory lap, we found ourselves pulling into the pits for repairs. Paul immediately went on TV and defended the speech, vigorously. But in the late hours, one of the networks made a line-by-line comparison of the two speeches and pretty much blew Paul's defense out of the water.

One word or one action was often the difference in our campaign of going from control to chaos. And managing the aftereffects was a challenge.

The moment Trump and Melania landed in New York, Paul got him on the phone again. I was with him. He put it on speaker. "It's worse than we thought," Paul said. "It appears that there are several excerpts that are used word for word from Michelle's speech."

Melania started crying. Through tears, she said she was less upset about the embarrassment for herself than she was worried that it might hurt her husband.

Trump stayed remarkably calm. "Baby, don't worry about it," he said. "You did phenomenal. You did a great job."

Paul said, "We'll continue to defend it, but we need to get to the bottom of it."

None of us had worked on her speech, which begged the question: Who did?

Trump's kids, including his second youngest, Tiffany, who was in college and who stayed out of the limelight most of the time, were all scheduled to give speeches, and all of them had worked with the campaign's speechwriters that were hired by Paul, Jared, Stephen Miller, and me. They had all been proofread. (But we immediately started proofreading them again, searching for any plagiarized passages, just in case.) The speechwriters we hired gave some material to Melania to read too. But almost as soon as we started the process, Melania said she was "all set." She would handle the speech with her own team from that point forward. So we had no idea who might be to blame for the plagiarism.

By 9:00 the next morning, the media started identifying *me* as the guy in charge of Melania's speech. My name was suddenly all over the news. Before that morning, my name hadn't surfaced publicly in the course of the entire campaign.

Weeks later, I would learn that Corey Lewandowski was the guy who planted that seed with the media. I knew he was still angry with Paul. Perhaps this was his way of seeking a little revenge for his June firing—but I didn't know that at the time. I was sure I was about to be fired. I called Paul to see if he'd gotten any kind of a heads-up, and he said, "Don't worry about it, everybody knows it's not your fault. You're fine."

But I wasn't so sure. To do something wrong and get caught for it is one thing. To be innocent and charged with something you had no part in at all is another. This was my reputation on the line. And to be fired for it could very well mark a disastrous end to my political career.

A few minutes later, my cell phone rang. It was Trump calling from his office in New York City. I picked up. I could tell he had me on the speakerbox. "Rick, I want to talk to you about Melania's speech. With everything that's going on with this speech, I wanted to call you. I want to let you know," he said, speaking slower with every word, "that you... are...not fired!"

He started laughing.

"Look, I know it wasn't your fault," he said.

I was relieved.

He seemed to be in a really good mood. He started talking about what a fantastic job Melania did. He said he recognized there were issues with the speech, but he didn't want any of us to focus on them because she gave such a great speech.

Before the day was out, a new round of press reports emerged saying that Meredith McIver was the one who wrote Melania's speech. Meredith is a full-time writer on Trump's staff. She's a grandmotherly type who stays completely out of the spotlight, who happens to be the ghostwriter behind most of Mr. Trump's books over the years—almost all of them after *The Art of the Deal*. But in the end, there was never a retraction from any of the media outlets or a specific press release from the campaign saying that I *wasn't* the one who wrote the speech.

Meredith wasn't fired for plagiarism, either. She had worked for Trump for far too long. I don't think it was her fault. I think she just fell on the sword a bit because the other two speechwriters who came aboard at the beginning—before Melania said she would handle the speech on her own, with her own people—had prepared a document drawing upon highlights from great speeches by First Ladies from the past. Meredith, and anyone else on Melania's team who worked on the speech, seemed to have worked from that preliminary document. Apparently, they did so without realizing that the passages they were reading were examples meant to *inspire*, not to *copy*.

This was the sort of chaos that happened on Trump's campaign far too frequently. There were miscommunications all the time.

In this case, the criticism directed at Melania calmed down, and she didn't take that big of a hit. There were plenty of media pundits who tried to use the plagiarism to say she was of poor character, mainly because she was easy pickings. But the people of America did not see her as some "politician's wife" who'd been at this for twenty-five years. There was a sympathy factor.

It's amazing to me that we didn't have issues with any of Donald Trump's other chosen speakers at this convention. Because his speakers list was *out there*.

The Monday night speakers, selected around a theme of "Make America Safe Again," included Willie Robertson, of *Duck Dynasty* fame; actor Scott Baio (yes, Chachi from *Happy Days*); and former Navy Seal Marcus Luttrell, who survived a Taliban attack and inspired the movie *Lone Survivor*. On Tuesday, for the theme of "Make America Work Again," Trump kicked things off with a speech by Dana White, the president of the UFC.

That's the Ultimate Fighting Championship, an organization which oversees and broadcasts massive mixed martial arts fights staged at Madison Square Garden and other huge arenas all around the globe. I wound up sitting with Reince Priebus and the CEO of the convention, Jeff Larson, for that one, and they didn't know who half of these people were. But so many of the speeches went smoothly and were so well received by the audience that they just went with it. After all the infighting and resistance, the party adapted to Trump—and wound up getting all kinds of positive publicity for it. For instance, that night, billionaire investor Peter Thiel spoke, and it was the first time in history that an openly gay man had spoken in a primetime slot at the Republican National Convention. For decades, the very thought of a gay man speaking in front of that audience was considered taboo. It was basically forbidden. But when it happened? Nobody blinked an eye.

To me, it was a great example of why change is good, and a great example of why even the radical change of electing an outsider like Trump to break up this old system was so very, very welcomed by the American public.

It will be up to the Republican Party, and to history, to determine if what they gave up while embracing Trump's brand was worth it in the end.

Trump's friend, real estate billionaire Tom Barrack, spoke that night. So did Kimberlin Brown, an actress from the soap opera *The Bold and the Beautiful*. Kerry Woolard, the general manager of Trump Winery, spoke too. The RNC didn't like that last one at all. They felt it was a brazen attempt at self-promotion by Trump, the private citizen and businessman, to pump his brand to an international audience. The party had to pick their battles.

I won't get into all the speakers for Wednesday's "Make America First Again" theme, or Thursday's "Make America One Again" theme—yes, a theme of unity from Donald Trump. But many were just as unexpected and "outrageous" as the speakers on the first two nights.

And then there was Ted Cruz.

An hour before Cruz's allotted speech time on Thursday evening, President Trump made one last demand (through Paul) for Cruz to endorse him during the speech. And Cruz still brushed him off. So Trump said, "I want him out. He is not speaking."

Paul begged Trump not to do it. He insisted that he himself had made the deal to let Cruz speak, and he understood if Trump was angry with him, but Cruz was the runner-up in the primaries and caucuses. It was tradition. The delegates expected to hear from him, and it could look really bad for Trump—as if he weren't a team player on the night they were talking about *unity*, of all things—if he were to cut Cruz's speech at the last minute.

"Fine," Trump said. "But he can't sell it. Never could. This will be bad for him."

Later that evening, just before Cruz started his speech, Trump came over to Rocket Arena and I brought him down to our holding suite. He was watching the proceedings on a TV. But restlessly, he said, "Come on, Rick, let's go have some fun." We headed to the family suite area where his kids were seated. I accompanied him up through the hallways to show him how to get there. I assumed he would want to know where to look during his own speech so that he could point to his family in the crowd later that night.

"It's over here," I said, leading him to an entryway into one of the audience sections. "It's right through here. So when you're on stage, you'll just look up and to the right."

"Oh," Trump said. "I see."

Cruz's voice was echoing through the arena and spilling out into that empty hallway, and at that moment, more than a few Republicans on the floor started booing him. In his speech, he told the delegates to "vote your conscience," in what seemed like a blatant dig against Trump.

Trump peeked out through the stairwell opening at the arena full of people, and then he looked back at me with a mischievous look in his eye.

"*Watch this*," he said.

Before I could say anything, Trump walked straight out into the well-lit arena and started descending the stairs near the Trump family box, slowly. A few audience members in the vicinity spotted him immediately. They started cheering. All of a sudden, every head in the arena turned to see what was going on, and as soon as people saw him they started shouting and hollering from all the way down on the convention floor. He waved to them. Like royalty. Cruz kept looking at the cameras and talking, oblivious to all of the shouts and commotion, clearly not connected to the crowd at all, or he would've noticed too. Then the cameramen figured out what was going on, and the production manager killed the lights on stage and cut away from Cruz's speech to show Trump mingling in the audience, all smiles and hand waves and thumbs up for the cameras and crowd.

I was standing right behind him, and I just turned my head and laughed.

The timing of Trump's spontaneous walk-on completely distracted from everything Cruz was saying. It destroyed the man's big moment on national TV. It happened right as Cruz was getting into the closing section of his speech, which I'm sure he thought was going to be a home run. But Trump drew so much attention that Cruz basically got ejected from the stage. The producers turned his mic off, and Cruz walked away with his head down, as the crowd kept chanting for Trump.

Where is Ted Cruz today? Supporting President Trump.

That one moment did him in. It took the wind out of his presidential-hopeful sails, and he's never been able to get that wind back.

Once again, Trump proved that he could draw more attention than anyone else in the room and outplay any politician in the game. And for those who crossed him or refused to play by his rules, there would always be a price to pay.

CHAPTER 7

Shifting to the General Election

Trump Being Trump

WE WOKE UP THE MORNING AFTER TRUMP'S ACCEPTANCE SPEECH to a ten-point bump in the polls. The feeling of what we'd accomplished can only be described in one word: euphoria.

It lasted for only a few hours. Before he headed to the airport, he stopped for what was supposed to be a ten-minute press conference aimed at thanking his campaign staff and supporters. But after he called all of us up to stand on stage with him, in plain view of the cameras, he launched into a tirade about Ted Cruz. He talked endlessly about a *National Enquirer* conspiracy story that Cruz's dad was somehow involved in the assassination of John F. Kennedy. And we all had to stand on stage while he did it.

His ten-point bump, the policy issues he discussed in his speech—any of it could have served as the perfect press-friendly launch pad into the general election, and instead Trump's random, conspiracy-laden ruminations on Ted Cruz's father became the media narrative of the day.

By the time it ended, my phone was blowing up. Paul, Jared, even Ivanka called me directly, asking, "What the hell just happened?!"

It was just so frustrating. There was no need for it. No *reason* for it.

And afterwards, we all tried to analyze, "*Why?*"

The best conclusion that we came up with was that the rallies and the impromptu press conferences were his outlets. After being kept from those outlets and being scripted so much over the course of the previous week for the convention, I think he just needed to unleash his frustrations. He needed to let off some steam.

The more we thought about our weekly schedules, we realized we were always better off when we gave him as many opportunities to speak in front of a crowd as possible. He would stay more positive and upbeat. He was more energized. He would stay on message, most of the time. We were almost better off scheduling three or four rallies in a single *day* than we were giving him three days off in a row.

If we didn't follow that unique set of rules? He might wind up taking what was supposed to be a ten-minute moment and turning it into a ninety-minute unfiltered rally, collapsing all the goodwill and support we'd built in a spotlight week, after months of effort.

It was an exhausting experience. All candidates' staffs have to deal with unplanned, unexpected scenarios and be able to adapt at a second's notice. But with Trump, more unplanned things happened in a week, or sometimes a single *day*, than would happen during any other campaign.

But no matter how much we learned about how to deal with his particular quirks and habits, the overriding message we received was this: "He wasn't going to change." And at this stage, few of us expected him to.

He was going to say what he was going to say, and say it when he wanted to say it. So we learned to deal with it, as opposed to trying to prevent it. We *couldn't* prevent it.

No one is *ever* going to prevent it. Because no single event will ever override the cumulative, overarching effect that his authentic, unfiltered voice has when it comes to engaging his supporters.

In every instance that he said something "un-presidential," it typically created a stir between us with the media, because they wanted to blow up every one of his words to show he's "not fit to be president." But in every instance, Trump himself knew better how to deal with the situation than anyone else. Better than his family, better than his advisors and close friends. Sure, he would get swept up in the moment occasionally and take something too far, but years before he ever thought about running for office, he had already tried and tested what the public would accept. He put himself out there, constantly, on TV and in the New York tabloid newspapers, under the relative safety of being a "businessman," or a "celebrity." So while no one took him as seriously as they would in a political role, he had the luxury of spending decades learning what buttons he could push and what buttons he couldn't push in ways that no other politician could ever match. *Ever.* No politician could possibly have a chance to practice that way, and the political operatives around them would never dare to push as far as Trump pushes. On any subject.

He truly knows the media better than anybody else in the game. He knows their timeframe for creating news, and how long it takes for people to digest it. And when he brought that skill set to the world of politics, he changed the paradigm of political reporting. To be honest, over the course of the 2016 campaign, he changed the news cycle itself. Stories that used to unfold for three or four days now played themselves out in less than twenty-four hours. There was always something new to talk about, one more outrageous thing that he said, and no one on TV seemed to be able to control themselves enough to keep quiet about it—even though all of that publicity benefitted *him*. All of it. No matter how outrageous or un-presidential it seemed, it was unearned media attention, which amounted to free advertising. And that was fantastic for the Trump brand.

Not to jump too far ahead in the timeline here, but do you know how much the Clinton campaign spent on TV ads during the 2016 campaign? $253 million.

Want to know how much Trump spent? $93 million.

She outspent him nearly three to one, and traditionally the TV ads serve as a barometer of whose campaign game is stronger, and who will win.

Trump's time on TV, and the amount of time everyone on TV kept talking about him, far outweighed any advertising dollars spent. (As I mentioned earlier, our estimate of Trump's unpaid media time over the entirety of the campaign came in at more than $5 billion.)

Likewise, over the course of the campaign, Hillary Clinton held about 450 fundraisers, netting her some $595 million in donations.

Trump? He only did fifty, and yet, in those fifty, he raised about $258 million—almost half as much as Clinton raised, and she had to do nine times as much work. The time taken away doing fundraisers was time that Clinton could have spent with the voters. And in this case, it impacted Clinton's ability to connect with people—especially the on-the-fence Independents and Bernie Sanders supporters of all stripes that she needed in order to win.

While the Democratic National Convention played out over the following week, fraught with plenty of party infighting and even violent protests outside of the Wells Fargo Center in Philadelphia, we had a chance to sit back and watch what felt like a Democrat implosion—all while putting in some time to start figuring out how to get over a few obstacles on the road to the general election.

Paul had been planning ahead all along. He had already charted out various courses to victory, looking at electoral maps, and thinking about where Trump needed to go to beat Hillary Clinton in the race for the 270 votes needed to win the presidency. But getting there would take a lot of money, and fundraising was a big issue for us. Trump didn't like to do fundraisers. It wasn't his thing. He hadn't held a single fundraiser during the entire primary season. The closest we came early on with fundraisers was when we got him to do "roundtables" with a handful of potential donors just before his rallies, at the rally sites themselves, in states like California where he didn't travel as often. That was it.

He'd already spent $55 million of his own money during the primaries, and we would surely need hundreds of millions to beat the Clinton machine. Trump either didn't want or didn't have that kind of money to spend. So we needed to start fundraising quickly.

We had not seriously focused on fundraising and did not have a formal fundraising apparatus in place, which meant we needed to set up PACs, then meet with major donors and coordinate with the RNC, which usually plays a big part in the overall fundraising operation for the nominee. But even with Reince and the RNC in our camp, there was still a lot of animosity and hesitation among party Republicans over donating to Trump.

We would fight straight through September over issues related to how any money raised in conjunction with the RNC would be spent, because there were still lots of Republicans who didn't believe Trump could win. If he didn't win, that meant they wouldn't be able to ride his presidential coattails into office. So they wanted to see the bulk of the money raised with the RNC's help go to down-ballot races, to help congressional candidates (House and Senate) who didn't have the funding or media presence they needed without a "strong" Republican at the top of the ticket.

Those discussions did not go well with Trump. He wanted names. He wanted to know who the remaining "Never-Trumpers" were (even if they weren't part of the more organized Never-Trump movement). He wanted to make sure they did not benefit from his hard work.

Once the money started coming in, there were two major areas I believed we were going to need to pay attention to in order to win.

One was data analytics, the key to pinpoint-targeting our online advertising and outreach to specific groups and individual households based on a wealth of demographic and personal data that's available online. Data analytics give Facebook, Twitter, Amazon, even Google itself the ability to deliver just what you want, directly to you, in terms of advertising, news topics, and search results every time you open your laptop or pick up your phone or tablet to browse the Web or use social media of any kind. Using those resources for a campaign made sense to me.

Two, we needed a strong ground game and robust grassroots operation in as many key states as possible. On the day of the election, you have to get people out to vote. You could have 65 million people supporting you in polls, but unless they get out and vote, it doesn't count. That's why candidates have to invest heavily at the state and local level, in yard signs, phone banks, door knocks, absentee ballot programs, early voting programs—they all become important, and at this point Trump had very few state operations in place. He had plenty of supporters at the state level, obviously. But the funding, the resources, the structure just weren't there. The fact that he did so many rallies was fantastic. Building up voter intensity is a *huge* part of getting people to the voting booth, and Hillary Clinton would downplay that aspect of the ground game to her peril. But Trump needed to do more. And that would require lots of help from the RNC.

The other essential buckets involved in our general election strategy included:

Budget: In an extraordinary move, Trump put his kids, Don Jr. and Eric, in charge of the campaign budget, keeping all of the money matters close to the vest and in the family.

Communications: Reaching people online through digital advertisements, driven by data analytics; refining campaign messaging (which was driven by Trump's own words); refining his speeches and getting Trump to speak on some broader topics where necessary; increasing the number of surrogates, both "regular" surrogates to go on secondary shows, like CNN's Don Lemon show in the late evening, and "super surrogates," people with high profiles who could go on prime-time television outlets, including the nightly news and the Sunday political shows (*Meet the Press*, and so forth).

Debates: Not only prepping Trump for the three televised presidential debates with Hillary Clinton, which was a challenge because he didn't want to prep, but also negotiating the terms of those debates with the Presidential Debate Commission, to nail down the dates as well as various nuances, from stage arrangements to audience size to the format of questions to selecting moderators, which took months.

Transition: An important and necessary part of any nominee's strategy involves getting fully prepared to actually move into the White House and take over the leadership of the country in a smooth transition of power at exactly noon on January 20 of the following year. It's a massive undertaking that was not a focus for the Trump campaign, in part because Trump saw it as bad luck, and just because our staff was so small. Trump put Chris Christie in charge of the transition initially, but we barely spoke of it over the subsequent months.

The War Room: Immediately after the convention ended, we began work to establish a safe, secure spot to use as a true campaign headquarters from which we could run our communications, polling, state operations, research, and high-level discussions in private, with an assurance of no outside interference or eavesdropping.

We set up the War Room on the floor directly above the fifth-floor campaign headquarters we'd already been using. A single stairwell connected the two floors, so we could keep tabs on anyone who came and went and easily control the flow of people going up or down. That space was already partially finished because it's where the famous "Boardroom" was built for the filming of *The Apprentice*.

As all of the construction, fundraising, negotiating, and planning got underway, Trump brought two new players into the fold to help with the campaign going forward.

The first was Kellyanne Conway, a pollster who was already on our campaign working for Paul, and who had worked for Mike Pence for years. Trump liked the way she talked. He liked the way she looked, the way she carried herself, and her approach to breaking down polls. Kellyanne had a keen ability to break down a number of the key issues in terms of how women viewed them. This was important because women voters were a critical component to winning the election. We put her on TV as a surrogate, and she was perfect in Trump's eyes.

I noticed that Trump seemed to listen to her and respond to her in a way that he generally reserved for Ivanka, or for Jared. It's like she was some kind of Trump whisperer. She was quick to understand how he processed issues and situations, and she knew how to navigate his moods. That was great for Paul, because Kellyanne and Paul saw eye to eye on the way a campaign ought to be run in terms of overall messaging and key strategic efforts.

The second hire, in mid-August, was Steve Bannon, the founder of Breitbart News, a site that Trump regularly went to for information. Bannon is also a skilled political operative. He was hired as the campaign's CEO to oversee the entire operation from a top-down position, which he assumed would also give him control of the campaign budget. When he found out Trump had instead given budget control to Don

Jr. and Eric, he wasn't happy. He basically started his position with one hand tied behind his back.

Bannon came recommended by Rupert Murdoch, the billionaire creator of Fox News Channel and head of News Corp, the company that owns the *New York Post*, the *Wall Street Journal*, HarperCollins publishing, Sky News, the *Times of London*, and dozens of other global media properties.

Murdoch wasn't involved in the day-to-day campaign activities, but he was quite involved in influencing Trump and Jared behind the scenes. They had weekly calls, and Trump saw Murdoch as a compatriot, a colleague who understood and advised him on what he believed was the most important element of his campaign: the media.

Murdoch was absolutely one of Trump's top outside advisors.

It's interesting to me that Bannon came recommended by Murdoch because Bannon's views were so well known. He's a nationalist who preached against globalism, and this resonated with much of Trump's voter base. He was opposed to the sort of power and control that existed among the elites, especially the Washington elites, and specifically at the RNC. His rumpled, often disheveled appearance, with multiple untucked layered t-shirts and button-downs, seemed completely out of place in Trump Tower's Fifth Avenue glitz. But Trump followed Murdoch's advice, and once Bannon showed up, he quickly solidified his importance as a critical player in the campaign.

It was clear to me that Paul and Bannon were never going to see eye to eye. But with Bannon focused entirely on media and boosting Trump's optics on TV, at the same time Paul focused on political tactics and the ground game, the two of them could have made an unstoppable team.

We would never get a chance to find out.

CHAPTER 8

Trump's Campaign Shake-Up

An Unconventional Campaign Model That Worked

O N AUGUST 14, RIGHT AFTER BANNON CAME ABOARD, THE *NEW York Times* reached out to Paul, saying they were getting ready to run an unflattering story—not on Trump, but on Paul himself. A reporter at the *Times* had been given a document from Ukraine, reportedly copied from a "black ledger," that allegedly showed evidence that long before the Trump campaign started, Paul had taken payouts of more than $12 million in cash from the Party of Regions, the ruling party in power at that time. The problem is that the story was completely made up by an opposition politician named Serhiy Leshchenko.

Three years later, investigations showed that the "black ledger" was fabricated. Paul's signature on that ledger was not actually his. And the "pages" supposedly shared with the *Times* were unverified copies, not originals. Furthermore, the parties who were interviewed by the *Times* at the time have since confirmed that they were handed the photocopied pages by sources they did not know. And the man who sent the fake ledger pages to the *Times* was one of Paul's clients' major political opponents in

Ukraine, who has since admitted that the ledger would not stand up as credible in a court.

In the middle of a presidential campaign, there was no time for Paul to prove any of that. The damage was done. The *Times*, which apparently did little due diligence as to the sourcing of the ledger pages, ran with the story despite Paul indicating that the story was fraudulent. The story made other unfounded accusations about Paul's financial and lobbying activities too, which sent shockwaves through Washington regardless of whether the story was true or not.

Paul let Trump know what was happening before the story hit and told him, "We're not going to respond to this. It's a completely fabricated story with no basis in fact."

I knew then that Trump had lost confidence in Paul Manafort.

If Paul had gone to Trump, told him the story was complete nonsense, and that he was going to attack the *Times* for printing it, Trump would have supported him. If Paul fought, I'm positive Trump would have respected that more, even if the story were true. (To be clear, it was not.)

But in this instance, Paul was weighed down by an old school mentality and never fully realized how much the media had changed in presidential politics since he'd worked on Bob Dole's campaign back in 1996. Paul's position was that he should never put the focus on himself and distract from the candidate. This was breaking a cardinal rule of presidential campaigns. Instead, Paul decided he would attempt to minimize the impact on both himself and Trump by having his attorney make one short statement and then letting the story fade into the background.

In the new, Twittering, non-stop twenty-four-hour-cable-news-cycle world, that strategy did not stand a chance at working.

On August 18, Paul called me near midnight. Jared had just called him, he said, asking him to meet for breakfast in the morning to discuss the story and developing situation. Paul said, "It's not blowing over. I think I'm going to suggest that I take a leave of absence and come back once things cool down."

The next morning, Jared told Paul that Trump did not believe he was going to be able to overcome "the Ukraine issue," and that he wanted Paul to resign and step aside. Paul attempted to explain, once again, that the ledger was fabricated. He could prove it. But none of them had time to endure a long fact-finding mission.

Jared wouldn't give him the time.

Paul suggested a leave of absence, but Jared said, "That's not going to work. The announcement is coming out in about thirty minutes."

Thirty minutes later, the campaign released an announcement saying Paul had resigned.

In reality, he was fired. Not by Trump himself, of course. But by Jared.

Jared came to me later in the morning. "I just want you to know you've done a phenomenal job for us," he said. "You have your hands in so many areas of the campaign. We still want you to be deputy manager reporting to Kellyanne and Bannon."

Kellyanne had been promoted to campaign manager.

I went to Paul's office. He had just settled into his new space on the fourteenth floor. He told me he was "gone" and Jared did not entertain the idea of a leave of absence. I told him I wasn't sure if I wanted to stay with the campaign without him. For the last ten years, I had watched Paul develop winning strategies and execute them near flawlessly. I didn't know Bannon at all.

I questioned whether or not Trump would have a fighting chance without Paul. I believed Trump had what it took—his messaging, his stamina, his presence—but as Paul and I knew, there was a lot more to presidential campaigns than just that when it comes to actually winning.

"Trump can win this. Trump can absolutely win this," Paul said.

I still wondered if this was my cue to bow out.

"I absolutely believe Trump can win," Paul reiterated. "I think you should stay. You know how he operates, you know how he thinks, you know the campaign. I can understand if you want to leave, but you should seriously consider staying."

I felt bad for Paul. I knew the *Times* story was false. I was *there*. There was no phantom $12 million in cash. But the more I thought about it and the timing of it all, the more it became clear to me that Paul was fired for more than just the Ukraine story. For Trump, the issues with Paul went right back to the very beginning—to Paul telling the RNC that Trump would "pivot" and be "more presidential" after the convention, and the other little clashes along the way.

Paul was the type of political operative into whose hands most candidates place their chance at success or failure. He was used to managing a candidate, building and following a strategy, scripting everything out, and Trump just wasn't that type of individual.

Paul had never really encountered a candidate like Trump, and Trump never had any interest in putting his fate or future in anybody's hands except his own.

On Monday, August 23, I met with Bannon for the first time ever, one-on-one. He had already set up an office on the fourteenth floor. So had Kellyanne—she moved right into the office that Paul had only recently set up for himself.

Bannon was very matter of fact. "All right, give me a download. Give me the lay of the land," he said.

I had learned that Bannon grew up in Richmond, where I currently live, so we talked briefly about our shared roots before I gave him a rundown on how we had managed to operate the campaign up to that point. We also talked about a few special programs that Paul had organized as part of his overall strategy, including:

- Building a strong outreach campaign to unions. Many blue-collar workers liked and respected Trump. A number of union representatives had already ensured Paul that as long as Trump didn't take a position on Right to Work, they would encourage their members to vote for Trump (unofficially)—even though "officially" they were giving their endorsement to Hillary. This would make a big difference in certain battleground states.

- In addition, the unions agreed to hold back resources normally used for "get out the vote" efforts on the Democrat side. This was significant but easy for them to do, they stated, since Hillary had not inspired them.

- Building a real National Economic Council for Trump, and a real National Security Council, to advise him—especially as we got closer to the debates.

- Putting together some consistent, formal coalition groups and outreach programs.
- And continued bridge-building with the RNC.

That last one was going to be tough. Having Bannon at the helm didn't go over well with the RNC at all. Priebus and Bannon didn't get along. They played nicely when needed to but fought each other behind the scenes on many issues.

Bannon also had a totally different style of working compared to Paul's. For instance, he would stay at work until 2:00 a.m. but then wouldn't come into the office until 10:00 a.m.

That actually worked well with Trump's schedule. Even though Trump was up and reading the news and making calls in the early morning hours, he rarely left his residence before 10:00 a.m. to make his way down to the twenty-sixth floor.

Bannon's presence also synced with Trump. Bannon was good at building narratives and deflecting issues. But more than anything, Bannon found an immensely powerful voice through Trump and his agenda of "America First." As an ideologue, Bannon could not have found a more perfect union. Trump provided the army of supporters that Bannon wanted so desperately to use to promote this shared agenda and similar policy goals.

With all of this internal shuffling going on, the media kept reporting that Trump's campaign had fallen into chaos. But it hadn't. It's actually pretty normal for a campaign to go through personnel changes and shuffling as the focus shifts from the convention into the general election. It just seemed more chaotic than usual because of how quickly, and publicly, Paul had been ousted, and the fact that the Trump campaign had such a small staff to begin with. But the core of the campaign remained the same. Social media director Dan Scavino and director of strategic communications Hope Hicks remained. Stephen Miller was still speechwriting, and in so doing was influencing the strength of Trump's "America First" policy points along the way. (Miller and Bannon had similar ideologies, so they got along from day one. Miller had used Breitbart to promote some of his policy positions well before his role started with the Trump campaign.)

Jared continued to solidify his role as de facto campaign manager and confirmed that I would remain as deputy campaign manager.

However, I suspected that the scrutiny of Paul would extend to me in my current role. Also, I was hesitant that Bannon and Kellyanne were bringing their own people into the campaign. I expressed my reservations to Reince, who then offered me a position as liaison with the RNC. Reince thought it was the right path for me at that stage, and I was eager to get out of the spotlight. Eventually, I took the role along with working on specific issues for Jared and Bannon.

Primarily, I was working with Brad Parscale to keep strengthening our digital campaign game.

It was widely acknowledged that Barack Obama's strong digital game was what put him over the top in 2008. And ever since then, the RNC had put a lot of time, money, and research into building a data operation that could overcome whatever system the Democrats had built. A lot of that work was done through a company that former George W. Bush campaign advisor Karl Rove had built, and it was assumed that once the party unified in 2016, whoever the nominee was would pick up the RNC data operation.

But we never really fully unified, although both sides worked genuinely to build bridges. And the campaign wasn't interested in using the RNC's system at all. Throughout the campaign, Jared made it clear that he wanted to build our own proprietary system, which we believed would be far more effective than anything the RNC had to offer.

That decision alone caused a lot of revised tension because the RNC had spent so much money on previous data operations and wanted everyone within the party to use it.

Our system was built on an incredibly small budget, primarily by Brad—a guy who had been hired over the internet to build Trump Organization websites, mainly for Trump's hotels and golf courses. Brad had never even been to New York before I flew him in for the first time in May, even though he had worked for the Trumps for about six years.

Born in Kansas and largely raised in San Antonio, the 6'8" tech whiz had no experience in politics when I called in early April to see what he'd been up to and what he might be able to offer. He was surprised to hear from me. "This is great," he said on the phone. "I've been trying to talk to people about this stuff. This guy Corey has *buried me.* I have literally no budget, and there's been no interest in what I have to offer the campaign so far, and I'm telling you, I think we can win this thing!"

Brad is passionate about what he does, and his enthusiasm was so genuine, the campaign was happy to let him run with his ideas. And he did. His company in San Antonio, Giles-Parscale, had worked for the Trump Organization for several years. His non-political understanding of digital data operations proved invaluable over the time of the campaign (and continues to this day).

In 2012, while working in Ukraine, I had worked with Obama's data guys and learned a ton from them, so I knew instantly that what Parscale had to offer was solid and a necessary pillar of how we would win the election.

He was already doing some online polling work, for free, that the Trump team in the early stages had basically ignored. For instance, back on March 8, when Corey Lewandowski was telling Trump he was going to win the Idaho Republican primary by ten points or more with no issues, Brad compiled polling data all on his own that showed Trump losing by twenty points. This data was never shared with Trump.

And Trump lost the primary by seventeen points.

Brad was the only one, in public or private, who got it right.

He wanted to show me how important data ops could be in the campaign in 2016—way more important than it was in 2008 or 2012, he surmised, just because of how the use of the internet and social media had changed so drastically in the last few years—but he didn't have to sell me. I was in complete agreement.

I had tried to convince Paul that we needed to spend bigger on digital after the convention, but he was reluctant because Trump was reticent about data and polls. He wanted to use the rallies as advertising and let the media continue to give us free time. He supported some tried-and-true TV and radio advertising, but we had a limited budget. Now that Jared was in a better position to influence and make decisions, he fully agreed with the digital data plan and became its chief sponsor.

Data analytics is basically the ability to break up and segment various demographical data and organize it into buckets, which in the political sphere allows campaigns or political operatives to identify core groups of people to target by the issues they support, and how they show their support, combined with all sorts of economic data. Ten years ago, I couldn't find out where a person shopped. There was no way to do that. Today? I can easily put together a digital profile of almost anyone, based on the digital footprints you leave behind through credit card usage, store membership info, discount membership info, and more, to find out not only where you shop, but how much you spend, and what you spend your money on, plus what kind of car you drive, how much your house is worth, and more. Most people don't want to think about it, but there is so much data out there on you, and how you operate, it's disconcerting.

I can then target you as a political voter, specifically, based on all of that data.

How?

First, we determine if you're an ardent Democrat or Republican or whether you're sort of on the fence based on historical voting. We especially wanted to target people on the fence, because they're the "unknowns" at the voting booth.

Then, to put it in simple terms, if you're someone who goes to Walmart and buys guns, I'm sending you ads on gun rights: "Hillary is going to take away your guns!"

That's powerful. Think about it: the way to get to voters in Richmond, Virginia, (or anywhere else) in 2006 was to send mailers, usually a postcard, to the entirety of Richmond, knowing that more than 50 percent of those cards would go in the trash because they were sent to voters of the opposite party. It was a waste of money and resources.

With data analytics, I can get the data on an individual household, and almost pinpoint exactly how they're going to vote or if they are likely to vote. That's a game-changer. In 2016, we gained the ability to succinctly identify what issues matter to you, then send targeted advertising directly to your computer or phone.

With a campaign operation as lean as ours, if Google charged me a certain dollar amount for a hundred thousand ads, and I had great data analytics resources, then instead of sending out those ads generically to a hundred thousand people, I could tell Google I wanted the ads sent to one hundred thousand specific IP addresses.

And here's why that was even more powerful in 2016 than it was in 2012. Back in 2012, if you were watching TV and the ads came on during your favorite TV show, you might have muted the TV or gone to get something to eat, but more likely, you just sat there until the ads were over. In 2016, most people who were watching TV when the ads came on opened their laptop or looked at their phone, where we hit them with our Trump ads, targeting people directly on an issue that specifically mattered to *them*. And it was at a fraction of the cost of regular TV ads.

So instead of sending some guy watching football an anti-abortion ad, we sent him an ad saying, "Here's what Trump will do for you on economic growth."

For immigrants—and I'm talking *legal* immigrants here—Trump's anti-immigration stance didn't always play so well. His public comments were just too harsh for many. But we were able to turn the tide on that in part by targeting immigrants specifically with our data that said, "If *illegal* immigration keeps up, you're going to lose your job—because *illegals* are taking your job!" or "Health care costs are going to go up, because of the increased cost of caring for people here illegally."

Our polling showed that this type of information helped us massively with the Latino vote, and more—because we were able to make the distinction between Latinos who were here legally, and those who weren't. And that got voters fired up.

It worked. And there is no doubt that it was a major key to Trump's victory. It enabled our campaign to channel Trump directly, unfiltered, to every individual that we wanted to target. We could send out upwards of 150,000 digital ads per day. And if candidates want to win in the future, they should learn from the Trump campaign's digital example. Because while we never had a team of more than twenty people in digital ops, Hillary had over two hundred people in hers. And she *lost*. At every step of the game, she lost.

And here's one big reason why: as we headed toward the general election, Brad made the rounds to Google, Twitter, and Facebook, and talked to them about how we could make our digital effectiveness stronger. It is fair to say these companies are motivated by money, and presidential elections create a lot of revenue. Each of these companies readily offered to help us directly, by embedding some of their own employees inside our campaigns. They were not offering partisan help. They wanted to help both sides accomplish whatever digital goals they had. Equally.

We accepted their help immediately.

Hillary's campaign received the very same offer, from all three companies—and her campaign turned them down.

The Google, Twitter, and Facebook staffers were able to show us what was working and what wasn't in online advertising, which is very different from TV advertising. Where TV targeted mostly to the over-sixty crowd still featured high production values, with waving flags and amber waves of grain in the background, the digital audience didn't care about any of that.

We went out with cartoonish ads that looked a little bit like *South Park* characters, and people resoundingly responded to them. We did impromptu video shoots with Trump, filming ten-, twenty-, and thirty-second ads. All Trump, all authentic.

If we had stuck to using the RNC structure and political firms to target our digital ads, I'm not sure it would have been nearly as effective because we never would have taken those kinds of "risks"—not knowing, of course, that the bigger risk would have been to keep things more traditional.

As I mentioned earlier, our campaign spent $93 million on TV ads. But we spent *half* that much on digital ads and got eight to ten times the impact of traditional advertising. Sinking money, time, talent, and effort into our digital game gave us a huge advantage.

I'm not the only one who thinks this. In interviews after the election was over, members of Hillary's campaign admitted that if they had shifted more budget to digital operations earlier, they might have been able to curtail our digital drive.

In 2016, I would offer that we were just crossing the line in terms of digital becoming more important than TV. And in 2020, I think digital will far surpass anything that TV ads have to offer.

Which means the Biden team, and the Democrats in general, had better have improved their data game substantially long before this book comes out if they want to have a shot at beating Trump. Brad and his team are not running a shoestring operation anymore. They have resources: lots of money, more staff, and deeper relationships. Brad has had three years to build a sophisticated digital platform and there is no doubt that it will be formidable.

Trump did not care to get too deep into any of these details. He cared about winning vs. losing. Bannon understood that aspect of Trump, right from the start. But since he was media-driven himself, and since he understood from the inside out how to manipulate the media in ways that aligned perfectly with Trump's messaging, he wound up being the perfect guy to take Trump to the next level. And he was able to do so from behind the scenes.

While Kellyanne Conway quickly became the leading face and voice of the campaign on TV, Bannon stayed in the shadows.

I remember spotting him in his office one week when no one else was there. Trump was traveling, and Kellyanne and most of the other senior staff were on the road with him.

I asked Bannon why he wasn't traveling too.

"No, no, no," he said with a laugh. "The dark lord stays in the tower upon high."

CHAPTER 9

Trump's Rhetoric

The Democrats' Russia Narrative Rages and WikiLeaks Strikes

I THINK THERE WERE MANY REPUBLICANS, AND PLENTY OF DEMOCRATS, who fully expected Trump to tone down the rhetoric after we moved into general election mode. That's what politicians do. They change. They curry favor. They bend, in order to appeal to the masses.

The general feeling among Washington elites was, "How could Trump possibly keep talking the way he's been talking and acting the way he's been acting and ever expect to become president of the United States—especially now that he's facing the formidable Clinton dynasty?"

This is the classic example of failing to know your opponent.

Understanding Trump isn't difficult. You have to acknowledge that he has a very unique set of skills that traditional politicians do not have.

He is not a chameleon like other politicians, and he's never going to put his finger in the wind and try to measure the mood of the people before making a decision. He is the final decision-maker. He thinks that his answers, based on his instincts, are the right answers to just about any question that arises.

When it came to the campaign, he went with his instincts time and time again, often against all of our very experienced and well-thought-out recommendations, and often what he did turned out to be the right thing. It got him where he wanted to go. It certainly got him further than anyone ever imagined he could go.

Trump's unpredictability and authenticity came with the baggage of him saying whatever he felt, often in inappropriate moments. He never stopped to think that his opinions were supposed to be reflective of or representative of the thoughts of millions of Republicans or other American voters.

Stopping to think carefully about what to say is what *politicians* do, and Hillary was very much the penultimate politician, which is why she rarely came across as "authentic" by comparison in most polls. And here's where that really hurt her: being inauthentic affects a candidate's trustworthiness.

Tony Fabrizio monitored this closely in our internal polling throughout the campaign, and by September, Hillary's negative on trustworthiness was a whopping 85 percent.

By comparison, Trump's negative on trustworthiness was only 65 percent, which is still terrible, but nowhere near as terrible as Hillary's number.

In his entire career, Fabrizio had never seen candidates with such significant negatives on trustworthiness make it this far in an election cycle. Polling data showed that we now had two of the *most* untrustworthy people he'd ever seen in this race. And one of them was going to be president!

Here's the really telling part, though: historically, Fabrizio's polling data had always shown that whoever's competing against someone with a negative trustworthiness rating, whether Republican or Democrat, has the upper hand. Which meant that Hillary wouldn't have been favored as a strong candidate against *any* opponent she faced.

Hillary's trustworthiness was so abominable that Fabrizio came to believe, based on that one piece of polling data alone, that Trump would be able to annihilate her going forward. And so much of our plan, to Trump's joy, was to attack her on her character, and the polling data made it easy to do it.

Also, remember this: almost nothing that happens in the election cycle really matters to voters until September. That's when the majority of voters start to pay attention for the first time. For all the Sturm und Drang, the breathless reporting on cable news, and the headlines that seem *so important* in the year-long run-up to the election, the only things that actually stick with the vast majority of voters when they go to the polls in November are the things the candidates do and say in the all-important fall season.

And what did Hillary do to open the fall season of 2016?

On September 9, she made her infamous "basket of deplorables" comment.

At a fundraiser in New York City, she told the audience, "You know, to just be grossly generalistic, you could put half of Trump's supporters into what I call the basket of deplorables. Right? The racist, sexist, homophobic, xenophobic, Islamophobic—you name it. And unfortunately, there are people like that. And he has lifted them up."

She went on to say that the other half of Trump's supporters "feel that the government has let them down" and are "desperate for change."

"Those are people we have to understand and empathize with as well," she said.

But it was the first part that resonated. Jason Miller, who had come on board as the senior communications advisor with the campaign, quickly put out a statement: "Just when Hillary Clinton said she was going to start running a positive campaign, she ripped off her mask and revealed her true contempt for everyday Americans."

Hillary wasn't talking in nuance here. She was talking in generalizations, and by creating that "deplorables" term, she *alienated* people— including some Democrats who fit the description. She came off as an elite politician who was talking down to half of America. And Trump benefitted from that immensely.

At a rally the next day, people showed up with "Deplorables" written on the front of their shirts. And Trump seized on it. The word turned into a mantra for people who were in blue-collar occupations, who didn't have a lot of money, who lived in rural areas—people who were already angry over politicians who had lost sight of them.

"Deplorables" became a rallying cry. Hillary took what Trump was already delivering in terms of voter intensity (that very key factor that gets people to the polls) and made it *worse* for herself. She made his voters angrier than ever.

Privately, the racist and xenophobic allegations bothered Trump. "I don't understand why they keep saying I'm a racist," he would say. "I'm not. I've done more for African Americans than Obama did...." His bravado didn't help him, of course, but he viewed the "racist" allegations as a personal assault.

He had a number of friends and acquaintances, many of them minorities, who knew him, who came out in the press and said that he is not "racist."

But it would not go away.

In politics, certain topics linger, and once the political press grabs hold of them they *never* go away.

I think the greatest example of this came when Trump was confronted with the notion that he and his campaign were somehow working in coordination with Russia, and specifically Vladimir Putin.

On Friday, July 22, after our convention had ended and just before the Democratic Convention began, WikiLeaks released twenty thousand emails that had been stolen during a hacking of a DNC server earlier that year. The emails were embarrassing for a number of powerful Democrats. They showed that there were multiple discussions among the DNC elite of how to ensure that Hillary Clinton became the nominee, and what they could do to keep Bernie Sanders from winning the nomination despite his massive groundswell of support all across America.

The emails were so damaging, and so embarrassing, that DNC Chair Debbie Wasserman Schultz was forced to resign before that start of the convention that Monday.

Our campaign had no idea those emails were coming, despite what anyone might think. It was a complete surprise—good for us, and bad for the Democrats.

A few reports surfaced quickly saying that investigators believed that the DNC server had been hacked by Russian operatives, who may or may not have been working for Vladimir Putin, but there was no conclusive evidence. The hacking was still under investigation.

But on July 24, on the eve of the convention, in the middle of the firestorm that was erupting between the Hillary and Bernie camps that would spill over into violent protests in Philadelphia, Hillary Clinton's campaign manager, Robby Mook, went on Jake Tapper's show on CNN and said that certain unnamed "experts" were now saying "that the Russians are releasing these emails for the purpose of helping Donald Trump."

He then connected that statement to a notion that Trump and the Republicans had changed their platform during the Republican convention to be more "favorable" to Russia (which wasn't true), adding that "when you put all of this together it's a disturbing picture, and I think voters need to reflect on that."

It was an astonishing accusation.

It was the first time that the Clinton campaign officially went on record saying that Trump was being helped by Russia. The inference was that Trump and the Republican Party were somehow working with Russia to get Donald Trump elected, to sway U.S. policy to benefit Putin. It was an outrageous charge. Some of Clinton's surrogates had been hinting at this supposed relationship and saying as much for a few months. But now that the damaging emails were out there, it seemed very clear to us that this talking point was a deflection—just one more unfortunately all-too-common act in the wicked game of presidential politics.

We believed it was a deflection from the embarrassing facts the leaked emails revealed.

In reality, it was more. Two years later, in the course of discovery during the Mueller investigation, emails revealed that certain members of the Clinton campaign and other high-ranking Democrats met in person at the White House with members of the National Security Council on January 23, 2016, and concocted a plan to accuse members of the Republican Party of working with Russia. The plan was a way to get ahead of a story, to deflect from Hillary Clinton's own history of taking major donations from Russian sources, which they worried might have a negative impact on her as the campaign moved forward.

One of the people who helped hatch that plan was Sidney Blumenthal, who's the equivalent of a Roger Stone figure in the Clinton world, a dark arts political operative. It was subversive, and it worked. Their candidate managed to escape any serious inquiry into her dealings with Russia through either the Clinton Foundation or the State Department throughout the campaign.

Coincidentally, one of the Republican operatives they aimed to accuse of working with Russia was Paul Manafort. The accusation was built around the fact that Paul's client, Viktor Yanukovych, had ties to Moscow, yet it ignored the fact that Yanukovych's aims were to align Ukraine with the European Union—not with Russia. Paul's work all along had been aimed at bringing Ukraine into the European Union, which aligned with U.S. policy in the region, even if Yanukovych wasn't the choice of Ukraine president that some U.S. diplomats supported. (See Postface for more detailed information on our time in Ukraine and its relevance to U.S. politics.)

Paul was not working in any way to bolster Russian interests.

To the media, it did not seem to matter. The connection was drawn.

After their plan was put into action, and now that the Clinton campaign had turned it into a very public issue, Trump's response was to go out and basically egg it on. While laughing at the absurdity of it all and calling it one of the most ridiculous "conspiracies" he'd ever heard, Trump tweeted, "If Putin wants a relationship, I have no problem with that."

As I've discussed earlier, he *didn't* have a problem with that. He wanted to sit face to face with Putin and negotiate with him in America's best interest. He wanted to talk to Putin and others specifically so the U.S. could benefit from better relations. But the media immediately used it against him, suggesting that Trump was soft on Russia—and implying that there must be a reason for that. They used statements he made about Putin being a "strong leader" as an indication that Trump "looked up" to Putin.

I can tell you firsthand: Trump doesn't "look up" to anyone.

The perceived lovefest between the two actually started with Putin, on December 17, 2015, when some of the first polls came out showing Trump as the Republican front-runner.

"He is a very flamboyant man," Putin said at his annual year-end press conference. "Very talented, no doubt about that. But it's not our business to judge his merits, it's up to the voters of the United States. He is an absolute leader of the presidential race, as we see it today. He says that he wants to move to another level relations, a deeper level of relations with Russia."

"How can we not welcome that?" he continued. "Of course, we welcome it."

Trump responded with praise of his own.

"It is always a great honor to be so nicely complimented by a man so highly respected within his own country and beyond," Trump said in a statement. "I have always felt that Russia and the United States should be able to work well with each other towards defeating terrorism and restoring world peace, not to mention trade and all of the other benefits derived from mutual respect."

Later, in February, Putin called Trump "a genius," which of course elicited a favorable response as well.

I find it funny that Putin seemed to know what Trump cared about— adulation—and used it early and often to gain his attention. Anyone with a sizable public platform could have accomplished something similar.

Flashing forward to after the election, when Trump was president and was finally set to meet with Putin in person for the very first time, he said to the press, "I think President Putin and I will get along…but who knows? Maybe I don't have a good relationship with Putin and this thing goes sideways."

If he had made statements like that all along, maybe people wouldn't have assumed that he was actually coordinating with Russia. But instead, Trump being Trump, he kept defending against the allegations the way he would any other far-less-consequential attack—from a celebrity, or a gossip columnist, or a political rival.

He spoke in soundbites because he believed that talking "too much" was detrimental to his brand, but when he did, he always seemed to leave out a part of what he was thinking.

In this case, that made a difference.

I do not believe that Trump understood just how damaging it would be to deal with the political press in the same way he'd dealt with the tabloids in New York or the entertainment shows on TV. I don't think he realized how dangerous it was to deal with the Washington elite in that manner, either.

Trump was never soft on Russia. During the campaign, I went back and looked at his tweets from 2014, after Russia invaded Crimea, and he was talking about putting sanctions on Russia even then. His talk was actually stronger than what President Obama was delivering as president at the time. But the media—reflecting the Clinton campaign's talking points—weren't interested in looking at the deeper story, or analyzing the accusation beyond the face of it. Robby Mook planted the public seed, and a perception and storyline grew from there. He cast his bait, and the media bit hook, line, and sinker.

And since the media were biting as hard as they were, Trump saw it as a chance to keep his name in the news, to generate more of that valuable unearned media that was pure gold to him.

On July 27, in Miami, Trump threw an impromptu press conference before heading to his plane. None of us were ready for it, none of us were warned about it, he just stopped and talked—as he sometimes did.

Perhaps I should have been prepared for what came next, given what he'd said earlier in the day. He had been watching TV, where the talking heads were going on and on about Russia, and whether or not Vladimir Putin was working to interfere in our election to help Trump win. "I don't understand," he said. "These people are losing their minds over this issue. We're gonna have some fun with this."

When he stepped in front of the cameras, I wondered if he might tell them about the night we'd just had. After a super successful campaign rally, Trump met with a number of Gold Star families in what I thought was one of the most heartfelt and powerful meetings he'd ever had. In an impromptu moment, a veteran stood up and gave his Purple Heart to Trump, as a gift. It was incredible.

He could've spoken about that. He could've spoken about how successful his Miami rally had been. But instead, he started talking about Hillary's still-missing emails: "Russia, if you're listening," he said, "I hope you're able to find the thirty thousand emails that are missing. I think you will probably be rewarded mightily by our press."

It was a flippant remark. It was Trump jabbing at the press for their latest obsession, and toying with the Clinton campaign for starting this ridiculous storyline in the first place.

That wasn't how it was received.

From the *New York Times* to CNN to the inner offices of the FBI, wheels started turning—over whether or not Trump had just sincerely asked an enemy nation to dig up potentially damaging information on his opponent in the race for the presidency.

The thing that was most infuriating about this topic is that the Russians, and many other countries too, have been interfering in our elections for years. They've been using our own social media against us. They've created their own data analytics programs to study our behaviors and to exploit our divisions. Automated bots and Russian troll farms are responsible for planting untrue stories and inflammatory comments all over Facebook, Twitter, and Google, that are specifically meant to drive a wedge between Americans on all sorts of issues, from politics to race relations to the safety of vaccines. There are reports now showing that the "anti-vaxxer" movement that caused so much anger in this country was made up almost entirely of Russian trolls. The movement wasn't real. This means that we're dealing with a new form of propaganda-style cyber warfare that we still don't have a handle on, and the more unrest and infighting the Russians sow, the weaker the "United" part of the "United States of America" looks to the world.

U.S. Intelligence has been aware of this for years. Reports in 2015 and 2016 informed the Obama administration that this kind of cyber-driven "election interference" was happening in the current election cycle. But almost nothing has been done to stop it.

And the more it's allowed to proceed, the more the division sown by those bots and trolls helps Putin gain and keep *power*.

Did Russia interfere in the U.S. election in 2016? Yes. Overwhelmingly, *yes*. But did it interfere in the presidential elections of 2004, 2008, and 2012 as well? Absolutely.

So what does "interfere" actually mean?

It means what I described above, and not much else. Look at any of the dozens of government agency and intelligence reports on this matter, and that's exactly what you'll see.

Does "interference" also mean that Putin was working with Trump, or me and Paul, or anyone else on the Trump campaign to coordinate in some way to steal the election from Hillary Clinton? Absolutely not. There is not now nor has there ever been any evidence to suggest this was the case. (I'll talk more about this later.)

Was Putin working to hack voting machines and change America's votes at the ballot box? Maybe. Those efforts had been made by the Chinese and North Koreans in the past as well. But as Obama said back in April of 2016, there is no way to hack, or "rig," an entire American election "in part because [voting] is so decentralized, and the numbers of votes involved. There's no evidence that that has happened in the past, or that there are instances where that will happen this time."

Plenty of prominent election experts, hacking experts, and intelligence experts all agree on that subject.

As more than one political operative in Ukraine told us later, Putin would have benefitted more from having Hillary Clinton become president. She was predictable—a known quantity from decades of being in U.S. politics. He knew her weak points and how to handle her, the way he knew how to handle Obama, and Bush. Instead, Putin wound up facing an unknown quantity in the White House. And Trump wound up placing more sanctions on Russia than were placed by any other U.S. president since the Cold War ended, including Obama after the annexation of Crimea.

Despite all of that, the story would not die. And maybe that's because through Trump's election, and the reaction to it, even despite the risks of the unknowns, and the sanctions, Putin wound up getting what he desired anyway—the seeds of separation, division, and infighting that he had been attempting to sow in America for years.

The idea that Putin would somehow coordinate with Trump, or attempt to work with his campaign, is absurd. No leader in his or her right mind would ever think they could get away with such a thing in today's world, when all eyes are on everyone, everywhere, all the time. But the good news for Putin was he didn't *have* to. He didn't even have to risk *trying* to coordinate with Trump or his campaign, because America itself was already doing the work for him.

Throughout the campaign, Trump truly saw the "Russia collusion" talk as a joke, as something to laugh at, as something to egg on and toy with, because he knew it wasn't true. He didn't know Putin. He wasn't working with his people or his government. If anything, he thought, Hillary's own ties to Russia would come back to bite her before the election was over.

So, the fact that the media kept hammering the Russia issue well into fall when his primary comments on the matter had already come and gone way back in July, when the vast majority of the electorate wasn't even paying attention, made him wonder just how desperate Clinton must be.

He was sure that before long, the media would catch on to some other topic and it would all be gone.

In retrospect, he couldn't have been more wrong.

CHAPTER 10

A Candidate and Campaign Tested

*Debates, Hillary's Weakness Shines,
and Trump's October Surprise*

I N September, as Trump continued to tackle the campaign trail,
going to rally after rally, hammering "Crooked Hillary" with everything her record provided for ammunition, we turned our digital
operation to the task of raising the money needed to get Trump over the
top in every way.

And since our coordination with the RNC was strained, we decided
to focus our efforts intently on another avenue of fundraising: small-dollar
donations.

By definition, small-dollar donations are campaign contributions of
$200 or less.

Obama started the small-dollar donation game in earnest during his
2008 campaign and improved upon it in 2012. But the Bernie Sanders
team perfected it in 2016, using internet campaigns to pull in more than
$130 million—more than half of his entire primary campaign fund—from

a formerly untapped electorate made up mostly of younger voters, the vast majority of whom donated less than an average of $27 at a time.

Once we knew that Hillary was Trump's one and only opponent in the run for the presidency, we decided to try to capitalize on the small-dollar trend too.

Our messaging to potential Trump donors was as targeted as our messaging to potential Trump *voters*, and no sooner did we begin our efforts than we realized just how good our messaging and targeting machine had become: we found we could raise $50 million in donations from a single targeted message—in under two weeks.

In the first quarter after Trump secured the nomination, we raised $239 million from small-dollar donors.

How did we do it?

Data analytics and digital advertising.

But for all of our attention to data research and internal polling, the one type of research we didn't budget for was "opposition research." Trump never thought we needed it. There was ample "research" out there on Fox News and Breitbart that proved Clinton to be as "crooked" as Trump claimed she was. There was plenty there for voters to sink their teeth into if they Googled the Clinton family or their various campaigns and organizations.

But Trump also knew he could attack his opponent on her record, on Benghazi, on the sweetheart deals she made to sell uranium to Russia (the Uranium One deal), and on all sorts of policy stances at every turn. He would never run out of a political history to attack because Clinton had been in politics for so many years.

Clinton, on the other hand, didn't have *any* Trump political record to attack. So she hired at least two opposition research firms (that we knew of) and had them working full-time to try to dig up dirt on Trump. *Real dirt.* Something that could bury him.

Try as they might, they never found any sort of a smoking gun issue that could take him down.

If they had, the Clinton campaign would have used it. Of that, I have no doubt.

As we rushed toward the first of three presidential debates on September 26, we were confident that Hillary wouldn't come in with any surprises up her sleeve. This meant that Hillary would have nothing to stand on but her own considerable political strength—and that worried some of us. Trump had held his own in debates with other Republicans, mostly because he threw them off their game so easily. They never had time to prepare for the sort of personal attacks he laid on them, or the nicknames that stuck, or the way he would abrasively call out, "That's a lie!" right in the middle of one of their answers. They weren't prepared for any of it.

But Clinton had months to watch and learn from all of those debates and other campaign events. She knew what she was getting into. And she had some of the best old school political minds in the game working in her camp.

If she pursued a strategy that attacked Trump in his weak spots, particularly on foreign policy, some of us weren't sure if he'd have the knowledge to counter the assault with detailed facts.

We pleaded with him to prepare for that first debate. To practice. To watch tapes of Hillary in action. To sit down with the panel of economic and national security experts we were putting together, just for him. To listen to some of the foreign policy experts we'd lined up, specifically to bring him up to speed on some of the major issues around the world that he might not be aware of. But the closest we got to giving him any kind of debate prep for the first debate was setting up an iPad with excerpts from the Bernie vs. Hillary debates from the last few months of the Democrats' primary season. Even then, he was more interested in laughing at the ways Bernie slammed Hillary than he was paying attention to certain topics or policy issues.

"I'm not a debater," he said. "Stop worrying. You have nothing to worry about."

Of course, he was right. The night of the debate, he came up short on his knowledge of some policy issues. He wasn't as prepared for some of the questions the moderators asked. But none of that really mattered. While Clinton stuck to a script of clearly well-prepared answers and mini speeches, Trump turned the tables with off-the-cuff remarks and an authenticity that made her look stiff and stilted. When talking about the economy, she launched into a long story to the effect of, "When I think about the economy, I think about sitting with my two-year-old granddaughter last night, reading her a bedtime story, and thinking about her future...." The same old shtick the public has heard a million times. Trump didn't do that. He hit her with one-liners and jabbed at her record. He talked broadly about how he'd build the "best" economy because he knew how to do that. He didn't say too much because he knew how to stay true to his brand.

He treated the debate like a boxing match. Or a street fight. And he came out looking like the winner, authentic and strong, especially to his supporters.

As we prepared for the second debate, he decided to bolster his policy knowledge a little bit, just so he wouldn't have any weak spots for Hillary to hit. But the bulk of the preparation, which he wanted to put off until the last few days before the debate itself, never happened. Because on October 7, we got hit with an "October surprise."

A videotape surfaced of Trump, on a bus, thinking he was having a private conversation with *Access Hollywood*'s Billy Bush, talking on an open mic about seducing a woman he knew was married, and explaining to Billy that his fame allowed him to approach any women he wanted, to kiss them, to do anything he wanted to them. (I'll leave out the vulgarity.)

The portion of tape that was released was audio only. The camera was outside of the bus when it happened. But there was no doubt it was Trump on that tape. It was his voice. It was Billy Bush's voice. They had video of him just before and just after, getting on and off the bus.

And it was *awful*.

We quickly learned that the tape came from some senior executives at NBC, who leaked it to the *Washington Post* after it was found by a producer at *Access Hollywood* (which is owned by NBCUniversal). The timing of the release was completely suspect and intentional, as far as we were concerned. We later learned that NBC was aware of the tape and its contents well in advance of the date it was eventually leaked—further confirming our suspicion that the timing was no accident. They saved this to use when the chips were down when Hillary was starting to dip in the polls after Trump's successful first debate.

Trump didn't try to deny it was him, or that he'd said exactly what we heard on that tape.

He was at Trump Tower with Ivanka, Jared, Eric, and Brad when the news broke. And what was described to me was something that none of us on the campaign had ever seen before: Trump actually looked defeated.

Trump dropped his head in his hands and asked, "How bad is it?"

Jared answered, "It's really bad."

"What do we do?" he asked.

No one in that room had any idea. And as the news trickled out to each of us, there weren't any answers to be had, either.

Trump actually voiced the unthinkable: "I might have to get out," he said.

It was the darkest moment of the campaign.

As you've already read, there were major establishment Republican players, both inside and outside of the RNC, who were sick and tired of Trump and everything he represented. They'd already worked hard to derail and oust him at the convention by maneuvering delegates to not support him. They'd failed. But this? There was no way they would let this stand.

Phone calls and text messages rebuking Trump flew. Speaker of the House Paul Ryan came out saying he did not want his daughters to be exposed to this kind of behavior from a president. RNC Chairman Reince Priebus got so many calls, he went directly to Trump that night and said, "You have to get out. You have to drop out of the race."

The RNC's emergency plan was to run Mike Pence as the replacement Republican nominee. It would require a complete manipulation of the RNC by-laws, but many of the people that wanted Trump out were determined to make it work. This was just over a month before the election, and Trump's name was already at the top of ballots that had been printed all over the country. Reince knew that undoing all of that would take enormous, unprecedented shifts, triggering a complicated, complex, and controversial process that could damage the party long-term. And if Trump fought it, in his mind it would certainly result in the Republican candidate losing. He knew that the only way that it could even *start* to work was if Trump voluntarily dropped out.

But when confronted with that ultimatum, Trump did what he always did.

Trump refused.

"No way," he said. "I'll fight this."

Priebus should've known that would be the reaction if he tried to tell Trump what to do. It didn't matter how bad things were; Trump's response to aggression is always to dig in his heels and fight back.

At that point, Priebus had no other choice but to go to Pence himself and tell Pence to ask Trump to step down.

He wasn't the only one who came calling. Pence got calls from Paul Ryan, from Mitch McConnell, and more, all asking him to do what was right for the country.

Pence was the establishment's last hope.

Internally, we turned to our pollster, Tony Fabrizio, to go out and get us a quick sense of how much damage this Billy Bush tape was doing—and the polling turned out to not be as bad as we thought it would be. Trump took a hit with support from women; he took a hit with college-educated men, but for the most part, his base remained intact.

Pence and Trump had a phone call, and Pence decided not to ask Trump to step down. He told him he would stand by him. He remained loyal.

Pence did this despite strong protests from his wife: Karen refused to interact with Trump at all at that point. She was angry, which makes sense given her religious values, and having daughters, but she was also angry at Mike. She didn't want to attach her family to Trump's coattails, and especially after this happened. But Pence is an ardent believer who practices forgiveness. He was also an experienced politician and knew his VP role was a long-term stepping-stone, one that would give him the infrastructure and relationships that can only happen as VP.

After this, Pence was all in. There was no turning back. If this dark moment cost Trump the presidency, Pence would go down with him.

But the decision to carry on was ultimately made entirely by Trump and his family.

Trump decided that the tape needed to be addressed. He couldn't just sweep it under the rug. So he and his kids decided he should make a video and release it to the press. No questions. Nothing live that could leave anything to chance. Just a video.

"What will he say? Will this be an apology?" the press asked me.

"No," I said.

Trump wouldn't apologize. He *doesn't* apologize. The press and the public would just have to wait and see.

Publicly, Trump put up a front and refused to budge, as if he were confident he could overcome this.

Privately? He knew this was bad.

When he released his statement and the press kept at it, as more and more people called for him to step down and drop out of the race, Trump talked to his family.

"I don't know what to do," he said. He asked them, "Can we still win?"

Steve Bannon and others looked at the data and contemplated the next steps: Trump and Hillary Clinton both had low trustworthy ratings. But at this juncture, Trump was at 56 percent, while Hillary was at 82 percent. This means that a large majority of potential voters saw them both as liars, sure, but the vast majority still had a lower opinion of Hillary. If either had a higher rating or had any likability from the other side, then things might have been different, but when starting from a point that low, Bannon figured it only made sense to dig for the bottom even faster than the other side could.

It was the only way to salvage the election and win.

Bannon, along with some help from others, hatched a diabolical plan meant to change the conversation. They ran it by Don Jr., and Eric, and both got on board.

Jared and Ivanka did not.

Jared is Jewish, and Ivanka had converted to Judaism before they married. Together, they always abided by the traditional rules of Shabbat (the Sabbath), by not doing any work and discontinuing the use of all electronics from sundown on Friday to nightfall on Saturday.

Bannon used their religion against them. He brought his plan to Trump on Saturday when neither Jared nor Ivanka was present, and he knew they couldn't be reached.

Trump agreed to Bannon's plan, and once the balls were in motion, there was no way to stop it—despite Jared and Ivanka's vigorous objections when they learned of the plan that Sunday.

I didn't know a thing about it until the day of the debate. Almost no one did. It was a plan to not only deflect attention from Trump's "locker room talk" misogyny but to throw Hillary Clinton completely off her game.

On Sunday, October 9, Bannon planted four of "Bill Clinton's women"—four women who had famously accused and/or sued Hillary Clinton's husband for sexual harassment, rape, and other offenses—in the audience at the presidential debate. They sat directly behind Trump's kids, directly in the eyeline of where Hillary stood at her podium.

Hillary and her team caught word of what was happening when Bannon scheduled a press conference with these women two hours before the debate was to start. Right before the debate began and the cameras went live, the women showed up at the venue and moved toward their seats.

Clinton reportedly had come into this debate feeling more confident than ever that she would be able to beat Trump at his own game. With the Billy Bush tape still so fresh, she was ready to call Trump out as the ugly, misogynistic man she and lots of other women thought he was. But seeing those women and watching her husband squirm under the reminder of his own bad behavior took the wind right out of her sails. Once she was off her game, Trump saw her weakness and turned the tables. He was the one who went on the attack. He reminded her and the voters that through all of her husband's bad behavior she was no friend to women either. She had gone after these women and torn up their reputations. I don't think Clinton ever expected her past actions to come back and haunt her like this.

Trump went into that debate wondering just how badly the Billy Bush tapes had hurt him, but by playing the wicked game in some of the most wicked ways imaginable, he wound up winning round two of the presidential debate fight. Did the pundits think he won? Not necessarily. But he didn't care. Trump *knew* he won. *We* knew he'd won because he put Hillary on the defensive, and she never recovered. In our internal polling that came back after the debate, Tony Fabrizio showed us absolutely that

Trump had come out on top in this fiasco of a weekend: Trump's numbers were down, yes. But only slightly. And after a fiasco the size of this one, that was a major win for us.

The Democrats had thrown the worst at him, and he survived the blow.

Most surprisingly of all, his numbers with women, even college-educated women, had only fallen marginally.

Trump was going to survive this.

He hit the campaign trail again, and instead of pivoting toward a more friendly attitude, or trying to play nice and extend an olive branch to women voters everywhere, he went after Hillary harder than ever before.

He hammered the email issue. He hammered just how corrupt he thought she and Bill were, with all the crooked money flowing through the Clinton Foundation, and the sweetheart deals she'd given away to our enemies and others while she was secretary of state.

In this final run-up to the third debate, just weeks before the election, he led his crowds in chants of "Lock her up! Lock her up!" again and again.

We anticipated a backlash, and a slew of women—twenty-eight in all—came pouring out of the woodwork after the second debate, accusing Trump of assault and harassment. Trump hit back at every one of them and blamed the attacks on the Clinton campaign pulling dirty tricks.

The whole episode was grotesque. It was difficult for parents to talk about with their children. But this late in the campaign, there were only two presidential candidates in the race. Voters on both sides had to look beyond their candidate's transgressions, or alleged transgressions, in the name of picking a winner for their side, knowing that candidates represent bigger issues, such as Supreme Court nominations and other important policy initiatives.

While the media and the Clinton campaign kept spinning their wheels over the same old attacks, we turned our attention to the next debate.

The third debate's primary subjects were agreed to long before any of this happened, and the topics of focus were the economy, Supreme Court justices, and foreign policy. We knew the topic of foreign policy was one area where Trump's knowledge base was still thin, and that if anything might hurt him worse than these accusations from his personal and professional life, which all happened well before he stepped into the political ring, it would be the fact that he didn't have a handle on it.

And if anyone could slaughter him with foreign policy knowledge, it would certainly be the woman who had endured hours and hours of congressional grilling on Benghazi and who had more foreign diplomatic connections through her work with her family's foundations than just about any other politician on the planet.

Because of all of this, we knew that this debate was going to be crucial. And with days to go, Trump finally realized it too.

The stakes were as high as they could be.

So he agreed to listen and prepare.

First, we put him on a conference call with his new National Security Advisory Council, which was a stellar list of twenty-two mostly Conservative "hawks" (very strong pro-defense). Then we set up an in-person meeting between Trump and just nine members of the council because we knew there was no way he would have the patience to listen to all twenty-two members speak in person.

We set the meeting for October 17, 2016, in the twenty-fifth-floor conference room at Trump Tower. One month before the election. Two days before the debate.

The conference room is large, located one floor below Trump's personal office space, and is encased in glass, with a stunning view over Fifth Avenue and Central Park. It sits just next to the offices of Don Jr., Ivanka, and Eric, and in it sits a large, Boeing scale model of Trump's jet. There was also a TV screen in the middle of the main wall, which allowed us to illuminate the room with Trump campaign banners.

More impressive than the room itself was the caliber of advisors who showed up fully prepared to advise the Republican candidate and would-be president. They were all in place right before Trump walked in, smiling and shaking hands with everyone one by one as he always did before he took his seat.

The overall theme we were trying to achieve in that meeting was the one Trump would carry into the debate: "Hillary Clinton is the architect of failure and ruin."

K. T. McFarland, a Fox News political commentator (who worked briefly as a speechwriter in the Reagan administration before making a run for the U.S. Senate in New York in 2006), was the person who came up with that one-liner, based on the long list of failed policies that played out under Clinton's and Obama's watch in Syria, China, Iran, Egypt, and so forth. And throughout this one-hour meeting, with that one-liner in mind, the various advisors spoke as to what was happening in all of those countries, and more, including the current state of affairs with ISIS, Russia, NATO, North Korea, nuclear weapons, rebuilding the military, cyber warfare, and human rights. (Human rights were at the bottom of the agenda, purposefully, and we wouldn't even get to it in the meeting. It was generally agreed that no one, including Obama and Clinton, had been able to accomplish much of anything on human rights in China or anywhere else, no matter what tactic they used.)

Steve Bannon and I briefed most everyone in advance of the meeting that they would have to keep their talks to four or five minutes each, and that there was no point in bringing in any printed materials to leave behind because Trump wouldn't read them. "He learns by listening, not by reading," we told them. It was just the truth. Even at that crucial stage, Trump still rarely read anything more than half a page in length. I drew up a multi-page master set of everyone's talking points to share with the team but prepared a separate brief listing the foreign policy topics for Trump that wasn't even a full page in length.

In advance of the meeting, Trump told us he wanted to better understand the machinations of Washington. He wanted to know specifically what powers he would have as president vs. what powers Congress held, and we assured him that this group would be able to answer any questions he had.

Bannon opened the meeting by addressing Trump directly, saying, "We just wanted to get this group of people together and hit you with a number of things that Hillary's probably thinking on foreign policy."

Trump always wanted to know, "Why am I learning this? Is this a waste of my time, or is it useful?"

Bannon made it clear that it was useful, as did Jeff Sessions, the senator from Alabama, who kicked off the meeting with a sweeping review of the failures of Clinton and the Obama administration when it came to foreign policy.

It appeared that Trump liked what he heard. But beating up on Clinton and Obama was an easy task.

Mike McCaul, a congressional representative from Texas, spoke next, running down a long list of security threats in the Western Hemisphere. Then came McFarland, who covered nuclear weapons and Russia.

By the way: there were no fans of Russia in that room or on the broader committee. This group was more hawkish on defense than most Republicans, and some of these folks were much farther Right than Trump on all key foreign policy issues. But when it came to handling Russia, China, or North Korea, Trump still could not understand what we had to gain by having no dialogue with the leaders of those countries: "Why wouldn't you at least sit down and talk to them?" he said. "I'm not saying negotiations are going to go our way, but you've got to talk to them!" He could not comprehend why, in the political and diplomatic worlds, simply asking for a meeting with the leader of any one of these countries might have significant consequences. He truly believed that he could walk into the White House and "solve all the problems," the same way he did in the business world—no matter how many times any one of us tried to explain to him that this was an entirely different playing field.

Trump didn't say a whole lot about this during this particular meeting, though. He mostly just sat there and listened.

Giuliani was there but didn't speak much. Bannon stayed in the room, as did I, and Kellyanne Conway came in and out a few times while the discussions were happening. But none of us interjected.

Peter Hoekstra, a former member of Congress from Michigan, handled a brief on cyber warfare and terrorism, with more points on those topics added by General Robert Magnus, former assistant commandant for the U.S. Marine Corps. The rest of the agenda was handled by Mike Flynn, who Trump still liked and thought he knew well, the former lieutenant general and director of the Defense Intelligence Committee under President Obama, and Keith Kellogg, another lieutenant general in the army. As I said, it was an impressive group, and their presentations on these important matters were succinct, powerful, and on point. Trump shook his head at times, but that was about it.

Trump quietly listening wasn't what any member of this council expected, and it certainly wasn't the way these types of meetings tend to go when a politician has a chance to get in the room with such high-level experts in their respective fields. But finally, when everyone was done speaking, Trump nodded his head a little bit. He paused. Everyone prepared themselves to answer whatever question may come. And Trump said, "How do I declare war?"

The question was met with a moment of stunned silence, something that often happened in meetings with Trump. We were all in a room with the Republican nominee for president of the United States, which meant everyone was deferential. No one was going to gasp, or stand up in horror, or go so far as to let an uncomfortable laugh slip out. But I'm sure some of them must have thought, "*That's* what he wants to know after hearing all of this? Who is he talking about? War with *who*? China? Russia? *NATO*? Is he talking about declaring war on ISIS?"

McFarland was the first to speak up. She had a way of talking to Trump that he seemed to understand and like, and she immediately swayed her answer in the direction of *process*. She walked Trump through the minutiae of our political system, the ins and outs of the complexities of formally "declaring war," which was an act of Congress, vs. declaring an act of "national security," which could be done by executive order. Mike McCaul joined in on that discussion too, and Trump nodded his head.

"OK," he said. He then asked a few short follow-up questions about the process that had just been described, and offered comments on other topics, including China and ISIS (which had instigated the war question), two topics he knew a lot about.

And that was largely it.

He stood up, thanked everyone for coming, and he and Bannon left the conference room. Many of the advisory committee members left the room shortly after, thinking, wondering—maybe *hoping*—that the technicalities of the process of declaring war was all he really meant by his question.

For some on the advisory committee, especially those who were just meeting Trump for the first time, it was an unorthodox approach to a meeting. No doubt it created some concern on their part since they knew very little about Trump's politics or personality.

On October 19, on the debate stage, Trump barely used any of what our advisors had shared with him. Instead, he stuck to his tried-and-true debate tactics of off-the-cuff remarks, attacks on Hillary's record, and being Donald Trump the way only Donald Trump can.

When asked about the assault allegations that had been levied against him in recent weeks, he came out swinging: he called his accusers a bunch of "nasty women."

When asked about the border, he talked about building the wall, adding that we needed to get rid of drug dealers and "bad hombres." (You can imagine how that went over with the Liberal crowd.)

And when moderator Chris Wallace asked Trump if he would follow the expected American tradition of conceding the election and supporting the new president if he lost, Trump responded, "I will tell you at the time." He then jabbed at Hillary's hiding of the emails again, and said that she shouldn't have even been allowed to run for the presidency because she had committed a "serious crime." So as far as accepting the results of the election and making a concession, he said, "I'll keep you in suspense, OK?"

Hillary responded as a politician would be expected to, saying Trump's response to Wallace's question was "horrifying."

"We've been around for two hundred and forty years," she said. "We've had free and fair elections. We've accepted the outcomes when we may not have liked them. And that is what must be expected of anyone standing on a debate stage during a general election."

The pundits thought Trump gave a terrible answer. The Democrats thought it was a terrible answer. The establishment in Washington thought it was a terrible answer—the sort of immature response that would keep Donald Trump from winning, for sure.

We knew that it wasn't a "terrible" answer at all.

In this election, 48 percent of the American public had already decided to vote Hillary, and 48 percent had already decided to vote Trump, no matter what. The people we were trying to reach through these debates were the roughly 4 percent of the American electorate who were still unsure who to vote for.

From the poll numbers we had, we believed that Hillary's debate performance that night wouldn't have changed her numbers much either way. Her record was too well known. Her brand was worn out. So any major change in the way she behaved would have been perceived as "desperate."

Trump, on the other hand, was still new, he was the outsider, and nobody really knew how he would solve a crisis or deal with foreign policy issues. So that third debate was more important for him. Voters on both sides of the aisle were tired of the same old political choices. Many of them were much more willing to say, "I voted for Reagan, and Bush, and Clinton, and Obama—why not give the new guy a chance?"

That was especially true for voters in the swing states, where it *really* mattered.

For voters who were undecided, and who weren't wedded to any single issue, Trump's breaking with protocol, his "fearlessness" when it came to challenging the status quo, his "refreshing authenticity," gave them reason to believe that maybe, given the fact that he had been successful at business, he would go in and do the much-needed job of bringing real change to Washington for the first time in their lifetimes.

If the Democrats had paid more attention to what voters saw in Trump, rather than focusing on what his detractors hated about him, perhaps they could have come up with some better strategies to defeat him in the swing states. But by the end of the third debate, it seemed clear to us that they weren't even bothering to try.

CHAPTER 11

Election Shock

The Final Stretch, Comey's Surprise, and the Night Trump Won

O**N THE VERY SAME DAY THE** B**ILLY** B**USH TAPE WAS RELEASED, THE** Democratic Party got an October surprise of its own: WikiLeaks made another huge drop of hacked DNC emails—this time a collection of conversations involving political consultant John Podesta, who had formerly served as Bill Clinton's chief of staff and who was now serving as Hillary Clinton's campaign chairman.

We didn't address it much at the time because we didn't have the time, bandwidth, or staff to deal with it. But the fact is, we didn't *need* to address it. It was the Democrats' problem, and we believed that more damage would be done by just sitting back and letting them try to spin their way out of their own hole. If we had injected ourselves into the conversation, it may have backfired; we quite possibly could have drawn even more false accusations that we were involved in the hacking, the leaks, or some kind of interference from Russia.

We weren't involved. We had no warning that the leak was coming. We played no part in it. In fact, both the DNC and the RNC had been hacked, so we were expecting the possibility of leaked emails on the

Republican side at any moment. We were hopeful that it would deflect a little bit from the controversy from Trump's "locker room talk."

But the coincidence of that timing was nothing compared to what happened just ten days before the election: on October 28, FBI Director James Comey sent a letter to Congress, announcing that the FBI had "learned of the existence of emails that appear to be pertinent to the investigation" into the private email server that Clinton used during her time as secretary of state.

Trump was on the plane on the way to a rally when the news broke. No one knew what to make of the announcement from Comey, but there was a great deal of speculation that the thirty-three thousand missing Hillary emails had actually been found.

If we had timed an October surprise to land on the Clinton campaign *ourselves* we could not have timed it better. It is generally known in political campaigns that voters typically don't change their minds based on new information learned in the last week before the election. It takes ten days or more for advertising, breaking news, or anything else to sink in with voters to a deep enough degree that it actually sways their vote. Which meant that this was basically the last day to make a significant impact on voters in any area other than voter turnout.

Once again, our campaign was taken aback to read the news, and we immediately decided that the best thing we could do about it was nothing. Just as we had done with the WikiLeaks release on October 7, we realized the best thing we could do was to stand back and watch. Let the Democrats deal with the fallout.

Jared, Ivanka, Steve Bannon, Kellyanne—everyone was in agreement on this, and they all impressed upon Trump that it would be best not to say anything about it at all.

At his rally that night, he didn't.

He held himself back—for almost twelve hours.

The next day, at a rally in Manchester, New Hampshire, Trump let loose. Invoking Comey's letter, and still suspecting that the FBI now had a hold of the missing thirty-three thousand emails, Trump said Hillary was "corrupt on a scale we have never seen before. We must not let her take her criminal schemes into the Oval Office."

People accused Donald Trump of sowing chaos, but this was a clear-cut example of our *government* sowing chaos entirely on its own. There were all sorts of conspiracies floated as to why Comey did it, but in the end, it may just have been a typical government agency bungle of the highest degree, made by a man whose ego would eventually ruin his credibility.

It turned out that the FBI didn't have Hillary's missing emails. All they had were some State Department emails that Clinton's campaign advisor, Huma Abedin, had sent from her husband's laptop. Her husband was Anthony Weiner, the disgraced New York congressman, which only added to the gossipy intrigue of the story. But it wasn't until November 7—the day before the election—that Comey and the FBI made the announcement that there was no evidence that would result in new charges against Hillary.

It was too late. The damage was already done. Hillary's lead in the polls in some of the swing states was cut dramatically because of Comey's erroneous judgment, and her untrustworthiness numbers popped right back to the highest they'd ever been.

Confidence in Hillary, and the Democrats in general, was further damaged in the middle of all of this when on November 6, *two days* before the election, WikiLeaks released yet another batch of DNC emails, this time showing that CNN contributor and Clinton friend Donna Brazile had leaked debate questions to Hillary's team in advance of the 2016 presidential debates.

For all of the accusations that were flying around about Trump, the only *evidence* of cheating in the election so far fell upon the Democrats.

The wickedness of this game is undeniable. On both sides. And in 2016, voters were sick of it. Voters were fed up with the status quo. In both parties, there were more voters than not who believed it was time to "drain the swamp." Whether or not people believed that Donald Trump was the right person to do it, it was clear that more and more voters believed strongly that Hillary Clinton and her cronies were definitely *not* to be trusted to implement big-change reforms in Washington, nor were they capable of doing what was necessary to restore faith in our government.

In order to win, Hillary Clinton needed to persuade the fired-up voters from the Bernie Sanders camp to come and vote for her. But Bernie supporters were a lot like Trump supporters, in their own way. They wanted to see revolutionary change. Radical change. A rejection of the same old broken system.

Would they come out for Clinton after reading the details of those November 6 emails? On the heels of the previous emails that showed how hard she and the DNC had worked to shut Bernie down? Would they get out the vote to support a candidate who was "untrustworthy" after supporting a senator from Vermont who had a track record of sticking by the very same policy goals for more than thirty years?

For that matter, would the millions of Trump supporters who showed up in our polling data, and who basked in Trump's celebrity and fiery rhetoric at rallies all across the country, come out and do their part and cast votes on Tuesday the eighth?

We scheduled our very last rally on the evening of November 7 in Michigan, a state that we believed Hillary Clinton had neglected to pay attention to at her own peril.

All of our travels were targeted based on the possibility of various paths on the electoral map that would get us to 270 votes. Paul had charted those roads for us many months earlier, and Jared, Brad, and Kellyanne made adjustments along the way. In one example, we took Trump to northern Maine five times in the run-up to the election, just because Maine was uniquely set up so that its three electoral votes could be split proportionally. The more populated southern and coastal parts of Maine were Democrat territory. Those two electoral votes were surely going to Hillary. But the one electoral vote from the northern, less populated, woodsy part of Maine was up for grabs. It seemed a little crazy, even to Trump, to put so much effort into just one vote. But Paul recognized that there was a potential road to victory that would have put the candidates at a 269 to 269 tie, which meant that one split-off vote from Maine might be the one electoral vote that would get Trump the win. On the slim chance that might happen, we pursued it and pursued it hard, as we did every other crucial electoral vote in every region in the country. (While it wasn't a tie-breaker, we did win that one Maine vote in the end.)

We might not have been able to predict what Trump would say once he got there, but our campaign used surgical targeting, backed by data analytics, in every decision we made for our candidate when it came down to the technicalities of where he needed to go.

We believed that making that last stop in Michigan was important as well. And it *was*. Not to win over new voters, necessarily. But to make sure the voters in that state were fired up enough to get out and vote for Trump the next day. It was a Union state. The Unions were backing Hillary. She thought it was a foregone conclusion. But if you've read this far, you're aware of some of the earlier strategies Paul put into play that we hoped would come to fruition because of this one last push.

Trump got back to New York City around 3:00 a.m., and Brad and I decided to take one last look at our polling data. There were just a few hours to go before voting stations opened on the East Coast. We carefully combed through every bit of information we had at that moment, and we both came to the same conclusion before we went to bed that night: "If our numbers are accurate, Trump wins."

The next afternoon, the exit polls were grossly inaccurate. The most popular polls in the country all said Hillary was winning—and they all got it wrong.

A full twenty-four hours after Brad and I checked the numbers, Trump's victory was confirmed when the media finally announced that he had secured enough electoral votes with his win in Pennsylvania to ensure his victory—and Hillary Clinton called Trump up to concede the election. Trump had just walked into a suite at the Hilton Hotel on Sixth Avenue, upstairs from an anxious but patient crowd of his supporters gathered in a sparsely decorated ballroom below.

It was probably the shortest concession call in history. "Congratulations, Donald" was basically all Hillary said. She had to have been in complete shock. Trump was a little more cordial. He said, "You waged a hard campaign, it was a great fight, you were a great opponent." But then he got off the phone and got busy preparing a victory speech that he hadn't really focused on.

By 2:49 a.m., he was downstairs in front of his cheering supporters, and the cameras, as the whole world watched in shock as he announced that Hillary Clinton had called to concede and that he was now president-elect of the United States.

For him, and for us, it was honestly a little surreal. It felt as if it was just a rally. Or a state victory party. The weight of it didn't really sink in.

He said, "I have the greatest campaign," and he called a bunch of the staff up on stage with him. In a funny moment, Brad Parscale walked near him behind the stage before the speech, and Trump told him not to stand close to him. He made him stand at the far end of the stage. Brad's a few inches taller than Trump, and Trump didn't want his height overshadowing him on camera. The optics, particularly at this moment, meant everything.

After the speech, the celebration started in earnest. We didn't wrap things up at the Hilton until nearly 5:00 a.m.

For all of us, it was the endpoint of a cascade of physical, emotional, and mental exhaustion—and when I looked at Trump before he left the stage and walked down the hall to the elevator to head back to Trump Tower, that was what I saw in him too. He wasn't full of elation. He looked tired. He looked like a man who'd just won a major negotiation or completed a major business deal that had been months in the making. For Trump, I think he was more concerned with the prospect of losing than the idea of winning. I don't think the gravity of what would happen next really hit him that night.

For us? The gravity of it all started to sink in as we walked back to Trump Tower in the chilly November air.

A group of us walked across 55th Street, right past the opulent and pricey Peninsula Hotel, just around the corner from Trump Tower, where we knew Hillary had spent the night waiting for the election results. It blew me away that the two candidates for president of the United States stayed less than a block from each other on election night. And I couldn't help but think, for her, the election was over; for us, the election marked a new starting point.

I wondered how Trump was ever going to tackle the challenges that now laid in front of him.

Trump had just over two months to get ready to take over the *presidency*—and the enormity of the task of installing a new government was overwhelming.

I went to bed that morning of November 9 thinking about how tough the next two months were going to be.

* * *

The Monday morning quarterbacking began first thing that Wednesday morning. And the analysis of how the established, experienced, "most obvious" candidate for the job lost the election would go on for a long, long time.

But from what we saw, the results of the 2016 election didn't come about just because Trump got more voters out where it counted (even though he did). The real conclusion is based on how many voters didn't come out for Hillary.

From what we gathered in polls and surveys on our side, it wasn't just the untrustworthiness that did her in. There was just something about her that a lot of people couldn't relate to. She didn't seem like a person most voters could have a comfortable, casual conversation with. She couldn't connect. And that's important in candidates. It was almost the same as the unrelatability factor in Ted Cruz on the Republican side.

As Trump put it, "She can't sell it. She never could."

She certainly couldn't sell it to enough Bernie supporters to help her win. In the end, just over 70 percent of the Bernie supporters we knew of came out and voted for Hillary. We estimated that Bernie had twenty million potential voters behind him, so that means just over fourteen million came out for their party's nominee. That mattered. There were some important states that we didn't win by much. Michigan was one of them: we only won it by 10,704 votes. It was calculated that fifty-one thousand of Bernie's voters came out and voted for Trump. If they had voted for Hillary, she would have won the state.

There were similar stories in a number of key states.

Which is extraordinary when you really think about it.

Around 12 percent of Bernie supporters actually voted for Donald Trump nationwide. The Democrats seemed to miss the one issue that was more important to them than anything else: shaking things up in Washington and getting the establishment politicians (like Hillary Clinton) out.

So why were the polls so wrong?

They had Donald Trump losing throughout most of the campaign, and especially on election day when he won by a whopping 306 electoral votes to Clinton's 232.

The thing about polls is that all of their predictions are based on previously available voting data and models that pollsters create. So how do you poll for the unprecedented, which is what Donald Trump represented in this race?

We found that 3.2 percent of Trump's voters misled pollsters about who they were voting for in 2016. We don't know if they told pollsters they were voting for another candidate to save face because they felt uneasy that they were going with Trump, or if, for some, maybe they just changed their minds at the very last minute, after the final polls were taken. But given what we know about voters changing their minds, that's incredibly unlikely.

So now we have to consider what we called "the Trump factor," this particular X-variable, in polls going forward. And the factor could skew either way. Pollsters can only take past results and guesstimate at what that number might be for either candidate.

In short, the polls going into 2020 could be more inaccurate than ever.

I think the divided parties have also caused people to lose perspective on just how important their vote is. The Republicans work hard to make sure their voters get out while giving the impression that the Democrats shouldn't vote; the Democrats do the same on the other side; and they both work hard to try to force people to *not* vote for third party candidates, saying those votes are being wasted. That's the wrong message to send. The more people vote, the more we have a shot at making positive changes in our country. Votes really do matter. In Wisconsin, the final tally for Trump vs. Clinton was 47.2 percent to 46.5 percent, and in Michigan, even closer with 47.3 percent to 47.0 percent. Whole elections can swing on one state's, or even one county's votes. Just a few thousand people can change the outcome.

In 2016, Trump won almost all of Florida, but the two counties near Miami that Clinton won were nearly enough to put her over the top in that state. One more county and the state might have been hers.

So that's another place where the polls can go wrong: the difference between what people say on the phone or online, and whether or not those same people get out to vote on election day.

There is also built-in bias in the political reporting of TV and newspapers that tends to skew predictions. Over several months of the campaign, I independently took my own poll. I asked all of my taxi drivers in NYC who they would vote for. Almost all of them (with the exception of four) said they would vote for Trump. While not completely scientific and certainly not done with some high-powered algorithm, that anecdotal evidence alone showed me that Trump wasn't hurting as badly as the media would have had us think in terms of votes from traditionally liberal cities.

As for why Trump won: there was a lot of initial blame put on President Obama because he didn't campaign for Hillary as early as he could have. Staying out of the primaries is one thing, but he didn't come out and endorse her until mid-June.

Trump's refusal to conform to political norms was a huge factor in his winning too. What the establishment saw as his weaknesses were actually his greatest strengths. As I mentioned earlier, people were looking for a revolution, a movement, and were willing to take a chance on a non-politician, an outsider, someone who didn't say the right things, over the tried-and-true, which had let them down throughout their lifetimes.

Trump's messaging game was also stronger, not just because of the rallies or his unearned media or digital operations, but because of where he concentrated his media buys and influence too. While Hillary and even the RNC wanted to stick with big network and big cable, CNN and Fox primarily, those audiences are actually fairly small.

At the Trump campaign, we found a hidden gem in Sinclair Media, a media company that had bought up hundreds of local TV stations in regional markets all over the country. Clinton didn't advertise through Sinclair. We did. We placed ads on the Sinclair stations that reached people in their homes, during the local TV news shows and local programming they watched the most. But more than that, we were able to have more local interviews, which we could control easier than dealing with the larger more bureaucratic networks. And by control, I mean we had more ability to influence which topics they would ask him about.

They would happily embrace this structure because getting an interview with the next president was a big deal to local reporters. They would then share those interviews with all of the other stations in the Sinclair empire. Not all of the stations played along. But most of them did, taking cues from the top down, sharing our pre-taped interviews on the evening news, and getting our messages out to audiences who did not watch CNN or Fox nearly as often.

I could try to add it all up and analyze it in a hundred different ways, and I'm sure plenty of people will do that for decades to come.

But in the end, our campaign had two unstoppable forces working in its favor. The first was Trump himself, a master of media and a candidate for our time given the backlash of voters against institutional politicians. And the second was the campaign itself. Because it was self-funded by Trump in the beginning and had to build so much from scratch, our campaign was leaner and more determined. Like a startup in a big corporate universe, we were able to come into the marketplace and disrupt the status quo, to be nimble, break with traditions, displace the patterns, and win big because of it.

Because we were so small, nobody saw us coming. Nobody thought we had a chance.

It's almost as if Hillary Clinton was standing at the helm of the *Titanic* of the American political system, and Donald Trump was the iceberg.

Hillary had 868 people on her campaign staff, plus the backing of the Washington elites, and the full support of the DNC system that she and her husband were such a big part of building over the last thirty years. They also had plenty of mainstream media support and so much more. But none of it was enough to lift her over the top.

At the apex of our campaign, we had 218 people on staff in total, *without* the Washington elites on our side, or the RNC, or most of the mainstream media.

Not only did Trump beat Hillary, he won the game.

He beat the system.

And his victory made a lot of people inside Washington extremely angry.

THE INAUGURATION
AND TRANSITION

CHAPTER 12

The Peaceful Transition
of Power

*The People's Inauguration and Washington's
Reluctance to Accept Trump*

THE REJECTION OF DONALD TRUMP IN WASHINGTON BEGAN THE day after the election. People in every corner of our government and across a spectrum of media simply could not believe that he had beaten the entire system and won.

And, thanks in no part to the endless beat of the media drum and the Russia narrative that the Democrats had been pushing all year, many people assumed that Trump must have had some sort of "help" in order to accomplish the unthinkable.

Using Trump's own words against him, a groundswell of media pundits, influential individuals in Congress, and staunch Clinton supporters inside the criminal justice system and elsewhere in the tangled web of bureaucracy in Washington, D.C., convinced themselves that the election had been "rigged."

Suddenly, the "Russia interfered in our election" story took on a new sense of urgency, and a devious twist, as an unfamiliar word crept into the lexicon of American political discussion: "collusion."

The simple knowledge that Russia used social media and digital advertising schemes to sow discord and chaos among the American people in an election year now spun into a darker tale: that Trump himself, along with his kids and certain members of his campaign staff, had colluded with Russians to interfere in the election and somehow assure that Trump won.

In the third presidential debate, Hillary Clinton said to the world that Trump was "Putin's puppet"—and a startlingly large number of people took her at her word, despite the fact that she showed no evidence to support that statement.

Unbeknownst to any of us at the time, in the dark crevasses of the Capitol building and in far-off corners of the FBI and DOJ, a handful of resourceful individuals launched plans to go out and find the evidence to support this alleged crime of international proportions. Their actions would grow into a tidal wave that would wind up drowning America in years of senseless infighting and hurting Democrats themselves far more than their efforts would ever hurt Trump.

At the very same time, the fact that Trump was now president-elect left all sorts of corporate leaders, Republican politicians, and diplomats from every corner of earth scrambling to try to curry favor with him, to get to know him, to get closer to him or anyone in his campaign or soon-to-be-formed administration. Since they had mistakenly written him off throughout the entire election year, many people felt they had a lot of catching up to do.

These two opposing forces—the simultaneous rush to reject and hurry to embrace Donald Trump—would play into every facet of the two major tasks that were now on Trump's plate: the transition and the inauguration.

The transition involved filling all of the various cabinet positions, political appointees at government agencies, ambassadorships, seats on presidential commissions, and the senior staff of the White House, all of which would have to be approved by the Senate except for executive office positions at the White House. Trump had never faced the idea of having a body of politicians "approve" of who he hired. He had no idea just how difficult a process it was going to be.

The transition process, by law, is something that both candidates are supposed to participate in by sending campaign team members to Washington, regardless of whether they win or lose. It is the basis for how our government effectively transitions power.

In most campaigns, the vetting and preparation for the transition begins no later than July. It takes that long to do the deep vetting that is required by the Senate, and that's when you're dealing with lifelong politicians stepping into those cabinet roles, people who had likely been through public vetting procedures already at some point if not multiple times in their lives. But Trump had promised his voters that he would hire "the best people" for those jobs, and in his mind, the best people were not politicians. They were businesspeople, leaders from the worlds of finance and real estate and industry, who had likely never been through any sort of public vetting before. Which meant the process would be twice as painful and challenging for them. For a private citizen to join the ranks of government, they would have to divest from their businesses and put assets and holdings into blind trusts before the confirmation process could even begin.

That process was supposed to begin immediately after the election.

The first day Trump put any serious thought into *starting* the vetting process was the day after the election. He did not believe starting the transition process was necessary unless he won. He was practical about it—not political.

Behind the scenes, Chris Christie had been planning to install many of his loyalists, not necessarily Trump's, since he had been selected to chair Trump's transition committee in early May. But three days after the election, Christie was fired from his role. (Steve Bannon was the one who actually fired Christie. And it didn't go well. Tempers flared on the fourteenth floor, and the meetings went for hours.)

When Trump fired Christie, he put Pence in charge of the transition instead. He was the most experienced politician he had on his team and someone who would recognize the ins and outs of what needed to be done. But the people Trump chose for the roles presented all kinds of protracted issues during the vetting process, whether it was hedge fund manager Steve Mnuchin for treasury secretary or investor Wilbur Ross for secretary of commerce—they all had issues in divestiture and in their private lives that the government was not prepared to handle.

One early casualty of this new private/government conflict was Andy Puzder, Trump's first choice for secretary of labor. He was the CEO of the parent company that owns Hardee's and Carl's Jr. fast food restaurants. He endured two full months of non-stop vetting and put his assets into blind trusts only to face pushbacks from Senate Democrats because of his stances opposing the minimum wage and favoring automating the workplace. He also faced pushbacks from Republicans because he had once employed an undocumented immigrant as a housekeeper and failed to pay taxes for her services. After enduring all of the scrutiny, he wound up withdrawing himself from the process when a previously undisclosed alleged domestic incident surfaced in his background.

That was all just for one position—and Trump had to fill twenty-seven.

Trump was then supposed to fill almost 4,300 additional government positions that would be vacated when Obama left office. That was just never going to happen—not because of any incompetence on Trump's transition team, but because he (and Jared) set a goal to shrink the size of the federal government.

The idea of shrinking government wasn't new. It was a long-running and very popular Republican platform goal. Ronald Reagan ran on the idea that he was going to eliminate the entire Department of Education and Department of Energy when he took office because those departments were so bloated and ineffective. But he never actually did it. The bureaucracy pushed back so hard, he could never get it done.

Trump promised his supporters that he was going to shrink the bureaucracy, and he was determined to actually follow through. But what he and Jared found during the transition was an enormous pushback from the bureaucracy itself. In areas where they planned to tighten the operations and personnel, they were informed that they *couldn't* just fire people. There were decades of contracts and policies that prevented government workers from being fired. It's pretty well known in Washington that the only way to get rid of someone is to promote them and move them to a different office. Trump didn't know this. Jared didn't know this. They expected to walk in and act as CEOs act. Both of their companies operate extremely successfully with a surprisingly small staff. They didn't want or need four thousand people to run the government. Trump wanted to run things with the minimum number of staffers possible. Jared's insistence was that one person could do the job that any five government employees were paid to do. And one way or another, they were going to make that happen.

But the media kept hammering every cabinet nominee Trump put forward and deriding the fact that Trump "couldn't" fill the government positions that needed to be filled. It simply wasn't true. People were coming out of the woodwork trying to get jobs under Trump. A whole bunch of well-known Never-Trumpers jockeyed for positions under his leadership. When it came right down to it, a lot of bureaucrats and politicians don't care who the president is. They care about their own careers and promotions in ways that far outweigh any particular political ideology or loyalty. Remember Ken Cuccinelli, one of the leaders of the Never-Trump movement, the man who threw a tantrum on the convention floor in Cleveland? He would later become the acting deputy secretary of the Department of Homeland Security.

Part of Trump's goal of making the government smaller and more efficient also meant hiring heads of various agencies who would fight the establishment, bust the bureaucracy, overturn the old policies and legislation passed by earlier administrations, and shrink the agencies of which they were put in charge—including the Environmental Protection Agency, the Department of Labor, the Small Business Administration, and Health and Human Services, all of which Trump felt were "greatly" hindering business interests in this country, and therefore hurting our economy.

Every single one of these hires got pushback from the government itself, from *both* sides of the political aisle. It didn't matter whether or not Trump's follow-through might actually fulfill the long-desired goals of so many American people to rein in bloated budgets and government overreach. When it came right down to it, those within government— including many Republicans—didn't actually want things to change. The fact that Trump was following through so quickly on campaign promises, and the way in which he was following through—by aiming to dismantle so much of what had become "established" in Washington—seemed outrageous to all sorts of people from both parties.

This was especially true in the State Department, where career bureaucrats followed protocols in a system all their own, from presidency to presidency, and those systems had not been interrupted for decades. The State Department was its own fiefdom. Whenever a new president came aboard, up to 70 percent of the ambassador positions around the world were by tradition automatically filled by senior bureaucrats in the State Department. There was no law about this. It's just the way it was. The way it had been done for a very long time. That was a tradition Trump did not want to continue—and there were those within the State Department who would fight him every step of the way going forward, clinging with everything they had to keep the status quo. (This issue would play a highly relevant role during the impeachment proceedings three years later.)

Outside of the State Department, ambassadorships were traditionally filled by the highest bidders to the incoming president's campaign coffers. The unspoken price to buy an ambassadorship under George W. Bush was $250,000 in political donations. Under President Obama, the price went up to $350,000. Trump wanted to award ambassadorships to friends and business leaders, Washington outsiders who would align with his way of thinking and his agenda, without any price tag at all. He received lots of pushback on his ambassador choices too.

As I've previously mentioned, Trump detested fundraising. He never wanted to feel beholden to anyone because of some perception that they "bought their way in." In fact, he never was. As anyone who's ever worked with him will tell you, no matter how rich you are, no matter what you have to offer, if you got on Trump's bad side or if he felt you were disloyal, you could find yourself on the outs.

His whole approach to bringing in outsiders, which was what the vast majority of the American people wanted and voted for, on both sides, in the 2016 election, and shrinking government, which is what Republicans have been *saying* they wanted for decades, could have been widely applauded, or at least tolerated to see if it worked or not. But over the course of the transition period, nearly every single thing Trump wanted to do faced pushback from the bureaucracy, from the media, and from Congress.

The inauguration didn't face as much pushback as it did scrutiny.

Trump had no idea just how involved the planning for the inauguration would be. The pressure to arrange a series of parties, balls, and fundraisers, the spectacle of essentially putting on a show of celebration leading up to the peaceful transition of power that America was so well known for around the world, would be intense.

One person who did understand it? Paul Manafort.

Paul was still supporting Trump behind the scenes. He wanted to see him succeed in every way. He called their mutual friend, billionaire real estate investor Tom Barrack, the founder of Colony Capital, Inc., and told him he should call Trump and volunteer to chair Trump's Inaugural Committee. Paul knew that Tom would take on the task with style and class. As friends for decades, Tom would take the day-to-day worries of the inaugural planning off of Trump's already overcrowded plate.

So Tom called Trump. "Sure. It's yours," he said. And with just over two months to pull the whole thing together, Tom hit the ground running.

Tom asked me to serve as deputy chair, to essentially run the operations—from liaising with Congress (which oversees the official Inauguration Day festivities in front of the Capitol) and various agencies including the Democrat mayor's office in D.C. (to oversee activities and safety around town and on the Mall) to coordinating with the Joint Task Force (comprised of members from each group of the armed forces—the Department of Defense), and continuing to work with the RNC.

I flew to D.C. on November 10 for my first organizational meeting with Tom.

He equated the planning of the inauguration to planning the Olympics but doing it in less than seventy days. This meant organizing concerts, dinners, menus, donor events, and parades; placing people in hotels; hiring over 350 staff; arranging church services and fireworks; coordinating with police departments; supporting groups from across America that wanted to participate; sending invitations; dealing with seating and ticketing requests from billionaires, millionaires, congressional members, supreme court justices, and cabinet members (former and soon-to-be);

placing photographers; handling media requests and interviews; and arranging for transportation, security, credentials, bathrooms, commemorative items, big-screen TVs, programs, fundraising, and decorations. Not to mention taking care of Trump's large family including his kids, grandkids, wife, and two ex-wives (who we placed strategically on opposite sides of the Capitol).

For the next two months, there was no downtime at all. But working on the Inaugural Committee was an honor that comes along once in a lifetime. To have a front-row seat to one of our nation's most important political events, particularly with the first outsider president our country has ever elected, was incredible. Despite being in and around politics for decades, I never had a greater appreciation and humbleness for what our Founding Fathers did for us to create our nation.

The first established inaugural committee followed the election of Franklin Roosevelt in 1933. Every president since has established an inaugural committee, and all of them follow a pattern steeped in tradition.

We established the fifty-eighth Presidential Inaugural Committee, Inc., in late November as a non-profit entity to organize and conduct the events and activities surrounding Trump's inauguration. And our committee began by following the traditional process—until Trump got directly involved, and the whole process changed.

Presidents traditionally hold a series of candlelight dinners leading up to the inauguration: intimate dinners with high-dollar fundraisers that the political parties use for additional fundraising opportunities (beyond selling seating packages for the Inauguration Day itself). Bush had five different candlelight dinners on the night before the inauguration, with between two hundred and four hundred guests at each event, and he and Laura went to each one of those dinners to say hello for ten or twenty minutes.

Trump didn't want to do that. He and Melania said they would rather be with all of their family and friends at one big celebration dinner and stay in one location for the entire evening. So Tom and I put the wheels in motion to stage one giant dinner at Union Train Station in D.C.—for more than 1,500 people.

Melania recommended we bring in a party planner, Stephanie Winston Wolkoff, to plan the details of some of the bigger events during the inauguration. Wolkoff was a friend of Melania's from New York social circles who had worked on such massive events as the Met Gala in New York City. Her adoptive father, Bruce, is the son of famed jeweler Harry Winston. She charged exorbitant fees, but she was expected to bring a level of elegance that the inauguration had never seen.

No president gets involved in the minutiae of planning details or budgets for the events. Except Trump did. He couldn't help himself. He wanted to know. He looked at some of Wolkoff's plans and grew irate. He went through a line-item budget at one point and saw that she wanted to rent fine seat cushions for the candlelight dinner, at a cost of $65 apiece.

"We're not paying sixty-five dollars for seat cushions," Trump said. "You can buy these cheaper than that!" And he was right. Unfortunately, what Trump did not know is that during inaugural celebrations, every vendor raises prices: hotels, restaurants, caterers, security firms, car companies. Everyone. And no matter if it is a Republican or Democrat being sworn in, the prices skyrocket.

Once again, Trump dove into the tiny details, from backdrops to staging, to the type of microphone he wanted on the dais, to the length of the tablecloths at the dinners, to the colors of the posters and other signage that would go up around town.

When it came to the inauguration itself, he wanted to break with tradition in all sorts of ways. This is where it got complex and problematic. Based on Article II of our Constitution, it is Congress that is authorized to determine when a president is sworn in, not the actual president-elect. Over time the ceremony became more official and eventually a Joint Congressional Committee on Inaugural Ceremonies (known to insiders at JCCIC) was formed in 1901 to oversee the ceremony and its proceedings.

Funny enough, in one meeting the JCCIC told us that everything had to run on schedule on Inauguration Day—something that wasn't always Trump's strongest trait. They said if Trump's swearing in didn't happen at exactly noon on January 20th, if he were running behind, they would be required to swear in the sitting vice president as the 45th President of the United States. Which meant that if Trump ran late, Joe Biden would have been sworn in, even if just for a few minutes, thus making Trump the 46th president. Tom Barrack relayed this news to Trump, who said, in all seriousness, "No, no. I like 45. It's a good number. I'll be on time."

Trump did want to change the way Congress led the ceremony, though, going head to head with a body of individuals that he largely shocked by winning, and to which he had no allegiance. For example, instead of one preacher to offer the invocation and one for the benediction, Trump wanted six different people with various religious affiliations on stage for the swearing-in ceremony, and every one of his requests sent the JCCIC into a frenzy. They pushed back on almost everything, and they had the final say on a lot of the proceedings.

One of the most significant moments where Trump changed the plan occurred just after he was sworn in. It has become a tradition that the incoming president visit the President's Room, one of the most ornate rooms in the U.S. Capitol, to sign an executive order establishing the members of the cabinet. Traditionally, the incoming president is flanked by the congressional leadership and it is a symbolic moment. It will come as no surprise that instead of being just flanked by the leaders of Congress, President Trump invited his entire family to join him in the room. It was both a humorous and historic moment. Many members of the leadership were taken aback at so many people in the room, and clearly, it was not part of the plan or the tradition to which they were accustomed. These moments created a great deal of friction with the JCCIC, but they wound up graciously going along with Trump's wishes and agreed to most of our recommendations and changes in the end. They adapted—to him.

Given Trump's ongoing rankling of the system, the RNC was worried about how he was going to pay for the festivities. They had already seen how hard it had been to get big donors to open their checkbooks during the campaign. They informed us that Bush raised $41 million for his inaugural celebration in 2001 and that Obama had only raised a little more than that in 2009. We saw our estimated costs balloon closer to $50 million pretty quickly. And we hadn't even talked about putting on a large-scale concert, which was something Obama had done to great success. Trump wanted more people to see this inauguration than had ever watched the inaugural celebrations and ceremonies before. He knew the optics. He knew how important it was to do everything in a big way so that audiences would show up in person and tune in on TV and online from all over the world.

Lew Eisenberg, the RNC finance chair, said, "Look, we're not going to raise more than forty-five million, fifty million tops. That's the absolutely high mark. I would set the budget for forty-five million."

By mid-December, after the donations started coming in, we knew we wouldn't have any trouble raising far more than that.

It wasn't that we did anything remarkably different than any other inaugural committee in the past. It's just that people wanted to get their foot in the door with this unexpected new administration. In politics, people believe that you only have a seat at the table if you contribute financially. People were nervous that they hadn't supported Trump before, so they were now anxious to contribute and be part of the win.

Even before we had a chance to put packages together to send out to big companies and potential donors to solicit contributions, big donors and big companies started calling *us*.

Since all of our fundraising information was out in the open, the media started pounding Trump for taking donations from big corporations, but it wasn't unusual at all. Obama's Inaugural Committee took corporate money. Bush's took it. Clinton's took it. We took it.

Trump wanted to know who was donating. But he didn't ask us how much any individual or company donated. He just wanted to know that he had support, and when we told him we were raising a *lot* of money, he was happy.

Wealthy casino owner Sheldon Adelson alone contributed $5 million. Everybody else was $1 million or under. Some CEOs gave separately from their companies. Some companies gave separately from their CEOs. But in the end, we had pledges of $110 million—and we collected a total of $107.4 million in donated funds.

The money was not for Trump personally, or for his political agenda. It was to fund the celebrations around the peaceful transition of power, an American event that our country does better than anyone else. And that is exactly where the money went.

For the opening night of the week-long festivities, Tom wanted to create something really special. We planned "The Chairman's Global Dinner," the first of its kind. Barrack wanted to "introduce" Trump to the international community. The event became the one ticket for the week that *everyone* wanted to attend. Trump's friend, Steve Wynn, offered to fly in a full-fledged stage production called "Showstoppers" from one of his Vegas hotels. There were events and other parties for past presidents that involved nothing but beer and some chips or pretzels on the tables. This, and all of Trump's events, were going to be done with more style and elegance, so people got excited about them.

We had world leaders who wanted to attend the Chairman's Dinner and the inaugural swearing-in ceremony, but we had to say no.

Under the Logan Act, a president-elect is not allowed to talk policy with world leaders until he or she is sworn into office. We wanted to avoid even the appearance that the Logan Act had been broken. We turned down some royalty, prime ministers, presidents, and others who absolutely wanted to attend just to get a sense of figuring out how they would deal with this outsider of a president and the relatively unknown members of his cabinet.

We were permitted to invite foreign ambassadors though because ambassadors are considered proper witnesses to America's peaceful transition of power. It had never been done on this scale before, at such a big event, and lots of them were excited to attend the Chairman's Dinner. We purposefully sat Trump at a table with some of his incoming cabinet and close friends (all American citizens) to avoid any questions of Trump meeting with foreign emissaries before he was officially inaugurated. Some of them would try to meet Trump that night, for the very first time. To say hello. To shake his hand. To take a photo. None of them had protracted conversations with Trump and nothing official. There were simply too many people there for Trump to talk to anyone more than a few seconds.

But the media (and a few Washington insiders) made a big deal about it. They noted that certain ambassadors from the Middle East were present, and the Russian ambassador was present. With Russia collusion talk bubbling in the background, and the ongoing crisis in Syria, this raised a lot of eyebrows. But most of the other "controversial" ambassadors were there too: representatives from China, Mexico, Ukraine, France, and Turkey. So was actor Jon Voight. So were a lot of wealthy businessmen.

Trump made it clear he wanted as many people as possible to attend the events during the week and to witness the inauguration too.

Trump wanted this to be the "people's Inauguration," and that's what we aimed to create.

The media wanted to spin things another way, to fight Trump on everything he did, from the outset. So when the weather was bad on January 20, and the crowd sizes on the Mall were less what they might have been were it not for the cold, rainy weather, it turned into a "major story" about how fewer people showed up to see Trump sworn in.

In reality, although the physical attendance was not as high as Obama's inauguration, on TV and on the internet, more people tuned in to see Trump sworn in than had ever tuned in for the inauguration of any other president in history. By far. Trump did not help the matter any by insisting that more people were at his inauguration. As a result, it blemished Sean Spicer's initial days as the White House spokesperson and he was never able to recover, leading to his exit.

The media also kept waving a red flag over the amount of money we raised for Trump's events and not so subtly tried to imply that the money must have been going somewhere it wasn't supposed to be going.

The heat of that story grew so strong and went on for so long, we later leaked our entire line-item budgets to two publications, just to try to quell the controversy. And to a large degree, it worked. It was absolutely clear where and how all of the money was spent. But just as soon as the media realized there was no more story about questionable spending, they spun the story into a complaint about how lavishly the Inaugural Committee spent. On everything.

As a quasi-government non-profit, we *had* to spend all the money we raised. It wasn't a choice. And given the success of every event we threw, and the success of the logistics, security, and everything else that went so smoothly on January 20, I can say without hesitation that the money was more than well spent.

We also kept the tradition of donating any remaining inaugural funds to charity.

The committee gave $1 million each to the American Red Cross, Samaritan's Purse, and the Salvation Army. Also, we gave $750,000 to the vice president's residence in D.C., which isn't funded by taxpayer money beyond utility bills and the exterior upkeep and is instead run by a non-profit organization. The same goes for the White House, which is why we donated another $1 million to the White House Historical Association, an act done by most inaugural committees.

We made some smaller donations to other charities too, and the total amount of charitable giving by our Inaugural Committee was around $5 million—the most of any elected president in the history of inaugurations.

That fact wasn't widely reported, and none of the actual facts stopped the constant harassment from the media, or certain members of Congress, and even some investigative units inside the Department of Justice. This certainly didn't make Trump feel welcome, appreciated, or respected at the outset of his presidency.

Trump is wont to exaggeration, sure. Hyperbole is part of his character. But when Trump complains that no other president has faced the kind of harassment and scrutiny he's been under from the start, I can attest that he is not exaggerating.

I can say that with conviction. Simply because I was a part of Trump's inaugural team, I wound up under more scrutiny than I'd ever faced in my life (up until that point). That scrutiny continued for the next three and a half years, including at one of the trials in which I testified, where I was accused by the defense lawyers of embezzling inaugural funds. I wasn't in charge of the inaugural fund. I didn't hold the purse strings or have control over the budget. I didn't have access to the checkbook. We had a CEO and board treasurer and we worked in conjunction with the RNC; we ran internal audits and did everything by the book. The only reason I faced scrutiny was because I worked for Trump and because a defense lawyer was attempting to bait me.

There was a tremendous amount of anticipation among the media and certain elites in Washington that Trump would fail. It felt to me that there was a *desire* to see him fail, just to prove that he didn't belong there or had no right to be there.

Many presidents have been investigated or attacked at some point for actions taken while they were president, because of how they handled controversies and crises, whether self-made, man-made, or natural disasters. But historically, we have never seen a president-elect so attacked while making his way to the presidency. Instead of Trump's transition and inauguration serving as the peaceful transition of power that our country had cherished since its founding, this period was a continuation of the divisive and angry, emotionally charged atmosphere we'd seen during the campaign, an atmosphere in which certain people and certain media channels could not get over the fact that Trump won, and therefore continued to make every effort possible to show why he should not be president. There was even talk about how the election could be nullified.

President Obama went through some of this type of scrutiny and opposition in 2008 and again in 2012, at the hands of certain right-wing radio hosts and talking heads on Fox News. But from what I saw up close, those attacks paled in size and scope to what was happening to Trump from a wide spectrum of sources all across the media landscape.

All the pushback angered Trump. The attacks riled him. He felt he wasn't being shown *any* of the respect that had been given to past presidents, of either party, including Obama, whom Trump thought was highly ineffective.

These constant attacks didn't hurt him, though. They only served to fire him up. They put him in fight mode—where Trump thrives.

And that played a direct role in how Trump would operate as he stepped into the presidency.

CHAPTER 13

President Donald J. Trump

WHILE TRUMP, HIS FAMILY, AND MANY OF HIS SUPPORTERS WERE watching the Inauguration Day parade from the reviewing stand along Pennsylvania Avenue, I stood ever so briefly in the Oval Office, alone.

I had credentials that allowed me access just about anywhere that day. We had planned some events in the White House for the family, and for some donors, and I was checking to make sure that everything would be ready. I had walked in through the main entrance on the north side, through the entrance hall, and then over to the West Wing. I passed by the White House press briefing room (where Franklin Roosevelt's indoor pool used to be located before they filled it in), as the White House staff scrambled to change out the furniture, the beds, and the carpets, and hang the gold-colored drapes that the Trumps had specifically chosen.

The Obamas officially moved out at noon. The Trumps were scheduled to arrive around four. The entire changeover of the White House happened in that tiny window of time. It was astonishing to watch the exchange unfold in a buzz of activity all around me, and then to stand in that office, by myself, realizing the magnitude of what had happened and what was *going* to happen in a matter of hours.

For me, it was a pretty solemn and impactful moment.

Lots of people take tours of the White House. But to be able to experience the Oval Office in this in-between state, after Obama had vacated but before any of Trump's personal effects arrived—to take it in for what the office *stood for,* instead of who held the office for a moment in time—was humbling.

America had a new president, and I wondered if Trump was ready for what he was about to face in Washington.

He had personally wanted to turn the inaugural parade into a full military spectacle, but the plan was nixed, and there was nothing he could do to change it. Our military liaisons loved the idea that the president-elect wanted to honor them on Inauguration Day. They broke into huge smiles when I first presented the idea to them. But Trump's vision of rolling tanks through the streets of Washington to show American strength was thwarted by the Department of the Interior, who insisted the equipment would tear up and destroy the pavement of the city's streets (including Pennsylvania Avenue). Then his plan for a military flyover, with a single F-16 fighter scheduled to sail over the Mall at precisely the moment he was sworn in, was thwarted too. We'd spent weeks negotiating with the air force and the FAA until they finally agreed to briefly lift the permanent no-fly zone over the Capitol and the White House, for just a few seconds, just for him. But on Inauguration Day, the weather wouldn't allow it. The visibility that day was just too poor for jets to fly safely.

The setbacks that day were just the beginning of the frustrations Trump would face in Washington over the next several years.

We spent countless hours discussing schedules and routes based on the idea that Trump was going to sign his very first executive order while he was in the presidential limo (known as "The Beast") on the way from the parade route to the White House. No president had ever done such a thing. It was aggressive. It was *different.* It would show the world he was wasting no time following through on his campaign promises.

His very first act, in addition to signing an executive order declaring January 20 a National Day of Patriotic Devotion, would be to order a systematic dismantling of President Obama's crowning achievement, the Affordable Care Act. After attacking it at every rally and in nearly every interview for the last year and a half, and on Twitter long before that, he was finally going to kill Obamacare.

It was, without a doubt, an opening salvo. A shot which would aggravate Democrats and get pushback from more than a few Republicans who believed in many provisions of the ACA too. Whether he fully understood the implications or not, he was starting a Washington war.

After all the work and coordination between teams, the limo idea was scrapped. It was ultimately decided it would be more powerful to sign that executive order in front of cameras, in the room in which I had just stood. And he did.

The very next day, he signed an executive order to push through the controversial Keystone Pipeline, fulfilling another campaign promise but setting up new fights far from Washington in an already tense situation between the energy industry and Native Americans. In Trump's view, it was part of his promise to achieve energy independence for our country. To others, it was akin to firing shots at our own people.

On the twenty-fifth he signed two more executive orders: one to begin construction on the wall, which would trigger the president of Mexico to cancel a planned visit in February, taking his fight to the international community already; and another cutting federal funding to so-called "sanctuary cities," which harbored undocumented immigrants from federal immigration laws. On the same day, he also called for an investigation into voter fraud, to get to the bottom of why Hillary Clinton won more popular votes than he did—a fact that bothered him as much as the criticism and speculative rumors that were being fired at him over charges of collusion with Russia.

And on the twenty-seventh, he signed an executive order on immigration that was drafted largely at the direction of Steve Bannon and Stephen Miller, restricting refugee admissions and immigrant and nonimmigrant travel from seven specific countries, primarily in the Middle East.

On paper, it looked as if Trump was accomplishing everything he wanted to in his first week in office.

In reality? He was on government turf now. And the opening days, weeks, and months of Trump's White House were a conflagration of chaos.

His first order, on the ACA, was immediately upended and mired by pushback from Congress, from the courts, and to an extent in the court of public opinion. A week after his Keystone Pipeline act, his staff let him know that it hadn't been implemented. The order had to be approved by FERC, the Federal Energy Regulatory Commission, they explained, which by law has to sign off on new policy initiatives.

"So get FERC to approve it!" Trump shouted.

His staff explained that they *couldn't*. FERC needed to reach a quorum first, and that quorum required Trump to fill two board positions, which would then need to get confirmed by the Senate.

Tom Barrack was present for that meeting and said he could see Trump boiling. He expected to see the pipe in the ground by now, and it hadn't gotten out of the starting gate. Trump couldn't believe that he had to appoint commissioners to confirm something he already signed.

Tom and I were in and out of the White House regularly through March, wrapping up tail-end details on the Inaugural Committee's work and other projects that Tom was involved in. So we both witnessed the frustration that came pouring out of the new administration's offices into the narrow hallways.

Trump ran into wall after wall, on everything he tried to do—including the wall. All of his stances on immigration were quickly dismissed by various courts and government agencies as unenforceable, in addition to renewing and hardening the media's racist and xenophobic accusations against Trump. It didn't take long before the immigration order he signed, which Bannon and Miller structured for him, was found to be largely illegal on its face because they never notified key agencies about the changes they wanted in the policy. They tried to change U.S. immigration law without including the Department of Homeland Security and the Department of Justice in the initial policy draft.

The signing of that executive order caused major rifts within the administration as well, because Bannon used the Shabbat strategy again. He got Trump to sign it on a Friday evening when Jared and Ivanka were honoring their religious practices and unreachable; and he used similar tactics again with Trump's declaration to withdraw from the Paris Climate accord down the road.

Jared and Ivanka were not happy, and the skullduggery on the inside was just the beginning. Bannon would eventually be cast aside, and Trump would realize that in almost any White House, the lust for power within the administration sometimes caused staffers and cabinet members to go at each other—sometimes hurting the president's agenda more than the opposing party ever could.

Trump *thought* he was doing what he does best: meeting all of the fight, scrutiny, and rejection of Washington head on. That's what he *does*. But maybe for the first time in his adult life, his old strategies weren't working. He found himself unable to accomplish some of his goals.

He had come to Washington with the notion, supported by millions of voters, that the entire government was going to be run through the White House. *His* White House. But as soon as he and his staff arrived, they were confronted with barriers they didn't even know existed.

Trump could have found and hired an expert on U.S. government bureaucracy to guide him, the way Paul had guided the campaign through the convention, an expert or two who knew the technical ins and outs of how the bureaucracy works, someone who could lead them around all of the bureaucratic obstacles to the victory they sought.

Instead, they hired people like Wilbur Ross, Linda McMahon, Steve Mnuchin, and Rex Tillerson. They're all very smart, accomplished people, but none of them really understood the process of how government works. They all faced a massive learning curve, just like Trump, but even more so, because they were trying to enact the directives that Trump had given them, which propelled them into an abyss of bureaucracy.

Trump's campaign promises were important to him. He felt he had made a promise to *do something* for the American people, and especially for his supporters. Reflecting back, Trump had said on numerous occasions that politicians "never keep their word."

The bureaucracy in Washington was suddenly making him look like one of those politicians.

What the bureaucracy didn't understand about Trump is that he would not roll over or give up the way so many presidents had done in the past, even on some of their biggest campaign promises. Trump would fight, find loopholes, push boundaries, and break every protocol and accepted behavior on earth before he would be defeated. It's what he's done in business and in his public life full of tabloid scrutiny, and it is what he would do in Washington: he would fight to the end to do things *his way*, no matter what the fallout and consequences might be.

His fight began before he stepped into office, and it will not stop until he leaves Washington behind—whether of his own accord or through the will of the people.

★   ★   ★

During all of my back-and-forth trips to the White House during Trump's first three months, I was given a new task that took me by surprise.

The day after he was sworn in, Trump announced the start of his reelection campaign. People thought he was crazy. Most presidents don't even think of doing that until two years into their term of office. *Why do it so soon?*

Here's why: it allowed him and Pence to start fundraising right away. To get a jump on the competition. And it was a bold and successful decision. Fast forward two years, and he had already raised nearly $500 million before a single Democrat threw a hat in the ring for the 2020 election.

Trump wasn't allowed to fundraise directly for his reelection while he was president. No president is. It is a conflict for a government official (even the president) to cross the line into campaign politics, which is why super PACs were invented. (A super PAC is an independent political action committee that may raise unlimited sums of money from corporations, unions, and individuals but is not permitted to contribute to or coordinate directly with parties or candidates.) There are strict lines between campaigning and governance. Those lines are never to be crossed, and they can't be, because the media is always watching.

Brad Parscale approached me just after the inauguration and asked me to help run a new super PAC for Trump. Along with Nick Ayers, one of Mike Pence's closest staffers, we established and co-chaired America First Policies.

It was a role with implications and responsibilities that would impact Trump's (and Pence's) future as a candidate.

Nick and I hired a small staff initially and worked out of the Trump Hotel until we could find office space of our own. We started planning a few dinners and fundraisers at the VP's residence at the Naval Observatory.

Meanwhile, the Russia collusion story continued to gain momentum in the media; and the Democrats' plan to ensnare Paul Manafort as one of several architects that allegedly used Russia to help Trump win had begun to take effect.

I was no longer working for Manafort. I hadn't been on his payroll since mid-2016. After leaving the Trump campaign, Paul shifted his work away from Ukraine and began working in several new countries. And in addition to working with the super PAC, I took a role with Tom Barrack at his company, Colony Capital, Inc.

I was still working behind the scenes, not in any official public role.

But in mid-March, a Buzzfeed story made note of the fact that I was making frequent visits to the White House. It was all aboveboard, for work I was doing with Tom related to the Inaugural Committee. But the Buzzfeed story implied otherwise.

On March 22, an AP story linked Paul Manafort to Oleg Deripaska, a billionaire who allegedly had extensive ties to Putin. Paul had worked with Deripaska in the mid-2000s, but in no way was the work he did related to anything involving Putin or the Russian government. In fact, it was in direct opposition to Putin's goals in the region.

It didn't matter. There was little room for nuance in this narrative. And given most Americans' slim understanding of foreign relations, let alone the complicated inner workings of oligarchs, business entities, and government agencies in Ukraine, the simple connect-the-dots story linking Putin and Deripaska to Trump's former campaign manager raised eyebrows all over Washington.

That same day, the *Washington Post* put the two and two of those stories together, under the headline: "Manafort Is Gone, but His Business Associate Remains a Key Part of Trump's Operation."

I gave a brief interview to the reporter on that story and tried to correct the AP's interpretation, which wrongly implied that working for Deripaska meant we were doing Putin's bidding. I told the paper that our work was focused on "supporting the private equity fund started by [Deripaska's] firm, and democracy and party building in Ukraine."

I was glad they used my quote. It was the absolute truth.

The truth did not matter.

Earlier that week, FBI Director James Comey announced that his office was investigating possible collusion between Russia and the Trump campaign. In the media's eyes, Paul and I were easy suspects because of our work in Ukraine. So was General Mike Flynn, because of his consulting work in Russia and lunch with Putin. So was George Papadopoulos, a minor figure in the campaign whom I had never met, because of his efforts and meetings with those attempting to arrange a meeting between Putin and Trump. So was Jared, who had loans through Deutsche Bank, which had Russian investors.

To those who bought into the theory that Russia and Trump had colluded to interfere in the election, the various unconnected dots seemed far too coincidental to ignore.

The fact is, if the same storyline had been applied to the Democrats and the Clinton campaign, all kinds of similar dots could have been found there as well: Bill Clinton giving a speech in Moscow in 2010 for $500,000; nine separate donors from Uranium One (a Russian/Canadian conglomerate) contributing almost $150 million to the Clinton Foundation; and John Podesta holding shares in Russian companies. Hillary Clinton had the most Russian connections of anyone through her work with the Clinton Foundation, and the much-reported-on (and some might say suspicious) large donations from Russian oligarchs that flowed into the Clinton Foundation while she was secretary of state.

If you applied this same logic to investigating certain Independent candidates, the media would have found the same. There were photographs of Green Party candidate Jill Stein sitting at the very same table as Vladimir Putin and Michael Flynn in 2015. Interactions with Russians, and Russian media, are not a crime. People like Flynn were highly sought-after public speakers on the international stage, just like Bill Clinton.

If the media or the FBI wanted to investigate Russia collusion on all fronts, they easily could have investigated the day the Clinton Foundation received a $2 million donation from Ukrainian oligarch Victor Pinchuk.

In September 2013, Hillary Clinton gave a keynote speech at the Yalta Economic Summit; that day she had planned on speaking out about the persecution of former Ukrainian prime minister Yulia Tymoshenko, as detailed in the advance copies of Clinton's speech; the very same day she decided to *drop* at Pinchuk's request that potentially damaging portion of her speech at the last minute.

Pinchuk was the biggest donor to the Clinton Foundation that year, donating $23 million in total.

Later, in 2018, I gave details of these events to the Special Counsel, and to my knowledge no investigation was ever carried out and it was omitted from their final report.

At the time, any narrative of who else may have helped Putin's interests or played any role in Russia's interference in our elections never played out. The media wasn't interested. Neither was the American public. Unfortunately, as accusations flew against Trump, he brushed them off. In some cases, he encouraged the story and toyed with the media throughout his campaign, and even after he became president because it fired up his base and he found it humorous how it set the media off.

Still, word got back to me that Trump and Jared were both concerned about the stories, and how my visiting the White House might be perceived in light of the current media tales.

When the story refused to die a week later, Nick Ayers raised the concern about me continuing on at the super PAC. So did Reince Priebus. And in a matter of days, I felt I had no choice but to remove myself from my co-chair role and involvement with the super PAC. The last thing I wanted to do was to hurt Trump, or Pence, by my continued association with the White House or the reelection fundraising efforts that were just getting underway.

I was still employed by Tom Barrack, and I had his full support. He knew all of the various players involved. He had known Stone, and Paul, and Trump himself for many years, and he knew the Russia collusion story was an empty one.

The Russia collusion narrative only accelerated in the media through April, but I was never contacted by the FBI about any investigation. So I wasn't worried about it. If Comey and his investigators came calling, I would happily tell them what I knew: that neither I nor anyone I worked with on the campaign, nor Trump himself, had any contact with Russians who could have influenced the election. There was no collusion. It was a made-up storyline. It was malicious, and it was absurd.

As the narrative continued to spin, I received a letter in May 2017 from the House Intelligence Committee, informing me that they were undertaking an investigation of their own. The House was still under Republican control then. This was supposed to be an investigation on Russia's interference in the election, which had nothing to do with "collusion," and it was extremely confusing to me. The letter was a general letter sent out to dozens of people, plus an attachment covering the things the committee wanted to talk to me about—and the attachment was two pages about Paul's work in Ukraine between 2010 and 2014. All of that work preceded the Trump campaign by more than two years. There were only two bullet points tacked on to the end, asking if I was aware of any collusion between the Trump campaign and Russia.

I called Paul, and he had received the same letter with essentially the same attachment. He said it was nothing to worry about. I was low on the list, he said. They wanted to talk to Steve Bannon, Don Jr., and himself more than they did anyone who worked under them. But he did think I should hire a lawyer, just in case.

Tom Barrack later received the same letter and generously stepped up and offered to support me and help pay my legal bills, since I wasn't independently wealthy and any lawyer capable of handling a government investigation would charge me exorbitantly. Tom knew Trump better than any of us and had no concerns about Trump or our campaign having worked with the Russians to sway the election. He saw this as a full-throttle partisan attack, but he knew the implications of it as well. He naturally wanted to protect us and himself, since he was so closely tied with a lot of us who had worked on the campaign, and he had just served as the Inaugural Committee chairman himself.

With everything else that was going on in the world, and in Washington, I found it hard to believe that this Russia story kept building and circulating. But it did.

Jeff Sessions, who had been with the Trump campaign since nearly the beginning and whom Trump had appointed attorney general, recused himself early on from anything having to do with the investigation of Trump and Russia. Personally, it was a disappointing decision. Sessions had not informed Trump of his intentions, which would have been the honorable and professional approach. Instead, he made the decision, announced it publicly, and *then* informed Trump of what he had done. With Trump, loyalty is paramount, which Sessions knew well. Trump went ballistic. He publicly derided Sessions for his decision and is still denouncing him to this day. (In July 2020, it cost Sessions a return to his U.S. Senate seat in Alabama. His primary loss was a direct result of Trump campaigning against him.)

Whether Sessions truly understood what he had done or not, his recusal allowed for many of those individuals inside the DOJ and FBI who were upset with Trump's election to activate the legal system against the president. Sessions's poor judgment paved the way for everything that happened next.

On May 9, Donald Trump had dinner with FBI Director Comey. The next day, he fired him—and the media speculation immediately turned to the Russia collusion investigation as the cause for the firing. Trump told people privately that he thought Comey was "a nutjob" and had considered removing Comey well before the FBI launched its Russia probe. While he appreciated what he'd done to derail Hillary Clinton ten days prior to the election, he didn't think Comey was loyal or capable. He was part of the Washington establishment that Trump was trying to fix. Regardless of the reason, Trump had a right to fire him if he wanted, with no questions asked. Deputy Attorney General Rod Rosenstein, who stepped in for Sessions in this case, did the actual firing, and he said the decision had been handed down by Trump, while the White House said Trump had fired him based on the recommendation of Rosenstein. Regardless, Rosenstein put Deputy FBI Director Andrew McCabe into Comey's job on an acting basis that day, until Trump could fill the role.

On May 16, Trump met with Robert Mueller to interview Mueller as the leading candidate to take over Comey's role as the new head of the FBI.

And on May 17, the very next day, Rod Rosenstein appointed Mueller as Special Counsel to investigate Russian interference in the 2016 election.

Even from afar, it all seemed questionable. The timing was just too strange. The decision to appoint a Special Counsel, and to appoint Mueller in that role, was not made in the span of twenty-four hours. There had to have been time and thought put into that decision, and Mueller likely would have known about the prospect of it ahead of time. Did he meet with Donald Trump under false pretenses? What was going on behind the scenes? No one could explain these actions, and it is clear today that Trump was unaware of them at the time too.

As this was unfolding, former Obama-era staff, including former attorney general Sally Yates and CIA director John Brennan, were testifying about Russian interference in the election before Congress on Capitol Hill. At the same time, Trump kept questioning whether Russia interfered *at all*—mainly because of his distrust of the U.S. Intelligence community—which only made things look worse for Trump.

In his appointment letter, Rod Rosenstein gave Mueller the ability not only to investigate any links between Trump's campaign and Russia but to investigate "any matters that arose or may arise directly from the investigation," and prosecute "any other matters within the scope."

Essentially, Rosenstein gave the Special Counsel the sweeping authority to investigate anyone and everything they deemed a part of their investigation, on any charges they could create—whether or not those charges were related to actual Russia collusion or Russian election interference in any way. The power granted to the Special Counsel extended well beyond the purpose of the Russia investigation and I firmly believe it was an abuse of power within our legal system—one of many which I would encounter over the next two and a half years.

At the time, it didn't worry me. I didn't think it worried any of us who had worked on the campaign. Many of us from the campaign still spoke to each other, and we all believed we were fine. Russia collusion simply didn't exist, and none of us imagined in the moment how that sweeping authority might be used against us, or how charges might be manufactured and manipulated.

In mid-May I received another letter, this time from the Senate Select Committee on Intelligence, saying the Senate was launching its own separate investigation—but in the end, neither the House nor the Senate ever called me in for formal testimony.

On July 25, 2017, Paul called me late in the afternoon and told me he had just met with staff from the Senate Intel Committee. Both of us were asked to submit documents and participate in an interview.

At this stage, the Russia collusion issue had become a central focus of Congress and many Democrat members were already making strong claims that Trump's team colluded with the government of Russia to win the election. However, since they had no evidence, they claimed that these investigations would get to the bottom of it.

Initially, I did not fully understand just how politically unhinged congressional members were becoming, but I was about to find out. It was a shining example of the wicked game in action. Paul said his meeting with the Senate Select Committee on Intelligence lasted fewer than thirty minutes, and that only staff were present.

He said the questions were not thorough and seemed more of an exercise to check a box. However, the Senate Intel Committee publicly made the meeting with Paul seem urgent and monumental.

The most disturbing facet to come from the meeting occurred later that day when U.S. Senator Mark Warner, from Virginia, angrily demanded that Paul must come back to the committee because he did not answer all of the committee's questions. Keep in mind that Senator Warner did not even attend the meeting. I wonder what questions he forgot to ask if he was not there. It was a disturbing example of politics influencing Warner's deceptive narrative.

There were three other small bits of information that Warner forgot to mention. First, he was back-channeling with Adam Waldman, a lobbyist for Oleg Deripaska, who is the same Russian businessman that Manafort worked with. Second, Warner was communicating with Waldman to have him set up a meeting with Chris Steele, the now-debunked source used by the FBI to peddle uncorroborated reports and evidence it was collecting. Finally, Warner actually knew Paul fairly well. He and his partner, Rick Davis, shared an office suite with Warner in his Old Town Alexandria building for several years. During one of Warner's reelection campaigns, he asked Paul to serve as his Republicans for Warner chair. Paul declined the offer.

In August 2017, the FBI had closed their case. They found no evidence of collusion between Russia and the Trump campaign. Two years later we learned that the FBI report was shared with the Special Counsel, and with the House and Senate, as soon as it was finished. But neither the Special Counsel nor either body of Congress put a stop to their own investigations. By fall, the narrative was still active. The media kept regurgitating the issue. They could not let it go.

At the time, I did not believe I was high enough in the hierarchy to have anything substantial to offer to the House or Senate, or they would have called me in to testify. Which meant I certainly didn't have to worry about facing any sort of action from the Special Counsel, either.

When Greg Andres, a prosecutor in the Special Counsel's office, sent me a subpoena asking for some documents, I voluntarily provided copies of those documents in September. At that time, he gave my lawyer the clear impression that I was not a target of the investigation.

I took him at his word.

THE MUELLER INVESTIGATION AND AFTERMATH

CHAPTER 14

Mueller's Investigation

What We Learned Then and Now

O N FRIDAY, OCTOBER 27, THE RUMORS STARTED FLYING.

Robert Mueller's Special Counsel investigation delivered a set of sealed indictments to the court. Reporters from every major and minor media outlet around the world started scurrying to figure out who Mueller had ensnared, on what charges, and just how close to the president they might be.

The speculation pointed primarily to Roger Stone. Some speculated that the indictments were against Paul too. That scared me—not only because of the proximity factor and how anything that happened to him might affect my own reputation but mostly just thinking about what it might mean for Paul and his family. I was certain Manafort and Stone hadn't committed any act of collusion. Other names were floating around too, including Trump's personal attorney, Michael Cohen, whom I didn't know well but who had been directly involved in Trump's business dealings, including a plan the media had unearthed to build a Trump hotel in Moscow, which of course raised more suspicions.

But nobody thought the investigations were ultimately targeting me. Including *me*.

I was busy attending my younger brother's wedding. It was an exceptional fall day in Charlottesville, Virginia, and we were surrounded by family and friends. My phone was turned off.

My brother and his bride had graciously asked all of our children to participate in the wedding too, and they were thrilled to be a part of it. The ceremony was outdoors, overlooking the sweeping Virginia mountains around us, and the reception was an elegant sit-down dinner, followed by dancing and the sounds of laughter and happiness.

At the end of the night, I checked my phone and was greeted with a barrage of texts from reporters wanting to know if Paul was one of the people indicted. All I could tell them was, "You know more than me."

The general consensus was, "I guess we'll find out Monday morning."

I wouldn't have to wait that long.

On Sunday morning, as we were unpacking from our trip, my phone rang. It was my lawyer. He asked if I was alone, so I stepped into my home office to take the call.

"What's going on?" I said.

"Rick," he said, "I'm sorry to have to tell you this, and there is no easy way to do it. I just received a call from Greg Andres. You are a target in the investigation, and you're going to be indicted tomorrow."

I was shocked.

I tend to be someone who takes news calmly. Even bad news. It is a trait that has helped me navigate working with others more effectively. So I sat down in my office chair and listened as my attorney explained the process I would have to go through in order to turn myself in to the FBI.

Looking back on it, I think my calmness that morning was in part because I couldn't have possibly understood what the ramifications of this indictment would be. There was no way I could have imagined what this was going to do to my life and to my family. Plus, I was innocent. This was *crazy*. I hadn't been a part of any of the things that the press or investigators or anyone else had insinuated the "Trump team" did. No one I knew during my time on the Trump campaign had "colluded" with Russia to try and sway the election in any way. We didn't need to. Trump did plenty to sway the press, the voters, and everything else in that campaign all on his own. Which is why I truly could not understand why the investigation had targeted me, and why they were "indicting" me.

"What are they accusing me of?" I asked.

"I don't know. The indictments are sealed. Hopefully, you can get a look at the charges before you're in front of the judge," he said. "But there's something else...."

My lawyer went on to tell me that he couldn't appear with me in court the next day.

He was dropping me as a client.

"Why?" I asked.

He said there was a dispute over payments between his firm and Tom Barrack. In my work for Tom, I knew that the law firm had been grossly running up its fees and that Barrack wasn't having it. Tom had been withholding funds while disputing the charges, but the timing of this news felt suspect to me.

"What am I supposed to do with no attorney?" I asked.

"They'll assign a public defender to you. It won't matter much at this stage, but you will need to find new counsel," he said. "They've offered to let you self-surrender, which means there won't be a public spectacle. It'll all be handled quietly. They want you to come into D.C. tonight, stay at a hotel, and the FBI will pick you up and bring you in for processing first thing in the morning. You have to surrender your passport as well. They'll send someone over today to get it."

"To my *house*?"

I could hear the sound of my children laughing in the living room. I was paralyzed.

"Yes. Someone from the local FBI field office will call you to set that up. Just turn it over. Don't say anything. I'll meet you later at the hotel tonight to go over what to expect in the morning. You'll be fine. Again, I'm sorry, Rick."

"Right. I understand. Okay, thanks," I said.

I hung up the phone, completely numb.

Two hours later, an agent from the FBI's field office in Richmond came to my house. Thankfully, he called me ahead of time and arranged for me to walk outside to meet him near the street, so our kids wouldn't be impacted. I didn't want to have to explain who he was, or what he was doing at the house on a Sunday.

He was polite. He acted as if he knew less about what was going than I did. I got the sense that he'd never been asked to pick up someone's passport on a Sunday like this, but he took it from me and said, "Thank you very much, Mr. Gates. Can I ask you to sign this form?" The only thing the form did was confirm that I had handed over my passport to the custody of the FBI, so I signed it. It didn't say anything about what the charges were, or why the surrendering of my passport was required—although I later learned that confiscating my passport was over the fear that I would flee the country.

Naively we thought this would all blow over quickly.

After an early dinner, I told the kids I had to go into D.C. for a morning meeting, which was not unusual on a Sunday night. I would sometimes drive in the night before in order to avoid the brutal I-95 commute. I checked into a hotel where I met my outgoing attorney, and he told me what to expect in the morning. And then I stayed up for most of the night running through everything I had ever done or said, and everything anyone else I had worked with on the campaign had ever done or said since I'd first been introduced to Trump in March of 2016. I was absolutely certain that no one I knew had colluded with any Russian to help sway the election. No way. Which made me question: Was this whole Special Counsel investigation a move to try and thwart the election results? Was this a political reaction to Trump breaking all the norms of the political system, and beating them so badly at their own game?

In the morning, two FBI agents took me to the Washington Field Office for processing. They did what my lawyer had promised: they took me in through an underground garage, so my family wouldn't ever have to see a public spectacle.

It was in the field office where I saw Paul for the first time in several months. We passed one another in an office lobby while paperwork was being completed. Then we were separated into two separate rooms waiting to be moved over to the D.C. Federal District Courthouse, less than two blocks away.

The FBI agents then drove us in two separate vehicles to the court-house, but once we arrived, we were positioned in the same area behind the magistrate's chambers. This was the first time we were left alone together.

"This is absurd," I said. "Why are we here? There's no Russia collusion!"

Paul looked pained and in shock to see me. "I know," he said. "I don't understand why you're here. I am really shocked. There's no reason you should be here. We're going to get through this. Don't worry, everything will be fine."

The only thing I knew with absolute certainty was that I was not guilty. So I stood tall as they walked me in the courtroom. I felt it was important to hold my head high, to let it be known through my body language that I hadn't colluded with any Russians.

On the inside, not knowing what I didn't know, having still not seen the actual indictment, not knowing what I was walking into—I was scared.

The outdated carpet on the floor, the worn wooden benches, and the fluorescent lighting of that run-down old courtroom hit me like a blinding light as we walked in. I'll never forget the smell of that place, and the buzz in the air, as I looked around the gallery and saw it was packed. There wasn't even any standing room left.

I had never seen the inside of a courtroom from this perspective before. I noticed sketch artists alternately staring at me and then looking down at their sketch pads, frantically scribbling, then looking over at Paul, and frantically scribbling some more.

The two of us were tied together in this, no matter what happened from here.

As the clerks and stenographer took their seats and a bailiff stood up and swung the door to the judge's chambers open, my heart raced.

"All rise...."

The magistrate judge, Deborah Robinson, a woman with more than thirty years on the bench, came in, and she started speaking agonizingly slow.

She began reading the indictments, one syllable at a time, and slowly but surely the truth of why I'd been targeted became clear: not one single charge in either of the indictments against us had anything to do with "Russia collusion."

Instead, it was a dizzying array of charges, on everything from taxes to FARA registration issues, and none of which had anything to do with President Trump, his team, or anything that occurred during the 2016 campaign.

I could not wrap my head around what she was saying. None of the charges against me were true, and I did not believe any of the charges against Paul were true, either. But the indictments had me tied to Paul's charges in a "conspiracy."

And that's when I started seething.

"This is political persecution," I thought.

I didn't want to believe it. I didn't want to believe that our political system was this corrupt on so many levels. Paul and I had seen plenty of corrupt politicians in other countries. But here? At this high a level? It was unthinkable. The multiple counts in these indictments were about financial matters: Paul's taxes, foreign accounts, and an issue with "FARA registration," which, as I later learned, carried no criminal sentencing guidelines and was usually treated by the Department of Justice as a clerical error, not a federal crime. There was nothing about Russia. Which could only mean one thing: all of this was politically motived. There was no other reason that an investigation into Russian interference in the 2016 election would dig up these unrelated charges against any two people, except for the fact that we happened to be people who worked for Trump.

When the judge asked me to enter my plea, I said with absolute certainty, in a clear, strong, and defiant voice, "Not guilty."

The word "conspiracy" immediately struck me. "Conspiracy" meant that more than one person was involved. The charges linked the two of us in "conspiring" to do these things they alleged we had done. And one of the charges—failure to properly register our political consulting work in Ukraine under the FARA Act (the Foreign Agents Registration Act of 1938), which was designed primarily to make sure *foreigners* openly registered their intentions as agents in dealings with the U.S. government— came with the demoralizing wording of charges of "conspiracy against the United States."

In no way were we ever working "against" the United States of America. In fact, we were asked in 2014 to voluntarily support an FBI investigation looking into the ways in which the Ukraine government worked and to help the FBI understand what had happened during and after the Western-backed coup of the Ukrainian government, which was controlled by the political party we represented. We were tasked with helping an FBI investigation. And we did. Gladly. We weren't under investigation then. If we were, then why had we heard nothing from the FBI or Department of Justice between 2014 and when this Special Counsel was appointed in 2017?

An experienced lawyer told me a little later on, "I don't worry about indictments that carry thirty or forty charges. That's just for show. It's to scare you. It is the indictment that has only one or two charges that scare me most because I know they really have something."

Even before I heard that advice, it occurred to me in that courtroom that the Special Counsel wasn't after *us*. They did this in order to try and force us to take plea deals, to cooperate in their investigation, and to give up information on their real target, President Trump.

They were trying to get to him by using us as pawns to get there, to incentivize us to turn on him and tell the Special Counsel what they wanted to hear.

The irony is that there was nothing to tell.

If they had simply asked me to come in and give them everything I knew, I would have done it voluntarily. Instead, I was now being targeted.

My court-appointed attorney, David Bos, who turned out to be one of the sharpest attorneys I'd ever met, and Paul's attorney both asked for bail in order to keep us out of prison while we waited for the next steps. There was utter confusion about this because courts in D.C. don't *do* bail. They don't have systems in place to even deal with bail.

Paul and I were released on our own recognizance the day of our arraignment, but we were both placed on house arrest. Although I was in D.C., our neighborhood back in Richmond had been swarmed by satellite trucks and newspaper reporters, staking out the house. My wife had to face that and try to shield the kids from that on her own. I was in despair thinking about them having to deal with the emotional trauma.

Two days after the arraignment, when we were back in front of a new judge, again facing these charges that had nothing to do with Trump-Russia collusion, the judge set my bail at $5 million. Secured. Which meant we needed to put up $5 million in collateral to cover the bail and be removed from house arrest.

Paul's bail was set at *$10 million.*

To put that into perspective, Phil Spector, the Hollywood record producer who was accused of murder, was released on bail for $1 million. Harvey Weinstein, one of the wealthiest and now most reviled alleged sex offenders to come out of Hollywood, a man whose behavior was so offensive that it helped inspire the #MeToo movement, was released on $1 million bail as well.

I didn't have $5 million in assets. I didn't have anything close to that. And my alleged crimes didn't come close to the level of crime that would ever warrant that kind of secured bail in any other circumstance.

My wife and I had to put our house up as collateral, and ask our parents to put *their* houses up, and we still didn't come close. We had to do this as the media started spinning wild tales about the business dealings Paul and I were a part of. The narratives were false and absurd. They seemed uninterested in reporting or checking the facts. We added our savings and kids' college funds up to try to secure the bail, and it *still* wasn't enough.

We had friends offer collateral, and even then it wasn't enough. This went on for an excruciating amount of time, and it became clear to me that it was a legal tactic meant to add pressure. The Special Counsel would agree with us to an asset we put forth, and then would oppose it in front of the judge—demanding real estate assessments, and time-consuming and costly legal documents. The judge eventually relented two months later in January and agreed to our bail package, even though I never came up with a fully secured $5 million.

On top of all this, the judge then required my wife to surrender her passport. I am not even sure that was *legal.* Initially, we could not figure out why this occurred but later discovered the reasoning was to prevent the possibility that my wife would flee the country with our children, and increase my level of flight risk. This seemed insane and just surreal to us. It was so out of the ordinary that the probation office in Richmond asked me what on earth they were supposed to do with her passport once we turned it over! They had never seen this before.

I hadn't done anything that the Special Counsel had been called to investigate. Yet my family was now in danger of being ripped apart. My whole life was in jeopardy. And to top it all off, on that second day in court, the judge placed a gag order on both Paul and me. Which meant I wouldn't be allowed to talk to *anyone*, let alone the press, about anything related to the investigation. Which further meant I had no way to defend my reputation in public or to tell the American people what exactly was happening.

Instead, as the chaos continued to unfold all around me and I saw so clearly where our country was headed if this Russia investigation continued, they deliberately silenced me. In one fell swoop, all because of the fractures and division caused by the singular election of Donald Trump, the United States government and the United States federal court system stopped my life in its tracks and forced me into a crucible. I was now a statistic in an increasingly broken political and judicial system.

They stole my *voice*.

I wouldn't get it back—I wouldn't get *any* of it back—until more than two years later.

★ ★ ★

Here are the facts that we know now—more than three years after my indictment.

The FBI's investigation into Russia collusion was launched by an agent named Peter Strzok, based on thirdhand information delivered to the FBI following a meeting that George Papadopoulos held with the deputy ambassador from Australia in 2016. The two met in London. They were drinking. And in that meeting, George made comments saying that a third party had told him that "Moscow" had "embarrassing information" on Hillary Clinton. The deputy ambassador told his FBI counterpart in Australia what Papadopoulos said, and that agent then relayed the information back to D.C.

The FBI requires proof in order to start an investigation. There are standards and thresholds for launching *any* investigation, let alone an investigation of political candidates. Strzok didn't have any such proof. In fact, in July 2020 the Senate Judiciary Committee released internal notes written by Strzok which stated, "We have not seen evidence of any officials associated with the Trump team in contact with [intelligence officers]. We are unaware of ANY Trump advisors engaging in conversations with Russian intelligence officials." But he launched the investigation anyway, under the code name "Crossfire Hurricane."

Strzok was a staunch supporter of Hillary Clinton, and vocally anti-Trump. He shared these feelings with a woman named Lisa Page, with whom he was romantically involved, via text messages. Page also worked for the FBI as an attorney and adviser to Deputy Director McCabe, a significant and senior role.

It all spun out of control from there.

Once the FBI opened a process to obtain more information, they were provided with a copy of the now-infamous "Steele dossier," a report documenting Donald Trump's dealings in Moscow, much of which has since been shown to be fabricated, and none of it proven true. The fabricated information in the Steele dossier—which was funded in part as "opposition research" by Fusion GPS, an organization connected to the Clinton campaign—was then used to obtain warrants to start surveillance on Carter Page, one of Trump's foreign policy advisors. (Carter was hired before Paul and I were on the team, around the same time Papadopoulos joined the team. I never met him.) The FBI falsely portrayed Page as a possible Russian spy in its warrant filings to the Department of Justice, when in fact, agents within the FBI, having already been informed by the CIA, *knew* that Page was working for the CIA in Moscow as an American asset. Also, we now know through testimony from the Clinton campaign's law firm member, Marc Elias, that invoices for Fusion's work were passed directly to Clinton's campaign manager, Robby Mook. The same Robby Mook who derided the Trump campaign in late July 2016 based on his accusation that Russia was, without question, helping to elect Trump.

As the investigation continued, the DNC began submitting information to the FBI through a Department of Justice official named Bruce

Ohr. (Ohr's wife, Nellie, happened to be working for Fusion GPS at the time.) That information included material on Paul Manafort's political, business, and financial dealings in Ukraine, as well as information about certain loans to Trump and others from Deutsche Bank, with possible links to Russian oligarchs and Vladimir Putin.

If the DNC had given that information directly to the FBI, it would have been considered biased or tainted, but because Bruce Ohr handed it off *inside* the FBI, it was deemed credible.

That information gave the FBI enough backing to continue the investigation, creating and building all sorts of unconnected dots that seemed to point back to some nefarious connection between Trump and Russia.

One of the "leads" that the FBI's Washington Field Office pursued was on General Mike Flynn, who was brought aboard as Trump's national security advisor after serving as a surrogate for Trump on the campaign trail. The office investigated Flynn for five months and determined that Flynn was not acting improperly with the Russians. They filed a memo closing the case back on January 4, 2017.

In May of 2020, the transcripts were finally released from the House Intelligence Committee's investigation into Russian election interference, and those transcripts revealed that out of fifty-three witnesses interviewed, not one provided any evidence of collusion between Russia and Trump or his campaign. And many of those witnesses were high-level Democrats who served under Obama.

Rod Rosenstein, the deputy attorney general, had access to all of that information when he gave Robert Mueller and his office of the Special Counsel the power to upend so many lives in pursuit of evidence for this alleged crime, for which the FBI had zero proof to begin with. On June 3, 2020, Rosenstein sat in front of a congressional committee and readily admitted that he had regrets about some of the decisions he made at the launch of the investigation. He admitted that some of the supporting documents against Carter Page (who was later ensnared for supposedly lying to investigators) were tampered with, falsified, or unverified by people within the Justice Department, and therefore those surveillance warrants should not have been issued.

At the hearing, Senator Lindsey Graham asked if Rosenstein would agree there was ultimately "no there there" when it came to the idea that "the [Trump] campaign was colluding with the Russians in August 2017."

Rosenstein responded, "I agree with that general statement."

"As we now know," Rosenstein said, "the eventual conclusions were that Russians committed crimes seeking to influence the election and Americans did not conspire with them."

But before his testimony, in a statement released to the press, Rosenstein said, "Even the best law enforcement officers make mistakes, and some engage in willful misconduct."

While he did not name names of who might have committed "willful misconduct," I expect those names will eventually come out and may include names I've already mentioned here, since the Department of Justice has been conducting a thorough investigation of this entire debacle at the same time I've been working on this book.

In the spring of 2020, the Department of Justice dropped its case against General Mike Flynn. It was an unexpected move by the DOJ, and a step rarely taken. Flynn, whose son had been threatened with indictment if he didn't cooperate with investigators, was ensnared by the Special Counsel in what amounted to a perjury trap. He pled guilty to lying to the government—just as I did. But the Justice Department in 2020 found that the "lie" he told was not connected to a criminal act, and therefore his "guilty" plea was invalid. They threw the case out.

Catching Flynn in a "lie" when he had committed no act of collusion with the Russians, which was the intended scope of the Special Counsel investigation, is what happened to *everyone* charged in the Mueller investigation. Everyone was hit with a "perjury" charge. It was a scheme. A tactic designed to ensure that when any one of us involved in this investigation was able to speak, we would all be viewed with less credibility. (I'll share details that support these statements in the next two chapters.)

None of this is to say that all FBI agents are corrupt, or the whole Department of Justice is corrupt, or the entirety of the Democratic National Committee is corrupt. What's remarkable is that it all just came down to a few powerful people in key positions. And not a single one of those people is still working in government today. They all left, were fired, retired, or resigned. Strzok and Lisa Page, McCabe and Comey, James Baker (the general counsel of the FBI, who was another key player), Bruce Ohr—they're all gone.

I expect there will be additional indictments from the investigation on all of this, and I have reason to believe that those indictments will be handed down before the election in November. Maybe they'll already have been handed down by the time this book is released.

I welcome them. We should all welcome them. Because what we know now, objectively, is that there was more collusion within the confines of our government to go after President Trump on these charges than there ever was any collusion between Trump or his campaign and Russia.

Martin Luther King, Jr. wrote a phrase that I wrote down very early in this process. He said, "Injustice anywhere is a threat to justice everywhere." I repeatedly recited this to myself over the last three years and took it to heart.

This quote is more profound today than it was when I found it.

The fact that Trump himself was the target of the investigation is not a conspiracy theory. We *know* he was a target because the Mueller Report states it. Trump brought suspicion upon himself because of the sometimes foolish and careless statements he made in public.

But from a prosecutorial point of view, the investigation itself and all of the charges unrelated to Russia collusion that were brought against me, Paul Manafort, Michael Flynn, Roger Stone, and others, were nothing more than a legal pyramid scheme, one in which prosecutors went after their primary target by targeting the people below the target.

They went after me in order to get to Paul.

They went after Paul in order to get to Trump.

They never found Russia collusion at any step along the way.

Through separate silos, one by one, they climbed through Flynn to try to get to Trump. They climbed through Roger to try to get to Trump. They tried to get to Trump on the business side too, by attempting to climb through Michael Cohen.

They never reached the top of the pyramid.

They never found what they were looking for—because it wasn't *there*.

After receiving the report from the FBI in August 2017 that concluded neither Trump nor anyone in his campaign colluded with the Russians to alter the election, the investigation should have been closed.

It wasn't. And the consequences are profound and disturbing: three years of deepening mistrust in our government, further divisiveness in our country, a presidential administration kept on the defensive, and humiliation on the part of the Democrats.

The investigation ultimately emboldened Trump.

It gave Trump even *more* power to continue to fight, to push back, to create and exploit more chaos in an already unstable political environment, to upend the norms and protocols in Washington, and to solidify his support not only with his large base but with more and more Republicans inside the Beltway.

CHAPTER 15

Lifting Mueller's Curtain

What the American People
Were Not Allowed to See

B Y SILENCING ME AND EVERYONE ELSE, THE SPECIAL COUNSEL WAS able to control the narrative.

That was part of their strategy.

I was part of their strategy.

In our case, the prosecutors wanted to get as much of their information into the public domain as possible. They wanted to shape the stories quickly. They used a tool known as a "speaking indictment," which goes beyond the usual statement of charges brought against a defendant and actually allows prosecutors to put information out about *alleged events* into the public domain. This means that they are allowed to speak publicly about unproven accusations. In our case it allowed the prosecutors to say whatever they wanted in the context of the ongoing Russia investigation without any accountability. This allowed the media to carry on with this destructive narrative over several years, and in my mind ruined any chance for a fair trial. It is another deceptive weapon used in the legal arena.

I had no idea how any of this actually worked until I was thrown into it. The judicial system operates by its own set of rules, and it is a wicked game all its own—not dissimilar and yet uniquely distinct from the wicked game of presidential politics.

I was about to get an education.

I had no legal choice but to stand back and take it while the media attacked me and my family with misstated facts drawn directly from the indictments and exacerbated by what can only be described as the abject failure of journalists to do their jobs.

To start things off, the media said I began working for Paul in 1980. Fact check: I was born in 1972 and would have been eight years old at that time.

Then multiple media reports confused me with Rick Davis—Paul's longtime business partner. Because we share a first name, I suspect, they routinely wrote about me working on campaigns I'd never worked on, and in countries I've never visited.

The media stated that I was worth tens of millions of dollars. Not true. I own one home, which wasn't worth nearly as much as the media (or the Special Counsel's narrative) stated. But the prosecutors and media kept trying to paint me as a peer of Paul Manafort's. I wasn't. I was his employee. Paul owned multiple houses, a closet full of expensive custom suits, and lived a lifestyle I could never afford. As I learned, he was much wealthier than I even knew. I had never been to his house in the Hamptons and had no clue of the lifestyle he lived there.

It's not a crime that Paul was wealthy. But after years of working for him, even I was surprised to learn certain details about his lifestyle.

The media consistently said that Paul and I worked for pro-Russian interests in Ukraine, which was the polar opposite of the truth.

And the media consistently overstated the seriousness of the crimes for which we were indicted—while neglecting to point out the fact that none of them were related to Russia, to Trump's campaign, or to the 2016 election.

There were twelve charges in the original indictment; eight of them impacted me, as the government attempted to tie me to Paul's charges in order to create a "conspiracy" charge which was needed to put pressure on Paul. The majority of the counts related to not disclosing foreign bank accounts, held by Paul. Additional charges were filed against Paul for not paying enough in income taxes. One of the foreign bank charges related to me specifically failing to report a foreign bank account. I had a bank account during the two separate times my family lived in the United Kingdom. I unknowingly omitted checking a box on our tax returns after Obama changed the law in 2010. I am accountable for that mistake.

Interestingly, the Special Counsel did not make a charge of "tax evasion." There is a significant difference between tax evasion and filing false tax returns. The latter means paying some taxes but not enough. Rarely are these brought as criminal charges. Normally there are remedies for those types of issues, and most individuals have an opportunity to resolve the deficiency. These matters should have been dealt with by the IRS, and not via sweeping indictments by Special Prosecutors.

Paul had foreign bank accounts for his businesses, some of which I learned later were never reported to the IRS because he was using a loophole in the tax code. The indictment claimed he had "hidden" $150 million in those accounts over ten years. He *had* failed to report that he had foreign accounts, but the amount wasn't anywhere *near* $150 million. First the Special Counsel had double-counted some of Paul's accounts, which they later acknowledged. Second these were business accounts and the Special Counsel was using a gross number, not the actual total after deducting media and advertising buys, polling costs, external consulting fees, staff, the leasing of office space, and other common business expenses. It was eventually concluded that the amount of taxes owed over a six-year period, which went unpaid because of the lack of reporting, was approximately $4.5 million. That is a large number for sure and inexcusable, but far less than what the Special Counsel calculated and the media reported. There was no accountability for their inaccuracies, but the damage had been inflicted and it fueled a media firestorm. Was this a mistake, or was it purposeful?

I may never find out, but some proof was offered to me by my financial adviser, who was interviewed by the Special Counsel about my finances. It would be more than a year after my indictment before I could talk with him. But he was explicit in recounting how the Special Counsel provided incorrect information to him about my net worth, and he stead-fastly corrected them on multiple occasions until they reached a point of frustration. Despite the interview and knowing that I was not worth anywhere close to $26 million, the Special Counsel continued to use this number in multiple documents that were part of the public narrative used against me. This information was categorically false, and the Special Counsel knew it.

Was it wrong for Paul to not fully report his income? Yes. Of course, it was. But how was any of this related to Russia collusion? It wasn't. The IRS never audited Paul or me. In tax investigations, an audit is a required first step. A chance to remedy any discrepancies found in an audit is step two. In this case, Paul would have owed a lot of money and owed interest and penalties on the amount he failed to pay. If he refused to pay the amount owed, then criminal proceedings might have proceeded. But none of those steps were ever taken—not before, during, or after this investigation. This was a misapplication of the law. Everyone should be treated equally under the law.

In addition to the tax charges, the Special Counsel stated that Paul and I had failed to register as "foreign agents" under a section of the law called the Foreign Agents Registration Act (or FARA). As I briefly mentioned in the last chapter, the law, which was created during World War II, was specifically meant to keep *foreign* agents who represent foreign governments from talking to members of Congress without first registering and declaring those activities with the U.S. government. American individuals and companies had to register when they were working on behalf of foreign governments when talking to members of Congress as well—just to keep everything clear. It sounds nefarious, largely because no one has heard of the obscure law. Rest assured that today everyone in Washington, D.C. and beyond knows about FARA. (Registrations increased by 50 percent following the Special Counsel's actions against members of Trump's campaign.) The allegation by the Special Counsel was that Paul did not register as a foreign agent despite working for a foreign political party.

But none of what Paul or I did during our decade working together in Ukraine was done in secret. There were hundreds of communications back and forth to the U.S. State Department, explicitly demonstrating that Paul was working with the Party of Regions, Viktor Yanukovych, and others. It was widely known. During his ten years of work in Ukraine,

Paul met with four different U.S. ambassadors on a frequent basis to communicate with them about U.S. policy goals toward Ukraine. Everyone in Washington was aware that Paul was working in Ukraine and for the most part knew what he was doing. In the entire time that Paul worked in Ukraine, and even after our voluntary interviews with the FBI in 2014, not one single U.S. government official enquired or directed Paul to file under FARA. Ambassador Geoffrey Pyatt certainly did not have an issue when he appealed to Paul in the summer of 2013 to "lobby" the Ukrainian government on his behalf to expedite the quarantine procedures for his dog when he moved to the country to take up his post.

During the course of the Special Counsel investigation, we learned that the FBI had opened a preliminary investigation on Paul. We were never aware of this before, or the fact that in 2014 the FBI agent conducting that investigation, Karen Greenaway, concluded that there was not enough evidence to pursue Paul. However, the investigation was reopened in 2017 by Andrew Weissmann a DOJ prosecutor who eventually moved over to the Special Counsel team—even *before* the Special Counsel was formed.

Paul was never paid by or worked for the government of Ukraine. He was working for the Party of Regions, a political party, and individual candidates, and he rarely ever spoke to members of Congress about that work. So, it was ambiguous under the law whether he (and certainly whether I by extension) needed to register under FARA or not. We sought legal advice in 2007 and 2009 and were told that registration was unnecessary. Even if it was ultimately determined that we did need to register, the decades-old precedent when dealing with American citizens allowed for retroactive FARA registration. There were no penalties. There was no jail time. In fact, it was not uncommon for American companies and lobbyists working overseas to register ten years after their work as "foreign agents" was completed. For example, Tony Podesta, the brother of Hillary Clinton's campaign Chair John Podesta, and former congressman Vin Weber, both working for public affairs firms that Paul hired in 2012, were allowed to retroactively file their FARA registrations in 2017. Yet Paul and I were held to a different standard, and the way the media framed the issue made it sound as if we had committed high treason.

The exaggeration and drama poured into the way the media talked about the alleged money laundering charges in our indictments as well, as if Paul and I were some sort of sophisticated bankers. The "money laundering" in this case amounted to Paul paying bills for goods and services from his foreign accounts instead of his U.S. accounts. Since the money in those foreign accounts was not reported to the IRS, they charged, it amounted to "money laundering" under the law. It did not mean that the money had been "cleaned" through a series of secret transactions, or filtered through any illegal channels—which is the classic definition of money laundering. Was there a reason that these charges, which stemmed from many years earlier, were being brought now? Absolutely.

These same gotcha games, process crimes, exaggerations, and bad-guy storylines were applied across the board, to every person ensnared in the Mueller investigation, and I could only begin to imagine what some of these other individuals and their families were going through.

At this juncture, I was desperate for advice on my options and next steps. I reached out to my mentor, Charlie Black, and asked him for help. He said if he were ever in my shoes, there was only one person he would call: D.C. defense attorney Tom Green.

Tom has been involved in more special and independent counsel investigations than any other lawyer I have been able to research. He is a Democrat, so this decision was not about aligning on politics, although I had been warned that our different political affiliations would cause a stir in D.C. circles. It was about finding an attorney with the reputation, experience, and the heart to help me understand what was happening to me. Tom helped me through this difficult time with compassion and wisdom. He went way beyond the scope of what a lawyer needed to do for a client, and some of the most significant relationships in my life today are a result of direct and indirect actions Tom took on my behalf. I will be forever indebted to him. Choosing Tom would prove to be one of the greatest gifts through this difficult experience.

The reason we were targeted is clear to understand and was explained to each of us by our various attorneys. All of the pressure by the Special Counsel was meant as leverage to force us to plea. Without a plea, the

Special Counsel could not get the step closer to Trump that they desperately needed in order to justify and continue their investigation.

I can't even count the number of sleepless nights my wife and I endured, spinning over everything, weighing legal advice, trying to figure out what to do, and how to make it stop, all while trying to protect our children. That was always our first and most important goal.

Did any of us deserve to have the law weaponized against us, just because we worked for Donald Trump? What if the shoe was on the other foot, and this was a Democrat? Anyone but Trump? Would there not be public outrage over the tactics that were being used to ensnare and pressure this group of people who worked or previously worked for the president?

Tom reviewed every charge the Special Counsel laid upon me. He knew Robert Mueller, personally, for more than forty years, and I felt he would be able to assimilate all of the moving legal pieces and help me plot our next course. He arranged to meet with a couple of the prosecutors from the Special Counsel's Office after they reached out to him. Following that initial meeting, Tom made it absolutely clear to me exactly what they wanted: even after the FBI report to the contrary, they were convinced that Trump was aided by Russia in the 2016 election and that he and/or members of his campaign played a role in that effort.

This is not how investigations are supposed to work in our country. Evidence is supposed to be gathered first, and *then* charges are determined. In this case, the Special Counsel proceeded to force a new investigation, despite being told directly that there was no evidence suggesting links with Trump's campaign. And they would use "every weapon that the legal system afforded them" to investigate this assertion, Tom said.

There was nothing that Paul and I were accused of doing that would justify what happened to each of us, either. Nothing in the indictments should have risen to this level of prosecution, and it wouldn't have, were the prosecutors not on the hunt for Trump.

And I knew there was going to be no easy out, no messing around, for either of us.

I'd been told that if we went to a first trial, even with Paul as a co-defendant, my personal legal bill would likely be in excess of $1.5 million. A second trial could cost even more.

I didn't have it—and the Special Counsel knew it. This was part of the pressure.

In addition, I learned that the conspiracy charges leveled against me meant that I would have to go to trial with Paul. There would not be separate trials. So the fate of me (and my family) was tied to a man that I did not know everything about. His lawyers were not fully sharing all of the information with my attorneys and they were insistent on taking control of the entire legal process.

Tom Green spoke to me about seeing families torn apart by trials.

"You don't want to put yourself or your family through a trial," Tom said. "In addition to the financial expense, there's just no way people do well in these things, mentally, emotionally, physically."

He kept talking about the "circus" a trial would be for my family, and to seriously consider the impact. What I didn't know at the time was that Manafort's trial would end up being a circus for all involved regardless. Tom's thought was that I should get out of this quickly, and with as little pain as possible. What *he* didn't know at the time was that this was going to be a Special Counsel investigation like no other.

"I think Manafort probably did some things. Maybe he inflated assets. Maybe didn't pay all of his taxes," he said. "I don't know all of it yet. I don't think the indictment is representative of what he really did, but you're under an incredible amount of pressure here. These guys are going to try and crush you. This is how the system works."

It was clear to Tom that the Special Counsel was likely withholding some discovery, but it would take time to work through the legal system. More prosecutorial tactics. They had buried us in paperwork. They wanted me to plea, and they would keep applying every pressure imaginable until I did. And the lead prosecutor in my case, Andrew Weissmann, was notorious for knowing how to manipulate the system to get the results he wanted.

I still wasn't ready to give in. This was gut-wrenching. But I had to protect my family from an investigation that was ultimately not about me.

Tom suggested that we simply go in and talk with the Special Counsel to see what information they specifically had that related to me and my charges. In legal terms, this is called a proffer process. The nickname for it in legal circles is "Queen for a Day." It's a provision where you agree to meet with prosecutors and tell them the truth about everything they ask, under an agreement that they can't use anything from that interview against you.

It would give them a chance to test how the evidence they had stacked up to the truth of the firsthand, eyewitness accounts I had to offer, and it would give me a chance to figure out what *they* had, and what they might have to offer in return for my cooperation.

In making our decision to take this step, Tom made it clear: "Immunity is guaranteed if you have anything on Trump, on Russia collusion or anything else."

"That would be great," I said, "but I have absolutely nothing. All I have is what I saw, and what I know."

On January 29, 2017, we drove to the office the Special Counsel had set up in Patriot's Plaza, along the Potomac River in Southwest Washington, D.C. Outside it was all brick, with a glass entryway. Inside, it was as pathetic and outdated as most government office buildings tend to be.

We came in through the garage, so no one would see me, and rode a freight elevator to the third floor. We went through a secure door into a small reception area. There were small lockers against a wall to store cell phones and other electronics.

As we followed the protocols and waited to enter our conference room, Bob Mueller walked in the main door. I was no more than two feet from him, and I think he was clearly surprised to see us.

"Good morning, everyone," he said in a quiet voice while looking across the lobby toward another door.

I remember it vividly because it was the only time I saw Robert Mueller throughout the course of the entire investigation. He never sat in on any of our meetings, calls, or trial prep sessions. Given his lack of participation, some believed, myself included, that Mueller was in charge of the investigation in name only and that it was Andrew Weissmann who was really driving the investigation.

We were eventually escorted to a small conference room and waited for the Special Counsel's team to join us.

We met with Weissmann and Greg Andres in a small interview room. Weissmann started with a long preamble about the purpose of a proffer and making sure I understood the importance of telling the truth. Looking at Weissmann, I felt nothing but disdain. I felt that he had manufactured and manipulated evidence to attack me and my family. Throughout this process, I would come to realize that Weissmann did not care about people. They were pawns to him. He was mentally calculating his next move at every moment. Unlike Andres, who was more beligerant, Weissmann would engage quietly, asking questions very deliberately and with a purpose that was sometimes unknown. He and Paul were very much alike in many ways. They were both calculating and strategic, but also manipulative and arrogant. They played their given fields like a chess game—always prepared and ten moves ahead of anyone else.

He had a famous history of using scorched-earth tactics in his work on the Enron case and elsewhere to get the convictions he was after. Without question, in my mind, Weissmann was the architect of the Russian investigation. His political bias was public knowledge. In fact, in 2020, Weissmann made known his political leanings again by agreeing to host a fundraiser for Democratic presidential nominee Joe Biden.

After being around personalities as strong as Trump's, or Paul's for that matter, it gets pretty easy to spot certain traits in people. And in Weissmann, I could quickly see that what drove him was the "win"—in the legal world, being better at this game than anybody else. He was dismissive of other lawyers, judges, the Supreme Court, you name it. Whenever he was in the room, other prosecutors and investigators deferred to him. It was automatic. He seemed to intimidate them. But even after doing some reading on his work on the Enron case, it was still shocking that someone could act so sinisterly. In both cases, Weissmann seemed to have a predetermined narrative and would go to any lengths to make the chess pieces fit into that narrative. I would come to learn that during the majority of his legal career, most of his major trial cases were overturned at some point over the years.

The first questions out of the gate were whether I had ever had conversations with Donald Trump about working with Russia to interfere in the election.

"No," I said. "Absolutely not."

Had I ever heard or overheard Donald Trump talking about those subjects?

"No," I said again. "Absolutely not."

They pivoted to asking me about Paul, and the frustration on their part was visible right away. At one point Andres exclaimed, "You're not telling us what we want to hear." Weissmann interjected quickly to shut down those comments. But that sentiment was reflected in later questioning as well in the months to come.

They focused heavily on the FARA registration issue, and they were confused by the nuances of how things worked in Ukraine—that we could have been paid to do work by a businessman who was simultaneously a politician, and how that could be legal. I had to explain it to them. They tried to pressure me over my decision-making power in coordinating with Paul, as if I might have participated in a scheme to not register under FARA for some nefarious reason. I didn't. I also explained to them that I was Paul's employee, not a partner. That seemed to surprise them. I wondered for a moment if they were confusing me with Rick Davis, just like the newspapers had done. I told them I had no legal rights or even verbal rights to make decisions for Paul on these issues.

They volleyed among asking about Paul, the campaign, and Trump, but it was very clear that they eventually wanted to focus on Paul. They asked if I knew about the letters Paul sent to "KK," Konstantin Kilimnik, and whether we had shared polling data with him, and I said, "Yes" to both. But I also explained why Paul was sharing that information, and my explanations only seemed to frustrate them further.

They asked whether Paul's intent in communicating with KK was to bring in Russians to help with the campaign.

"Absolutely not. That doesn't even make sense!" I laughed, educating them on the way Paul used to poke fun at the dismal skills the Russians had when it came to campaigning.

Not once did they bring up anything that accused Paul or me—or anyone else associated with Trump or his campaign—with Russia collusion. Not once. They never asked me to confirm any evidence they had or stories others had shared with them. They just pounded on Paul and fished around, asking me if I knew of any other connections between campaign staff and the Russian government or Russian individuals.

We left the Special Counsel's office around 6:30 p.m. on January 29 with a commitment to return two days later. During the second day of discussions, we again focused for a period of time on the subject of FARA. The Special Counsel asked me about a particular meeting Paul had a number of years ago with California Congressman Dana Rohrabacher, one of the few congressmen with a long history of advocating for advancing U.S./Russia relations as a way to counter China's strength in the world. He and Paul had a twenty-plus-year relationship, and the particular meeting Weissmann was referring to happened while Paul and I were working with Viktor Yanukovych and the Party of Regions. Lobbyist and former congressman Vin Weber set up that particular meeting, and the Special Counsel asked specifically what I remembered about it. I didn't remember much because Vin and Paul had done several meetings together. I was never at the meeting. They asked if anyone said anything specifically about discussions related to Ukraine. "They just said it was a good meeting," I responded. "I don't believe Paul or Vin said anything about Ukraine." The information I gave to them was secondhand. Then they asked me who said it was a good meeting. I responded, "Paul told me it was a good meeting. I think Vin might have said it as well. They both told me it was a good meeting."

We wrapped things up and planned to do a follow-up meeting the next day. But that night, as I replayed the discussions in my head, I remembered that it *wasn't* both Paul and Vin who said it was a "good" meeting. Only Paul had told me the meeting was "good." I thought I ought to correct the record just to be as accurate as possible.

The next morning, February 1, I told Tom about the issue at his office before we headed to the Special Counsel's office again. He thought I was being overly cautious by trying to correct such a minor detail, but he thought it would be an important action to genuinely show my sincere effort to be truthful. Tom went in ahead of me and told the Special Counsel about the matter before we started our second day of the proffer session.

Tom came back to the conference room, indicated that he gave the information to the Special Counsel, and said that we would be starting in a few minutes. A couple of minutes later Weissmann came storming into the interview room, visibly angry.

"We've got a major issue," he said. "You've *lied.*"

I was shocked

"What do you mean?" I asked.

"You indicated that after the meeting, both Paul and Vin Weber told you the meeting went well. Your counsel just informed us that it was only Paul, not Vin, who told you that."

"That is correct," I said.

"You lied to us!" Weissmann fumed. I could not understand why he was so angry.

Tom was stunned. He had just left the room with Weissmann and did not expect this reaction.

Weissmann continued, "We will not be moving forward with any plea agreement unless you agree to accept a Title 18, U.S. Code, Section 1001 charge," he said.

That is the specific charge for "knowingly or willfully making a false statement under oath."

Perjury.

"I will leave you and your attorney alone to discuss this matter," he said, and he left the room.

We both sat in stunned silence for about thirty seconds. Tom and I didn't even look at each other until I finally turned to him and said, "What do we do?"

I was close to deciding to plea so that we could start to put this all behind us. The proffer so far had shown that they didn't have anything on Trump and that all I was doing was clarifying some things for them in terms of what they thought they had on Paul and those associated with him, pertaining mostly to his work in Ukraine. Cooperating on all of that would surely be easier than going through a trial and enduring the financial burdens associated with it. My wife vehemently disagreed. She felt that you don't say you are guilty if you are not.

Tom looked at me and said, "Rick, I don't know what to say. I can't believe they're doing this. I think we have to move forward and take the plea. Let's move forward. I will talk to Bob [Mueller] directly. I will get the charge dropped."

At a later point, outside of the building, Tom told me he thought they were just trying to put the screws to me to get me to plead right away. He was sure they would drop the 1001 charge once I agreed. The basis for the lie wasn't there, he said. It had no bearing and no relevance to anything they were investigating.

I took him at his word, and we moved on.

Without evidence, intent, or admission the Special Counsel was allowed to determine what constituted perjury. They could bring perjury against anyone for any reason and they were not accountable to anyone. If you simply forgot a fact or a date you could be charged with perjury. If you made a statement and then attempted to change or correct it, you could be charged with perjury. If you were asked about a document but it was not shown to you, and you mangled the facts, you could be charged with perjury. Think about the grave impact of this unilateral, unchecked power.

To be abundantly clear: I pled to a lying charge before the U.S. District Court in D.C. I have accepted that charge and the consequences associated with it. I write the facts of what transpired that day now so that you can formulate your own opinion and draw your own conclusions from these events. Legally, I cannot say I did not lie.

After working through the perjury charge, the Special Counsel had me back at their offices to continue our discussions. I was on edge and even more intimidated. Weissmann used this to his advantage and soon said, "Please take a look at these emails."

I thought I was there to talk about some aspect of the Trump campaign, and suddenly I was looking at a series of emails between me and my younger brother. They were from a time when I had joined the board of a publicly traded company. My brother emailed my father thinking the fact that I was on the board might mean it was a good time to invest. It wasn't insider trading. Not even close. I didn't tell them to buy the stock. There was no pending news that I was aware of at that time that would have moved the stock price one way or another. But Weissmann, Andres, and one of the FBI agents asked all sorts of questions about the inner workings of that company, the timing of the emails, when shares of the stock were purchased and sold, and I couldn't help but think, "Are they really threatening my brother and father? And what happens if my father who's been through triple bypass surgery comes up with a different answer than me? Are they going to charge him with perjury?"

The threat was not direct or overt. It was much more subtle. But the message was unmistakably clear: I needed to step up and plea or the Special Counsel was going to target not just me, but those close to me. And it was only going to get worse.

In addition to the threats against my family, the Special Counsel continued to escalate the pressure on me to plead. They indicated that a superseding indictment was coming. In our case, the Special Counsel intended to separate and expand the financial charges which amounted to charging me with an additional twenty-three new counts—all of them related to the same charges but extended over a longer period of time. This was a common prosecutorial tactic. For example, a single charge of not claiming a foreign bank account could now be charged as not claiming a foreign bank account in 2010, 2011, 2012, and 2013. The potential penalty increased dramatically.

The pressure against me just continued to build.

CHAPTER 16

The Crucible

*Pleading, Lessons Learned, and the
Power of Faith, Family, and Friends*

THE SPECIAL COUNSEL PREPARED A DRAFT PLEA AGREEMENT FOR Tom to review in early February. The perjury count was on it. They wanted me to plea to one count of conspiracy connected to Paul's case, which focused on three separate charges.

"Conspiracy" stemmed from the paperwork I processed for Paul, which he used to apply for bank loans, even though I had no idea what the loans were for at the time, and even though his lawyers and accountants had approved it all.

In pleading to those charges, none of the personal charges against me would be pursued. Although I did not believe I was guilty of anything criminal, I decided I could live with it, just to put an end to this ordeal. But perjury? To admit to the world that I had lied to the government, after going to them and voluntarily correcting my statement, seemed outrageous.

I struggled with the decision immensely. How would I ever gain anyone's trust again with that kind of a charge on my record? My wife and I just did not feel right about it, so we put everything on hold.

We didn't know at the time that the Special Counsel was basically slapping *everybody* with a perjury charge. It was just part of Weissmann's effective but ethically questionable strategy. More than a year later, Trump's deputy national security advisor, K. T. McFarland, recalled some facts differently in her case, and when they tried to charge her with perjury, she decided not to move forward with any cooperation. In fact, K. T. would later write in her book that she was terrified at the threat of a perjury charge and her lawyer aggressively pushed back, resulting in the Special Counsel standing down. Reading that, it was hard not to wish we had handled things differently.

Flynn had been caught in a "lie," too, and it was widely known that the Special Counsel threatened his son with an indictment in their efforts to force Flynn to take a plea. They needed Flynn to get to Trump.

In his interviews with the Special Counsel, Papadopoulos recalled that something occurred in March that actually happened in January, and they said *he* lied too.

It was a pattern. In my opinion, it was a manipulation of the law and an abuse of the legal system.

They got every single one of us on a lying charge, and that does not happen by accident.

This is one of a number of reasons why Trump's lawyers refused to do any in-person interviews with the Special Counsel. They answered written questions. They did cooperate, to the smallest degree possible. But they refused to sit down with them because they knew Weissmann would've caught Trump in a perjury trap.

In February, when I didn't sign off on the plea agreement as quickly as the Special Counsel wanted me to, Tom called to inform me that they were about to hit me with the superseding indictment they used to create pressure a few weeks earlier. The indictment would come down on February 23. That would be the last opportunity to accept a "favorable" plea deal.

Between the first indictment and the second indictment, which would loop me into Paul's bank fraud charges, he said, all told I would be looking at a maximum sentence of 112 years in prison. That was an unlikely, worst-case scenario, but it messed with my mind to hear a number like that.

Tom once again laid a full-court press on me to go ahead and plead and make the best decision for my family. This was "all about protecting them," he said. Tom Green believed you could not beat the government, particularly given the toxic political environment, and in hindsight, I can't say he was wrong.

On February 12, Katelyn Polantz, a reporter from CNN who had recounted all sorts of wrong information about this case, went on national TV and reported, "A source close to the proceedings has said that Rick Gates is going to plead."

Paul freaked out. Don Jr. freaked out. Everybody freaked out thinking I was going to flip. And by flip I mean give the government what they wanted on Trump, whether or not it was true. The term is "to bear false witness." Suddenly there was speculation about what I was going to say, and who it might hurt. One national headline read, "Rick Gates May Be the Most Dangerous Man in America to Trump." All of a sudden the false headline about plagiarizing Melania's speech seemed like nothing.

That same reporter then revealed on CNN that I had already met with the Special Counsel in a proffer session. There were very few people on earth who knew about those meetings, which signaled to me that the Special Counsel had likely leaked it. Yet another pressure point to try to convince me to plea.

I thought back to something Tom Barrack told me as soon as I told him I was wrapped up in the Special Counsel's investigation. He said, "Rick, don't fight it. You cannot fight the government."

He was exceptionally direct and specific. And knowing that he had enough money to wage a war against government (or many governments) if he wanted to but immediately counseled me against it was a valuable sign for me.

In August of 2018, right after Paul's trial, I wrote a bold message in the daily notes I made to myself throughout this journey: "My conclusion of the whole trial process is it's a perversion of justice. Weissmann is mangling the law for his benefit to decimate people...and Mueller allowed him to do it."

I thought back to Martha Stewart's infamous case with the SEC years earlier, the one in which she was never convicted of insider trading, but instead went to prison when the SEC nailed her on a perjury charge.

You can't fight the government. It's just too much.

On Friday, February 23, I pled guilty to one count of conspiracy with three subpoints, all related to the charges against Paul: conspiracy to help Paul file false tax returns, conspiracy to help Paul not disclose foreign bank accounts, and conspiracy to help Paul not register for FARA. Plus the perjury charge. (Tom, regretfully, couldn't get Mueller to drop it even after pleading and making extensive attempts to contact him directly. In the whole period of the investigation Mueller never responded to Tom.)

Those three charges had to do with paperwork for Paul. I certainly never intentionally helped Paul evade anything. It was evident in the trial that his accountants and lawyers assisted him (they received immunity from prosecution in exchange for testifying against him). But if an action I undertook led to something illegal then I was willing to accept the consequences. To say that I wished I had asked more questions of Paul is an understatement. It's something I will forever regret. But the perjury charge? That was the hardest to swallow.

In the end, I pled because it was the best thing for me to do for my family. You have to make the best decision you can, based on the information you have at the time. That is what we did.

There is one aspect of this ordeal I still struggle with. Intent. In order for prosecutors to prove a crime, there must be intent. Legally it is defined as "the mental desire to act in a particular way." Throughout my plea discussions and interviews, there were several instances where I was being aggressively pushed to admit to "intent" with certain events including in some of the paperwork I filed at Paul's request. Whether I gathered records or processed (seemingly innocuous) documents according to his instructions, there was never any nefarious intent on my behalf. But the prosecutors were insistent that we were plotting to benefit Paul. Despite there being no intent, Tom felt it would be difficult to prove in a courtroom since Paul and I had to be tried together due to the conspiracy charge. He felt it would be difficult to unravel me from Paul's actions in the same trial. I am still shaken that prosecutors can push a narrative and box you in by the manner in which the charges against you are brought. You think you go in with truth on your side, and then you find out that it just isn't enough.

At my hearing, the judge asked me what seemed like a thousand questions—Are you on drugs or alcohol? Have you been pressured into any decision?—every possible reason to make sure I wouldn't pull out of the plea agreement later. They want you of sound mind and body when you agree to everything in the plea, so there's no overturning any of it later on.

As we've since learned from General Mike Flynn's case, the truth eventually comes out. The Justice Department eventually found there was reason to exonerate Flynn after he'd pled guilty—because he had basically been *forced* to plea, and the lying charge to which he pled was not relevant to the investigation. As of the writing of this book, he is still fighting it. An appeals court recently ruled in his favor, but more legal wrangling continues.

Surprisingly, Trump didn't react to my plea deal when it was announced. No tweets. No angry words at a press conference. No trying to distance himself from me or call me weak. I'm convinced it was for one simple reason: Trump knew that there was nothing he had to worry about from me because there was nothing there.

After I entered the plea, I had a week off to let everything settle. Weissmann and his team took a victory lap. And then, my cooperation with the U.S. government officially began.

One thing gave me hope at the time. I believed at the beginning that this would never go to trial. I naively thought that once all the facts were on the table, this would get settled. In the end, the political stakes were too high, and no one was backing down. It was all a game.

Mueller's team worked in silos. In my interviews and trial prep, the meetings with members specifically from the Special Counsel's office were with small and different groups of prosecutors and FBI agents depending on the subject matter or person of interest. This served the purpose of attempting to keep information contained even among the Special Counsel's prosecutors and other staff.

Early on I made it a point to observe the way many on Mueller's team worked. The manner in which they took notes and how they asked questions. Mueller's team did not always capture the information accurately, the record was prone to mistakes, and in some cases, information was not recorded at all. On several occasions, the prosecutors or agents would fall asleep during our sessions. I could tell which prosecutors had a better command of the material, and which members often struggled to grasp large swaths of content. It was evident which prosecutors were more impaired by their political bias, and those that did a better job of disguising it. There was a major deviation in the behavior of Mueller's prosecutors and the FBI agents assigned to his team. The FBI agents were more cordial, helpful, talkative. The prosecutors were cold, dismissive, and arrogant.

Over the course of the next two years, I sat down for nearly a thousand hours of interviews and trial prep with investigators, in all of the various silos in their legal pyramid scheme. They often spent eight-to-ten-hour days grilling me with every question imaginable, asking many of the same questions over and over, and they never brought one new story or one new piece of evidence to the table that had anything to do with Russia collusion or Russian interference in the 2016 election. Nothing.

They were looking for evidence of a crime they had predetermined.

The pressure never let up. It only intensified and they constantly let me know that if I deviated the slightest bit on any of my stories, they would throw the plea agreement out, and everything I said while under my plea would then be used against me in court.

It was the equivalent of political waterboarding.

This game was more wicked than I ever imagined.

Let me give an example of how the law can be twisted. During the course of the Special Counsel investigation against me, I was asked about my business expenses including meals, transportation, and other expenses for years. Their arguments were complex and convoluted, but one charge came down to this: if I took a meal on an expense report while heading back to my home from an out-of-state meeting via the airport, they legally deemed the reporting of that expense as "wire fraud."

Another example: Paul would regularly tell staff to purchase items for him. Often, he wanted sports tickets, office equipment, or the latest and greatest tech devices (no surprise, he liked having the best and newest of most things). But his company was small so there were no paper requests or purchase orders. These instructions were all verbal. Most all of his instructions were verbal. It is how he operated. In addition, he would say, "Pay your expenses," and I would transfer the money. Again, the sign-off was verbal. Hindsight is 20/20. I wished I had gotten his formal sign-off or signature on any of these actions. The Special Counsel used this information against me (and also Paul during the course of his plea agreement) and raised it during Paul's trial. The Special Counsel deemed this to be wire fraud too.

Here is where the justice system gets more twisted and maniacal. My interviews were all turned over to Paul's legal team, which *they* then used in their defense of Paul by attacking *me*. Since I was cooperating with the government, I had to stand by the Special Counsel's definitions of any "crimes" they said I committed. If I had said anything differently on the stand (while under oath) I would have been charged with perjury again.

I was used as a pawn by *both* sides.

The government has unlimited resources, and the ability to control the narrative. The Special Counsel was exerting pressure on each of us to get to the person above us. So let me ask you: Would you plead?

It was and is an unbearable crucible. Do you think you will never be in my shoes? Do you think there is nothing in your life they could not twist or use against you? Think again. Have you ever made a mistake on a form or application? Have you ever signed forms quickly without reading the entire document? What about the person you work for? Think about the way prosecutors can twist the law for whatever purpose they choose. It can happen to anyone.

No matter what you think about me, whether you agree with my politics or not, this should concern you. It should not happen in America.

★ ★ ★

During the course of my cooperation, Mueller and his team finally released their report to the attorney general, who in turn released a summary to the public.

So after two years of compromising people's lives and spending more than $32 million of taxpayers' dollars, what did Mueller show? The ending they were after never materialized. That ending had been disproven by the FBI back in August 2017. The best the Mueller Report would offer was a potential case for obstruction of justice, which Mueller himself wasn't willing to prosecute; obstruction of justice for a case that never should have moved forward in the first place. In the end, Mueller did the smart thing. He punted it to the leadership of the DOJ and Congress. Mueller balked and pushed it to others to clean up.

Mueller resigned from his Special Counsel position just over two months after the report was released. From what we know now, and from what we're sure to find out in the days and months ahead, the whole investigation was fraught with deception, political motivation, and corruption.

Not a "hoax." Not a "witch hunt."

Something much worse.

After enduring under the Special Counsel's control for years, to me the most intriguing aspect of their report was not the content in it, but what they left out of it. I can only speak from my experience, but suspect (and have heard) that others encountered the same plight. Information I provided to the Special Counsel was (in my opinion) purposefully withheld in the final report. And it makes complete sense. If you are trying to find a crime, but don't have the evidence that you hoped existed, the only way to salvage your credibility is to create and control the narrative. In political speak, we call it "spin."

From what I saw, Mueller's probe was actually controlled by Weissmann. He assembled the team and was in charge of the tactics. I also believe he was the principal author of the final report. I was later told that Weissmann originally wanted to be appointed as Special Counsel, but Rod Rosenstein recognized that he was too controversial and politically compromised. Rosenstein and Weissmann then agreed that Mueller should be appointed, and that Weissmann would be his deputy in charge of the day-to-day aspects of the probe. Remember, Weissmann reopened Paul's case from 2014 and was the source of leaks following a meeting with the Associated Press pertaining to information about Manafort's work in

Ukraine. Also, he was reportedly aware that Bruce Ohr possessed and transmitted false and misleading information from Christopher Steele to the FBI. These incidents all occurred prior to Weissmann officially joining the Special Counsel's team.

The point is that when you control the report you get to write whatever you want and imply, suggest, or allude to events or thoughts without necessarily proving them. This is the essence of politics and justice today—deceive, confuse, manipulate, and obfuscate—to convince others that you are right, and your opponent is wrong.

In my interviews, I walked the Special Counsel through every detail of the campaign—everything I've outlined in this book. I let them in on the details of Donald Trump's personality. I gave them insight into our digital advertising strategies and data analytics—a playbook that I'm cynically guessing might somehow have found its way into the Democrats' hands as we head into 2020. I let them in on the few details I had of Don Jr.'s misguided but meaningless meeting with a few rogue Russians at Trump Tower that amounted to nothing. They hammered me on every detail of Trump's foreign policy speech in April 2016, wanting to know the size of the room, the size of the stage, where each ambassador was seated, where Flynn was seated; same for Tom Barrack's chairman's dinner at the start of the inaugural week. They grilled me about one phone call that Donald Trump had with Roger Stone while we were driving, which I had overheard. I only heard Donald Trump's side of the conversation, and when he got off the phone, Trump said, "More bad news is coming." I had no idea what he was talking about. They asked me if Stone might have been talking about WikiLeaks. I said, "It could have been about a thousand things"—I did not know. There was extensive talk during the call about polling numbers with Trump (many of which had him down, but he felt were not credible). In their reports, the investigators said I responded, "It could have been" about WikiLeaks. They pinned an entire facet of Roger Stone's trial on a blatant misrepresentation of what I'd said, and I wouldn't get to correct that bit of information until I was put on the witness stand in his trial, and even then, it was mangled by the media. It continues to get mangled by the media, and in other authors' books, to this day.

They pinned a massive portion of Paul's plea proceedings on another misrepresentation of what I'd said as well, calling me in at the last minute a whole year later to clarify what kind of polling data we had provided to "KK" Just as I had told them originally, I re-explained that it was top-line polling data only, that it was outdated and unreliable, and that Paul was doing it to demonstrate his credibility in the presidential race to seek payments for unpaid prior work. It was never to pass the data to the Russians. The prosecutors grew agitated and panicked. And when they submitted a corrected motion on the matter to the court, the judge commented that I had actually helped Paul Manafort's case more than the government's on this issue. Much of this information was omitted from the final Mueller report.

The thing is, I wasn't trying to help *anybody's* case. I was just telling the truth.

Why do some in our justice department not seem to care about that?

By the way, KK was indicted by the Mueller Investigation too. He'll avoid facing his day in court by simply never coming to America ever again. But guess what we found out several months after the Mueller Report was released? KK was labeled as a "high value" U.S. asset of "significant importance"—not to Russia, as the prosecutors and the press so readily described him, but to *us*, the United States. He was mentioned in countless State Department communiqués, which I did not have access to until long after Paul's trial. And the fact that he was a Ukrainian operative, acting in America's interests, was well known to the members of the Special Counsel and the FBI long ago.

How could our American justice system do so much harm to so many people's lives, based on false pretenses and ill-begotten investigations that were political in nature?

Do these people and the politicians who backed them understand the immense harm they did?

Leading up to Paul's trial, I expected him to come out and vigorously defend himself. Part of me thought he and his lawyers were going to have a reasonable explanation for the accounting structures, loan paperwork, value of his assets, and so forth. He was incredibly smart and while I had seen him push boundaries, I had never seen him cross the line. But my stomach sank when I learned his lawyer stood up and said I was the mastermind behind all of Paul's problems. I should have expected it. The prosecutors did. In our prep sessions, they told me he would lay all the blame on me, but I didn't believe it until it happened. Part of me is still angry but mostly I saw a desperate man willing to say anything to save himself. I had to focus on the fact that this nightmare would be ending, and my family could move on with our life.

However, after Manafort's trial in August of 2018, the Special Counsel chose not to release me for sentencing. Just when I thought we had made it through the worst of it, the Special Counsel informed me that I was going to be required to provide testimony in two additional trials. Which meant that I would have to endure another year of cooperation, or more, in order to fulfill my plea agreement.

The agony and uncertainty paralyzed me and my family. I suffered from PTSD for months as anyone would in the process of being grilled for a thousand hours of questioning. I still do. I was fearful of saying the wrong thing or wondering if they would bring another perjury charge against me. I answered "maybe" to everything just to protect myself. I was constantly on edge, and the stress and pressure were more than anyone should ever have to bear. At every juncture, the prosecutors subtly let me know that I was under their control. The prosecutors wanted me to know that at any moment they could invalidate my plea deal. And I was deeply concerned they would send me back to trial. It is a weapon they used to leverage cooperators and ensure compliance. It is how the system works. It felt like a labyrinth in which I had no choice but to continue, and finding a way out was painful.

In January of 2019, while I was still in the thick of providing information and prepping for the trials of Roger Stone and Greg Craig—an attorney who had done work for Viktor Yanukovych at Paul's behest, whom the government also tried (and failed) to prosecute on FARA violations—my wife was diagnosed with breast cancer.

It was devastating. It felt as if the whole world was just collapsing on our family.

The stress of what the Special Counsel was doing to our family was killing us.

I'm glad I got to be home with my wife and kids during that time. I learned how to slow down and be deliberate. I learned to cherish what I had more than ever before. My wife's strong will inspired me and taught me to forgive and be forgiven. I have great faith in God, and I am certain I would not have made it through this ordeal without Him, our family, and dear friends who saw past the politics and loved us for us.

When the government finally decided they were finished with me in December of 2019, they praised me for my cooperation. The same compromised organization that leveled a perjury charge against me in my plea deal praised me for being so "honest," "forthright," and "truthful" in all of my testimony.

The judicial game is more than wicked. It's abhorrent.

Through the course of this process, I learned a great deal about the U.S. justice system. First and foremost, the justice system does not work on many levels. Second, while no one is above the law (and I agree with that principle), the law is not applied equally to every American. And third, justice is not about seeking or finding the truth. Truth is given no place in this arena. The legal wrangling inside a courtroom is more diabolical than any maneuvers I have seen in politics.

The press didn't show up for my sentencing hearing at the end of 2019 with the same fervor or numbers in which they had packed the courtroom for my 2017 arraignment.

The press is maniacal and twisted too. Journalism has been all but eaten alive by corporate greed, and the never-ending drive for clickbait and ratings.

The Mueller Report showed there was no collusion, just as the FBI had determined there was no collusion way back in August of 2017.

And yet, the day after the Mueller Report came out, it seemed nobody in Washington wanted to talk about "collusion" anymore. The Democrats and the media quickly pivoted away from the Russia narrative and focused on a new narrative instead. This one in Ukraine. A place I knew all too well. And this time, instead of taking it to the justice system, the Democrats and the media started talking about their case for impeachment directly to the American public.

The government's systemic organ rejection of Trump was about to start all over again.

No hard pills swallowed. No lessons learned.

No stepping back to assess what went wrong.

No thought of how painful this had already been for the American people, and how much it had damaged America's respect in the world. And now it was starting again: a hard charge forward with the goal of ejecting a sitting president, on accusations that would turn out to be just as thin as the empty tales of Russia collusion. The justice system had had its turn. Now here we were, with the State Department and Congress having their chance to step into the game.

Adam Schiff, Jerry Nadler, and others, in both houses of Congress, have done this repeatedly, using oration to link unconnected dots with circumstantial lines, turning stories into narratives to fit an agenda that isn't quite aligned with the truth. The Republicans do it too. There is plenty of blame to go around but no accountability.

The division and chaos that allowed the false narrative of the Russia collusion story to grow in the media, and behind the scenes at the FBI, and in the Department of Justice, were a reflection of just how divided our nation had become during the last political election cycle. And while Trump turned the relatively subdued Washington establishment upside down, forcing it to change from the moment he won the 2016 election, we cannot forget that this is in part what he was elected to do. He was the emblem of change so many voters yearned for, to counter a system full of political insiders who ignored the people they were supposed to protect and nurture.

What is this doing to our democracy when we're spending all this time trying to take down each other, while Russia teams up with Syria, and China takes world economic power away from us? Our insistence on attacking each other has completely demoralized and diminished our standing as a country in this world.

In 1779 Thomas Jefferson said, "Experience [has] shown that, even under the best forms [of government], those entrusted with power have, in time and by slow operations, peverted it into tyranny." And it still holds true today.

While writing this book, I was reminded of the many definitions and connotations associated with politics. Some, of course, are good and others quite negative. As a definition, "politics is the activities associated with the governance of a country or other area, especially the debate or conflict among individuals or parties having or hoping to achieve power." The etymology stems from Aristotle's book *Politiká* in Greek and means "affairs of the cities." But I found the most applicable description to our times from Bernard Crick, a British political scholar and theorist that offered this definition: "Politics is a distinctive form of rule whereby people act together through institutionalized procedures to resolve differences, to conciliate diverse interests and values and to make public policies in the pursuit of common purposes." And that is what our Founding Fathers intended for us—a government of compromise. Can you even imagine if our leaders, from both parties, subscribed to this way of thinking and acted in concert with these words? Can you envision all of the good that could be done for the American people?

Instead, during the impeachment proceedings that followed on the heels of the Mueller Report, the efforts by Democrats galvanized Republicans in Trump's defense like never before, and Trump raised more money for his reelection fund in the course of those few months than he'd ever raised in such a short period. He also gained more respect from his supporters in those months, for standing strong, while the Democrats did the opposite of what they intended: they filled Trump's supporters with even more fire, more intensity, which they will most likely take to the polls come November no matter what other failings and trials the president faces between now and then.

So the wicked game continues.

Afterword

EOPLE OFTEN ASK ME IF THE SPECIAL COUNSEL INVESTIGATION "destroyed" my life. My response to that statement is absolutely not. The actions the Special Counsel took may have changed my life, but they certainly did not destroy it.

Through my faith, I renewed my commitment to the most important things in my life: God, family, and friends. Building relationships and investing in people. These last four years led me to want to use my experiences and the trials that I endured to build people up and work toward promoting more tolerance in our political system, and equality and transparency in the justice system.

People also ask me if I regret working for Donald Trump.

I don't regret it at all.

What I experienced over the last four years is nothing short of astonishing. I was witness to some of the most thrilling, unique, and appalling historical events I could ever imagine. We *all* were.

I chose to grow from it, and to learn from it, and that has made all the difference.

As a result, I am nothing but hopeful for this country.

I hope you are too.

The diversity of our opinions and our tolerance for each other is what makes us great. The value we place on our humanity is what sets us apart.

Long before Trump started his bid for the presidency, the U.S. was fracturing. Divisive forces have pushed Americans apart, and the infighting is only getting worse.

We have a number of very serious problems in our country right now, but we are also a great country that has overcome every challenge, obstacle, or threat ever thrown our way. The Founding Fathers of our nation went to great lengths and made many sacrifices to secure freedom and liberty for each of us. The divisiveness that invaded that period of time as they plotted a new course for us was without bounds, but they overcame it. While we often forget the many details associated with key historical events in our country, America has been through incredibly challenging and perilous times. But in every case, our resilience prevailed. It is a testament to our bonds, which closely bind us as Americans. We can be different, look different, live differently, pursue and explore differently. And we are a grateful nation because of it.

If we really want to move forward and make things better for all people in this country, it's time to consider the opinions of *all* people. Let's start listening to each other. Because we all have a lot to learn from each other, and because we all cherish America.

The Unlikely Impact of a Former Soviet Country

D URING THE MANY YEARS PAUL AND I WORKED IN UKRAINE, I WAS often asked about the complex historical and political issues that impacted the country, and how our work was helping orient Ukraine to the West. The questions inevitably focused on the role Russia played during this time and its efforts to destabilize Ukraine. The significance of Ukraine as a geopolitical "bridge" between Russia and the West has traversed decades of politics and politicians.

Now Ukraine has ensnared both candidates running in the 2020 presidential election and has called into question the actions, past and present, of both men relating to their separate involvement in affairs in Ukraine. In order to adequately understand the impact of Russia on the 2016 election and beyond, we first have to go back to Ukraine.

★　★　★

It is hard to ever imagine that the little-known country of Ukraine would become the epicenter of U.S. politics today. But that is exactly what happened following President Trump's inauguration in January 2017.

For Paul Manafort, the importance and significance of Ukraine started much earlier—in 2005, when Paul began a consulting job that would span more than ten years of immersion into Ukraine's political system.

Ukraine is the "buffer zone" between Russia and the European Union, the last barrier separating Russia from expanding its empire into Europe. It is larger in size, by far, than any country in the European Union, and it is in a constant state of turmoil, torn between aligning with the West or clinging to its past history and culture as part of the Soviet empire. But the country is vastly rich in resources and currently controls a major part of the transportation system of natural gas from Russia to the European Union. So the strategic significance of Ukraine is immense and has not gone unnoticed by the United States, the European Union, or Russia for decades.

Paul had been hired in 2005 to help build a new political party after the Supreme Court of Ukraine invalidated the then-recent presidential election in 2004 that saw Viktor Yanukovych initially elected. An uprising known as the Orange Revolution, led by Viktor Yushchenko and Yulia Tymoshenko, led to Yanukovych's removal. Yushchenko was installed as president and appointed Tymoshenko as prime minister briefly from January through September 2005, and later from December 2007 until March 2010. Her actions during her time as prime minister later led to her trial, conviction, and imprisonment in October 2011 for a series of financial crimes and signing unauthorized agreements with Russia from which she personally benefited.

Yanukovych's party was all but obliterated and in need of resurrection. Through a relationship of Rick Davis, he and Paul were introduced to the wealthiest Ukrainian businessman at the time, Rinat Akhmetov, to figure out how to rebuild after the party's recent defeat. Paul viewed Rinat as the most forward-thinking oligarch in terms of supporting Western democracies. He established a foundation with former U.S. senators on his board and understood the importance of aligning with the West.

In less than five years from the time Paul started his work he created the largest organized political party in Ukraine's history, the Party of Regions, resurrected Viktor Yanukovych from the proverbial political grave (he was polling at less than a 13 percent approval rating), positioned the party to take control of parliament in 2007 along with Yanukovych as the prime minister, and in 2010 he got Yanukovych elected as president.

Paul knows political strategy better than any operative I have seen in the business. He was good at crafting the plan, but also adept at hiring the right team to execute the plan. He developed an experienced team of seasoned experts in American political campaign models (senior individuals in both Republican and Democrat parties). These individuals were proficient in media advertising, polling, electoral reform, speechwriting, election integrity, social and digital media, and messaging. But most importantly, they were all steadfast believers in democracy and worked toward helping other countries create stable democracies with Western-oriented values.

And this included Paul. His work for Viktor Yanukovych and the Party of Regions was designed to "Westernize" Ukraine, its government, its parliament, its elections, and its politicians. This effort was *not* to benefit Putin. It was exactly the opposite. His work was designed to move Ukraine into closer relations with the West.

As much as reporters and other critics have claimed over the years (including officials in the Obama administration) that Yanukovych was a puppet of Putin, this could not have been further from the truth. Of course, they had to communicate and work together. Over 30 percent of Ukraine's economy was dependent on trade with Russia at that time. Families were still living in both countries; they were neighbors. However, Yanukovych wanted to be Westernized. He saw the value and economic benefits of aligning with the United States and the EU.

To prove this sentiment, Paul worked early with Yanukovych to move him toward a pledge that Ukraine would remove all of its highly enriched uranium by 2012. In April 2010, Yanukovych committed to then-President Obama at the U.S.-led Nuclear Security Summit to turn over Ukraine's highly enriched uranium stock. And in December 2010, Ukraine handed over more than 110 pounds of the material—the equivalent of roughly two atomic bombs. This significant step was to demonstrate Yanukovych's alignment with Western governments. (Interesting point—Obama did not want to deal with the transfer of the uranium, so he negotiated to have it sent to none other than Putin, whom he trusted to dispose of it.)

Ukraine, however, needed the support of the West to help guide it forward. Normally, Western democracies would welcome another ally into their fold. But due to the relationship between Chancellor of Germany Angela Merkel and Vladimir Putin, Ukraine's fate hung in the balance. During our time working in Ukraine, one of the most significant issues was the transit of natural gas from Russia to countries in Europe. All natural gas had to travel through Ukraine in order to get to Europe. Over the years this became extremely problematic for aggressive industrial countries like Germany. Trade wars often broke out between Russia and Ukraine, and as tensions escalated, Europe suffered. Russia would literally turn off the gas pipelines, preventing gas from reaching all European countries that were dependent on the natural gas.

The inconsistency and uncertainty of the trade disputes between Russia and Ukraine led the European Union, with Merkel leading the charge, to negotiate directly with Russia. Despite the EU's earnest desire to welcome Ukraine with open arms into Europe's coveted trade zone, securing a consistent and constant supply of natural gas was paramount to EU countries to expand their economies.

So, what do you think Merkel did? She entered into an initially secret agreement to work with Vladimir Putin to build a pipeline called Nord Stream that would transit gas from Russia to Europe directly, completely circumventing Ukraine and depriving it of vast amounts of revenue. Merkel was acutely aware that this agreement would crush Ukraine's economy. Yet she convinced Denmark, Sweden, and Finland to join as partners. Over the years I have questioned these actions by Merkel in the context of her criticism of Yanukovych as pro-Russian. In fact, Merkel and Putin have a solid twenty-year personal relationship that dwarfs that of any other two major countries.

In January 2019, Richard Grenell, the then-U.S. ambassador in Germany, wrote a letter to a series of companies involved in expanding the Nord Stream pipeline. He argued that the companies needed to stop working on the project or the United States would likely use sanctions, which it did at the end of that year. In a show of defiance to the U.S. and unity with Putin, Merkel stated that she did not "agree with the approach of [U.S.] sanctions." So is Merkel pro-Russian? Pro-Putin?

Putin and Yanukovych, personally, did not like each other. Yanukovych was tired of being bullied by Putin over the years over numerous policy issues, including the directive by Putin for Ukraine not to enter into an Association Agreement with the EU, a major campaign promise Yanukovych was determined to enact. The agreement would have started Ukraine down the path to become a member country of the EU several years down the road. However, Putin made every attempt to stop Yanukovych from winning the 2010 presidential election, including a $10 million campaign contribution he made to Yanukovych's competitor, Yulia Tymoshenko, (the former prime minister mentioned earlier in the book). She was also backed by the Obama administration during the election. And Putin was assured that Tymoshenko was going to win.

But she lost. And the notion that Yanukovych was under the thumb of and controlled by Russia was completely wrong.

It would take almost three years of work to bring the EU agreement to fruition, which represented the bulk of work that Paul and I did at that time for the Party of Regions.

Looking back on 2014, Russia and Putin overplayed their hand. Putin did not want Ukraine to align with the U.S. and the EU. Paul was ardently pushing Yanukovych to sign the Association Agreement with the EU and start the framework for a Western-oriented relationship supporting democratic values. However, Yanukovych was also concerned about Ukraine's fledgling economy, which was highly reliant on Russia. Signing the EU agreement would drive Putin to cancel billions of dollars in trade deals. As a result, Ukraine requested financial assistance amounting to $15 billion from the West as part of the EU agreement and calculated by the IMF. The Obama administration (under the reigns of Victoria Nuland and then-ambassador Geoffrey Pyatt) had failed to build a relationship with Ukraine and Yanukovych's government, and therefore withheld the financial assistance necessary to bail out Ukraine from its pending economic and political collapse. The West was already angered by the imprisonment of Tymoshenko in 2011 and did not believe the financial funds would be used appropriately. As a result, it chose not to help Ukraine under these conditions. No surprise: Putin stepped in and offered to help Ukraine with financial assistance instead.

In November 2013, Yanukovych traveled to Vilnius, Lithuania, for the accord summit but in the eleventh hour failed to sign it. Less than three months later, he was ousted from power. Paul was devastated. He had worked as hard as I had ever seen him work to try and convince Yanukovych, the U.S. government, and key EU leaders to find a solution. Interestingly, Paul was largely ignored by U.S. officials, despite the shared policy interest, as a result of his political affiliation as a Republican and the disgust that certain individuals at the State Department had over him getting Yanukovych elected in 2010.

Looking back, I am disappointed at seeing the adverse impact politics can have not just in our country, but also outside. As a result of the U.S. not backing Ukraine in February 2014 by failing to provide the monetary assistance it needed, Ukraine collapsed. Many in Obama's administration rejoiced at that time, thinking another world leader not endorsed or supported by the U.S. government was successfully removed. But what the U.S. failed to calculate was that it roused the sleeping bear in Russia, and by doing so, more than thirteen thousand people have died in civil chaos. The country has been torn apart.

The politics that prevailed at the price of so many lives are hard to process. I recall Paul's severe discouragement at what had occurred by the actions, or in this case, the inaction of the U.S. government. In between the failed summit in Vilnius and his ouster, Yanukovych brokered a deal with support from the U.S. that would require him to honor the conditions of the opposition groups, agree to concessions on anti-protest laws, and appoint key opposition leaders to important government posts, all of which Yanukovych did. Nonetheless, it was not enough and Yanukovych was forced to flee Ukraine and relinquish the presidency after deadly protests for failing to sign the EU agreement.

To this day, it is not clear who instigated the deadly riots. Many in Ukraine say it was a rogue group of the opposition protestors. The Russians claim it was the U.S. government fomenting the unrest after it leaked legitimate phone calls between Nuland and Pyatt discussing regime change in the current Ukraine government (a strong sign that the U.S. was interfering in the internal affairs of another country). The West claims it was Russia that sent snipers to Ukraine to create chaos and mayhem.

Shortly after, Vladimir Putin invaded Crimea and placed it under Russian control. In the end, Paul felt that Victoria Nuland acted in bad faith and destabilized a critical region that now gave Russia a stronger foothold in Ukraine.

Several years later, new information about alleged U.S. involvement surfaced. The CIA trained and backed one of the anti-Russia groups involved (Right Sector) and its leader, Dmitry Yarosh. This was a group of right-wing nationalists that Yarosh mobilized and armed during the alleged coup. Yarosh went on to become a member of the new parliament after the coup until 2019 and even ran for president, albeit unsuccessfully in the 2014 election.

There is one more significant event worth noting during this same period of time in 2014. Paul was asked to initially help organize the campaign strategy for Yanukovych's successor, Petro Poroshenko. After Yanukovych fled the country, Poroshenko won the presidential election. Because of Paul's political success in winning campaigns in Ukraine, it was not surprising for Poroshenko's team to reach out. However, I thought it was fascinating that Paul would work with yet another president of Ukraine, one who would ultimately come to oppose Trump and his presidential campaign.

Why is all of this important? It ties directly back into the presidential election of 2016 and Putin's goal of destroying the American model of democracy. During the campaign and after, Paul received a stretch of negative publicity after being linked to a Russian oligarch, Oleg Deripaska, who allegedly has ties to Putin. It was suggested this was the link between Russia and the Trump campaign.

Let me try to connect some of the dots involving many of these players. In 2006, Paul's business partner, Rick Davis, who was also John McCain's campaign manager for president in 2008, introduced Oleg Deripaska to Senator McCain in Switzerland for a meeting. Later that same year, Davis connected the two men again onboard Deripaska's yacht to bring Deripaska together with possibly the next president of the United States. This was traditional relationship building. McCain was later upset with the perception it created when the media reported his interactions with Deripaska but not before. Following those events, McCain became critical of Paul's work with Deripaska. It was at this juncture that McCain did what all politicians typically do in order to win. He changed. He began an assault on lobbyists and the work they did. He removed several people (many his personal friends) from his campaign that were lobbyists and who had built careers on this type of work. Davis was flagged for his part and involvement with political lobbyists, but unlike Paul in 2016, he survived the attacks.

The dots do not stop here. While Deripaska has been labeled a Putin ally, in 2009 the FBI solicited his help to free an American operative captured in Iran. Deripaska not only agreed to the deal but spent almost $25 million of his own money to finance the American effort. The person at the top of the FBI who not only knew about the mission but was regularly briefed: Robert Mueller.

In sum, the same man (Deripaska) with whom McCain had no problem building a relationship, the same man whom Democrat Senator Mark Warner was attempting to backchannel with, and whom Mueller and the FBI had no problem courting for help; the same man that laughed at FBI agents when approached with the claim that Russian forces were helping Donald Trump win the 2016 presidential election, was the same man that was used to character assassinate Paul and me.

One of the most egregious and false narratives in Paul's career was that he was working for the benefit of the Russians. It is clear when actually looking at the facts that this is not true. Paul did not need the support of the Russians in 2016 to impact the U.S. presidential election for Donald Trump. It was the American people who impacted the election in 2016 in one of the greatest upsets in modern-day U.S. presidential politics.

But the impact of Ukraine will not end before the 2020 election regardless of who wins. Both Biden and Trump are enmeshed in Ukrainian affairs but for different reasons. Trump's impeachment was predicated on his actions relating to Ukraine, and Biden's family affairs have him entangled in allegations of corruption and interference during his time as vice president.

As the wicked game continues, and the infighting in Washington likely intensifies through 2020 and beyond, you can be assured that issues relating to Ukraine will surface again. And I hope more Americans seek to educate themselves too—not only about Ukraine but also about the inner workings of our own political system, which affects every one of us far more than we often recognize or want to admit.

Acknowledgments

MY TIME WITH DONALD TRUMP WAS AN EXPERIENCE LIKE NO other. It was not just because of the persona of the individual, although that certainly made it more interesting. But it is what he did to the presidential election process to break down years of political theory, traditions, and know-it-all politicians. (Yes, this is a positive.) His election instilled belief in the idea that anyone can be elected president of our country. He proved it. He broke the barriers and the static rules to show Americans that anyone can run and win the highest elected office of the greatest country in the world. I hope this inspires generations to come and encourages them to participate in the political process because their involvement does matter.

There are so many stories, anecdotes, and incredible moments that I could not include in this book simply because so much happens during a presidential election, a transition, and an inauguration. But without any doubt, it was one of the most humbling periods in my life. While they were not perfect, our Founding Fathers understood the importance of freedom and liberty and used the Constitution to ensure that our system of governance would be protected throughout our history. I have a much richer and deeper sense of gratitude for what they and those that followed have done for our country and the sacrifices they made that were required.

Over the last four years, the challenges have been particularly immense. Without the close support and counsel of family and friends, I would have been lost.

First, to my attorney, Tom Green, who treated me as a person always and not as a client, thank you. Your counsel and guidance helped me legally, but your huge heart saved me and my family.

To Anthony Ziccardi, Michael Wilson, and the entire team at Post Hill Press. You made this book happen and added excitement back to the project.

To David Vigliano for navigating more hurdles than anyone ever expected. Your experience, professionalism, and stellar reputation preceded you. I am grateful for your guidance, enduring the ups and downs, and help to make this a reality.

Mark Dagostino, although the project started much later than we both imagined, your commitment to this book never wavered. You were willing to listen and it is because of you that I am able to share my voice. Your insights and knowledge of the book world were invaluable. Your curiosity and enthusiasm made you a joy to work with.

Charlie, you have supported, mentored, and opened your heart to me for more than twenty-five years. You gave me my start and will never know how much I look up to you. You are, without a doubt, the kindest man in politics.

I am grateful to Tony for taking care of my family and helping me be the best version of myself. You are wise and full of compassion.

Casey Templeton, a gifted photographer.

Marc, you are one of the truest, most courageous, and strongest people I have had the pleasure of knowing. You have my gratitude and admiration.

To Shawn, who extended soccer, acceptance, and kindness. I am honored to be your friend.

Chris, our lunches have eased the burden immensely. I appreciate your friendship, laughter, and being a solid sounding board.

Scott, my college friend, and a true gentleman. Thank you for your steadfast encouragement, wisdom, blunt counsel, and for the inspiration for the title of this book.

Heather, your support and empathy meant everything to me. Your kindness, thoughtfulness, and ability to see good in people are unparalleled. I'd work with you again anytime, anywhere.

Mike, I am grateful for your relentless pursuit of making sure I had a friend in the Lord. I have learned so much from you in such a short amount of time. Your wisdom and tenacity to bring others together are humbling.

Tim, God works in amazing ways. Your friendship has been a wonderful gift. Thank you for your guidance, for helping me rebuild, and for keeping me focused on what is true. The band of brothers you have gathered in God's name, who has done nothing but provide encouragement, prayers, and support, has been and will continue to be a blessing.

Tom Hodgkins, who chartered these turbulent waters with me every day. Who gave time away from his family to support our family. Who sat with me and Drew on one of the hardest nights of my life. You supported me in ways that no one else would even consider. Your loyalty, sincerity, and positivity were most needed. Thank you for never wavering.

A special thank you to our siblings and parents who endured through this with us and gave us nothing but unconditional love and support. And to my younger brother Paul, who walked every step of this journey with me. I am humbled and proud to be your brother.

Finally, to Drew and Julee, Mike and Caroline, and Travis and Heather, our group of friends who banded together to hold us together. You weathered this storm with us, made sure we were fed, watched over our children, sat with us through court proceedings and surgeries, cried with us, encouraged us, prayed with us, and carried us through. You even made us laugh in the midst of it all. We wouldn't have made it without you. You are the very embodiment of selflessness. We love you.

It is hard to quantify the public humiliation and social ostracization that accompanies events of this magnitude. There have been moments where we felt so discouraged about humanity and other times that people's unexpected kindness filled our hearts. To all of those in our community who brought food, gave us messages of encouragement, and loved our kids, you will never know how grateful we'll forever be to you.

We walked through this journey in Faith. Many Bible verses encouraged and comforted me throughout this period, but one in particular I returned to time and again: Isaiah 41:10—*"Fear not, for I am with you. Do not be dismayed, for I am the Lord your God. I will strengthen you, and I will help you. I will uphold you with my righteous right hand."*